Economic History
of Canada

ECONOMICS INFORMATION GUIDE SERIES

Series Editor: Robert W. Haseltine, Associate Professor of Economics, State University College of Arts and Science at Geneseo, Geneseo, New York

Also in this series:

AMERICAN ECONOMIC HISTORY—*Edited by William K. Hutchinson**

ECONOMIC DEVELOPMENT—*Edited by Thomas A. Bieler**

ECONOMIC EDUCATION—*Edited by Catherine Hughes*

EAST ASIAN ECONOMIES—*Edited by Molly K.S.C. Lee**

ECONOMICS OF EDUCATION—*Edited by William Ganley**

ECONOMICS OF MINORITIES—*Edited by Kenneth L. Gagala*

HEALTH AND MEDICAL ECONOMICS—*Edited by Ted J. Ackroyd*

HISTORY OF ECONOMIC ANALYSIS—*Edited by William K. Hutchinson*

INTERNATIONAL TRADE—*Edited by Ahmed M. El-Dersh**

LABOR ECONOMICS—*Edited by Ross E. Azevedo*

STATISTICS AND ECONOMETRICS—*Edited by Joseph Zaremba**

MATHEMATICAL ECONOMICS AND OPERATIONS RESEARCH—*Edited by Joseph Zaremba*

MONEY, BANKING, AND MACROECONOMICS—*Edited by James M. Rock*

PUBLIC POLICY—*Edited by Michael Joshua**

REGIONAL ECONOMICS—*Edited by Jean Shackleford**

RUSSIAN ECONOMIC HISTORY—*Edited by Daniel Kazmer and Vera Kazmer*

SOVIET-TYPE ECONOMIC SYSTEMS—*Edited by Z. Edward O'Relley*

TRANSPORTATION ECONOMICS—*Edited by James P. Rakowski*

URBAN ECONOMICS—*Edited by Jean Shackleford**

*in preparation

The above series is part of the
GALE INFORMATION GUIDE LIBRARY

The Library consists of a number of separate series of guides covering major areas in the social sciences, humanities, and current affairs.

General Editor: Paul Wasserman, Professor and former Dean, School of Library and Information Services, University of Maryland

Managing Editor: Denise Allard Adzigian, Gale Research Company

Economic History of Canada

A GUIDE TO INFORMATION SOURCES

Volume 9 in the Economics Information Guide Series

Trevor J. O. Dick

*Assistant Professor of Economics
University of Lethbridge
Lethbridge, Alberta
Canada*

Gale Research Company
Book Tower, Detroit, Michigan 48226

Library of Congress Cataloging in Publication Data

Dick, Trevor J O
    Economic history of Canada.

    (Economics information guide series ; v. 9)
(Gale information guide library)
    Includes indexes.
    1. Canada--Economic conditions--Bibliography.
I. Title.
Z7165.C2D5   [HC113]   016.3309'71   73-17571
ISBN 0-8103-1292-1

Copyright © 1978 by
Trevor J. O. Dick

No part of this book may be reproduced in any form without permission in writing from the publisher, except by a reviewer who wishes to quote brief passages or entries in connection with a review written for inclusion in a magazine or newspaper. Manufactured in the United States of America.

VITA

Trevor J.O. Dick received his Ph.D. in economics from the University of Washington in 1970. He has published articles in EXPLORATIONS IN ECONOMIC HISTORY and the JOURNAL OF ECONOMIC HISTORY. He is assistant professor of economics at the University of Lethbridge, and serves on the Economic History Association's Committee on Research in Economic History.

CONTENTS

Introduction xi

Chapter I. Interpretive and Bibliographic Sources 1
  A. Interpretive Sources 1
  B. Bibliographic Sources 2

Chapter II. From Colonial Times to the Present 5
  A. Texts and General Works 5
    i. Texts 5
    ii. General Works 6
        The Maritimes 9
        Quebec 10
        Ontario 11
        The West 11
  B. Statistical Record 13
  C. Theses of Economic Growth 13
  D. Sectors and Industries 16
    i. Primary Industry 17
    ii. Secondary Industry 19
    iii. Tertiary Industry 21
  E. Economic Organization 23
    i. Industrial Organization 24
    ii. Labor Organization 24
    iii. The Role of Government 25
  F. Technology, Productivity Change, and Welfare 29
  G. Resources 30
    i. Land and Its Endowment 30
    ii. Population 31
    iii. Capital Formation 34

Chapter III. The Colonial Period to 1867 37
  A. General Works 37
    i. The Maritimes 37
    ii. The Canadas 39
    iii. The West 42
  B. Statistical Record 43
  C. Theses of Economic Growth 44

Contents

    D. Sectors and Industries 45
        i. Primary Industry 45
        ii. Secondary Industry 48
        iii. Tertiary Industry 48
    E. Economic Organization 50
        i. Industrial Organization 51
        ii. Labor Organization 52
        iii. The Role of Government 52
    F. Technology, Productivity Change, and Welfare 57
    G. Resources 57
        i. Land and Its Endowments 58
        ii. Population 58
        iii. Capital Formation 59

Chapter IV. Confederation (1867) to 1920 61
    A. General Works 61
        i. The Maritimes 63
        ii. Quebec 64
        iii. Ontario 64
        iv. The West 65
    B. Statistical Record 66
    C. Theses of Economic Growth 67
    D. Sectors and Industries 69
        i. Primary Industry 69
        ii. Secondary Industry 72
        iii. Tertiary Industry 74
    E. Economic Organization 77
        i. Industrial Organization 77
        ii. Labor Organization 78
        iii. The Role of Government 79
    F. Technology, Productivity Change, and Welfare 85
    G. Resources 86
        i. Land and Its Endowments 86
        ii. Population 86
        iii. Capital Formation 90

Chapter V. From 1920 to the Present 93
    A. General Works 93
        i. The Maritimes 96
        ii. Ontario and Quebec 97
        iii. The West 98
    B. Statistical Record 98
    C. Theses of Economic Growth 100
        i. The Role of Nationalism 101
        ii. The Role of the Tariff 103
        iii. Trade, Cycles, and the Balance of Payments 107
        iv. Quantity Theory vs. Income Expenditure 110
        v. Regional Growth Patterns 111
        vi. Quebec 112
    D. Sectors and Industries 113
        i. Primary Industry 113

	ii. Secondary Industry	118
	iii. Tertiary Industry	121
E.	Economic Organization	123
	i. Industrial Organization	123
	ii. Labor Organization	124
	iii. The Role of Government	125
F.	Technology, Productivity Change, and Welfare	134
G.	Resources	139
	i. Land and Its Endowments	139
	ii. Population	139
	iii. Capital Formation	141

Author Index 143

Title Index 153

Subject Index 165

INTRODUCTION

The coverage and organization of this annotated bibliography reflect my approach to research in the subject, and my perception of a bibliographic reference source useful for researchers pursuing their work in similar ways. This does not mean that many of the items included would not also be included if a different approach were used. Even the organization of the material might not differ greatly. What it does mean is that this bibliography should seem eminently sensible to an economist practicing as an economic historian, and who wishes not only to acquaint himself with the works and interpretations of other writers, but also to obtain detailed information about the past, useful in forming and testing hypotheses about the occurrence of past events. In these respects, I share the lot of all historians past and present who are bound by the perspective of their own particular time and training.

Canadian economic history is broadly defined to encompass the work of many different hands. Contributors to the literature have become increasingly diverse, both in their conception of the task of writing economic history, and in the skills they bring to bear on this task. The approach of the historian and that of the economist reveal research strategies that are different, though capable of limited integration. The historian typically pursues the uniqueness of an event for its own sake, seeking primarily to authenticate and document this uniqueness. The economist, as a social scientist, is primarily interested in hypothesizing how events occur or recur, and in mustering the evidence necessary to test such hypotheses. Between these two seemingly polar philosophical positions lies a vast range of scholarly efforts that differ from one another in only one essential way, the degree to which they self-consciously offer the reader an explanation, economic or otherwise, of past economic events. Each variety, no matter where it falls in this spectrum, adds something to our understanding of the past, if only by increasing our knowledge of the background conditions of Canadian economic growth. This bibliography, therefore, aims to include a wide representation of materials contributed by authors using different approaches. The list is not, however, exhaustive. Only those works that make a significant or distinctive contribution are included. The annotation accompanying the included items helps to identify the approaches taken by those authors whose works are notable examples of some well-developed, or developing, school or interpretation.

Introduction

The oldest interpretation is that of the Nationalist School, which focuses upon the political evolution of the relationship between colony and mother country. This school implicitly identifies the growth of political independence, particularly over commercial and fiscal policy, with the achievement of economic growth. Another interpretation may be called the Environmentalist School. At first, primary significance was attached to the frontier in economic development, emphasizing institutional similarities between Canada and the United States. This school underwent early revision, however, to draw a significant contrast between the two countries based on the distinctive contribution to Canadian economic growth made by metropolitan centers. The development and refinement of this interpretation became the major task of the Laurentian School, concentrating on the influences of geography, particularly of the St. Lawrence, and the development of a succession of staple trades. All of these interpretations have been painstakingly documented by their authors, and from the point of view of illuminating growth and welfare in the Canadian past, they share one characteristic, namely, they single out one or two strategic factors that assume overriding importance.

The Laurentian School, the latest and most highly developed, has recently shown some signs of fragmentation in the face of new developments in the social sciences, particularly in economics, but as yet, no common ground on which to base a new synthesis has been found. A recent interest in economic history among economists may eventually lead to such a synthesis. So-called new economic historians look not only to well-documented facts, but also employ the formal discipline of economics to develop relevant hypotheses made explicit in their writing, and to guide the accumulation of evidence, often quantitative, for testing these hypotheses. Typically, the results of this research suggest a greater variety and complexity of causes of economic growth than are implicit in much of the earlier historical research.

The organization of this bibliography is partly chronological and partly topical, reflecting my belief that many of the more traditional, particularly political, divisions of time have no particular economic significance, or represent little or no break in a fairly continuous process of economic change. Some temporal divisions, however, are useful. For example, colonial times betoken a framework of economic activity that is altered by the creation of a new national government capable of exerting a new influence on the economy. Somewhat less significantly, the colonial period is subdivided by the change from French to British hegemony. Of more appeal from an economic viewpoint may be a division at approximately 1920 between early national growth and the structural transformation of the economy later in the twentieth century. All temporal divisions, however, are made mainly for the sake of convenience rather than for their analytical merit. Works that span the entire period from early colonial times to the present are separated from those treating only shorter periods.

Whatever the time span under consideration, a topical organization of materials within this span reflects the view that the developing economy was made up of parts that fit together according to some economic logic. Organizational aspects

Introduction

of growth are distinguished from the history of particular industries or sectors producing goods and services; thus, industrial organization, labor organization, and governmental activities are treated as the component aspects of total economic organization. Industries are classified according to whether they are primary, secondary, or tertiary in nature, that is, according to whether they are resource-intensive with little or no value added, manufacturing with substantial value added, or services such as transportation and financial intermediation. Because economic growth may be viewed as a consequence of some increase either in resources or in the efficiency with which resources are used, works treating technological and productivity change and the distribution of these gains are distinguished from those documenting the discovery and acquisition of new resources. Another topic includes works whose primary object is to propose some thesis about how Canadian economic growth occurred. All works less specialized by topic are classified according to whether they are general, or suitable as texts. Works that contribute mainly to the statistical record of growth and welfare are distinguished as items of special interest to quantitative researchers.

One further organizing device that seems inescapable as one becomes more aware of the literature is the economic region. Much of Canadian economic history has been a story of the progress of diverse regions in the absence of thoroughgoing national integration. The treatment of individual regions is commonplace, and where a work is more clearly defined by the region that it treats than by any other dimension, it is so classified within the appropriate topic and time span. A regional orientation is implicit, for example, in the development of the "Laurentian School."

A danger of any classification is the temptation it provides to cross-file items because they appear to belong in more than one place. As a general rule this temptation is resisted except where it is obvious that the author's work has made a contribution capable of standing on its own in more than one of the areas identified in the bibliography. Items included in the section covering the total time span, or in sections listing general or textual materials, are not listed in less inclusive and more specialized sections. One purpose of the annotation is to cross-reference items that should be noted in more than one place in the organization of the bibliography.

Finally, one consequence of the logical topical organization followed here is that gaps in the existing literature become apparent; these gaps might not appear with alternative methods of organization. One use to which the bibliography may be put, therefore, is to draw attention to areas where further research may be especially productive in helping economists as well as others to understand growth and welfare in the Canadian past.

Chapter I
INTERPRETIVE AND BIBLIOGRAPHIC SOURCES

The works listed below are divided between items mainly interpretive, in section A, and those mainly bibliographic, in section B. Under A, the full spectrum of approaches to Canadian economic history is sampled. Under B, comprehensive and detailed reference sources are included.

I.A. INTERPRETIVE SOURCES

The schools of thought reviewed in the introduction are documented in items 2, 3, and 9 below. An extensive bibliography is included in 9. More specialized reviews are provided by 1 and 4. The latter includes important samples of the work of W.A. Mackintosh, H.A. Innis, and A.R.M. Lower, leading figures of the Laurentian School. The works of Harold Adams Innis, the doyen of Canadian economic historians, are systematically explored in 7, ending with a complete bibliographic listing of that author's writings. In 8, Paquet classifies and evaluates some alternative theoretic frameworks that have been, and/or might be, applied to Canadian economic history. In 6, the contributions of French Canadian historians in general are reviewed. Finally, in item 5, George and Oksanen discuss the more recent contributions of economic and quantitative analysis to Canadian economic history.

I.A. INTERPRETIVE SOURCES

1. Armstrong, Frederick H. "Canadian Business History: Approaches and Publications to 1970." In CANADIAN BUSINESS HISTORY, SELECTED STUDIES, 1497-1971, edited by David S. Macmillan, pp. 263-302. Toronto: McClelland & Stewart, 1972.

2. Careless, J[ames] M[aurice] S[tockford]. "Frontierism, Metropolitanism, and Canadian History." CANADIAN HISTORICAL REVIEW 35 (March 1954): 1-21.

Interpretive and Bibliographic Sources

3. Cook, R[amsey], et al. APPROACHES TO CANADIAN HISTORY. Canadian Historical Readings, no. 1. Toronto: University of Toronto Press, 1967. x, 98 p.

4. Easterbrook, W[illiam] T[homas], and Watkins, M[elville] H., eds. APPROACHES TO CANADIAN ECONOMIC HISTORY. Carleton Library, no. 31. Toronto: McClelland & Stewart, 1967. xvii, 292 p.

5. George, P[eter J.], and Oksanen, E[rnest] H. "Recent Developments in the Quantification of Canadian Economic History." HISTOIRE SOCIALE/SOCIAL HISTORY 4 (November 1969): 76-98.

6. Mandron, Robert. "L'Historiographie canadienne francaise, bilan et perspectives." CANADIAN HISTORICAL REVIEW 51 (March 1970): 5-20.

7. Neill, Robin [F.]. A NEW THEORY OF VALUE, THE CANADIAN ECONOMICS OF H.A. INNIS. Canadian University Paperbacks, no. 120. Toronto: University of Toronto Press, 1972. viii, 159 p. Bibliography, pp. 126-45.

8. Paquet, G[illes]. "Some Views on the Pattern of Canadian Economic Development." In GROWTH AND THE CANADIAN ECONOMY, chap. 3, edited by T[homas]. N. Brewis. Carlton Library, no. 39. Toronto: McClelland & Stewart, 1968.

9. Winks, R.W. RECENT TRENDS AND NEW LITERATURE IN CANADIAN HISTORY. Washington, D.C.: American Historical Association, 1959. v, 56 p.

I.B. BIBLIOGRAPHIC SOURCES

A considerable variety of bibliographic sources exists. Perhaps the most recent and comprehensive annotated lists are included in item 11 below. In addition to being a full-scale rewriting of Canadian history from earliest times, this recently published composite history by leading Canadian historians is especially notable for its careful documentation and detailed bibliographic references. Almost every volume contains chapters and accompanying references in economic history. For the specialist, these volumes are particularly useful in bridging the gap between secondary and archival sources. As a general reference guide, 6 is excellent and includes most of the standard bibliographic sources on Canadian history. It is also organized partly on a regional basis. Included are encyclopedias, dictionaries, yearbooks and handbooks, biographies, government publications, archives and manuscripts, theses, geographical guides, museums, societies and libraries, and other special topics, one of which is economic and social

Interpretive and Bibliographic Sources

history. The serials listed as items 7 and 5 were sequential publications, and contain about a dozen pages per issue listing publications and writings pertaining to Canada on such topics as economic history, agriculture, mining, forestry, industry, transport, labor, settlement and colonization, commercial policy, money and banking, and public finance. Historical items are included under many of these headings. Secondary, periodical, and government document sources are also covered. While the bibliographic listing found in 5 was discontinued in 1952, a similar listing, though less specific regarding the economy, is provided in all issues of 4 from 1920 to the present. A similar periodic listing including French language contributions can be found in the issues of 14 since 1947. The listing given by 9 is now somewhat out of date. A similar and more recent roundup of scholarship in economic and business history is provided by Bliss in 1, and this effort promises to be repeated on a regular basis in the future; see also the CANADA YEAR BOOK for 1939, (item 2 below), pages 36-40. The coverage of 3 is not as the title suggests, but rather a variety of historical and social research contributions of Canadian scholars, not all treating Canadian topics. Several bibliographic essays in item 10 are particularly relevant: "Economic History," Melville Watkins; "Labour History," Irving Abella; "The Economy," Ian Drummond; "Foreign Control of the Economy," A. Rotstein; and the sections on history, economics, and politics generally. Section IV of item 8 contains the more important works relating to the post-1867 economic history of Quebec, including French language contributions. See 12 and 13 for additional references dealing with the colonial period. The CANADA YEAR BOOK, item 2, aside from its main preoccupation with statistical documentation, lists sources of official government information and documents, statistical and otherwise. Finally, no attempt has been made to include in the current bibliography the unpublished work of university doctoral candidates. Most university libraries catalog these items in their reference collections, and item 15, especially pages 17-21, offers a useful guide to some of these contributions. See also 6, pages 48-49, for a guide to unpublished theses.

I.B. BIBLIOGRAPHIC SOURCES

1. Bliss, [John William] Michael. "Business and Economic History." In CANADA SINCE 1867, A BIBLIOGRAPHICAL GUIDE, edited by J.L. Granatstein and Paul Stevens, pp. 57-73. Toronto: Hakkert, 1974.

2. Canada. Department of Trade and Commerce. CANADA YEAR BOOK. Ottawa: Queen's Printer, 1905-- . Annual.

3. Canadian Economic Association. Committee on Economic History. "Annual Survey of Canadian Economic and Social History." Toronto: 1969-- . Annual.

4. CANADIAN HISTORICAL REVIEW. Toronto: University of Toronto Press, 1920-- . Quarterly.

Interpretive and Bibliographic Sources

5. CANADIAN JOURNAL OF ECONOMICS AND POLITICAL SCIENCE. Toronto: University of Toronto Press, 1935-52. Quarterly.

6. Clark, Jane. REFERENCE AIDS IN CANADIAN HISTORY. University of Toronto Library Reference Series, no. 14. Toronto: University of Toronto Library, 1972. 75 p.

7. CONTRIBUTIONS TO CANADIAN ECONOMICS: STUDIES IN ECONOMICS AND HISTORY. Toronto: University of Toronto Press, 1928-34. Irregular.

8. Durocher, René, and Linteau, Paul-André. HISTOIRE DU QUEBEC, BIBLIOGRAPHIE SELECTIVE (1867-1970). Trois-Rivières, Québec: Editions Boréal Express, 1970. 189 p.

9. Easterbrook, W[illiam] T[homas]. "Recent Contributions to Economic History: Canada." JOURNAL OF ECONOMIC HISTORY 19 (March 1959): 76-102.

10. Fulford, Robert, et al., eds. READ CANADIAN, A BOOK ABOUT CANADIAN BOOKS. Toronto: James, Lewis, and Samuel, 1972. xi, 273 p.

11. Morton, W[illiam] L[ewis], and Creighton, D[onald] G[rant], eds. A HISTORY OF CANADA. Canadian Centenary Series. 18 vols. Toronto: McClelland & Stewart, 1963-74.

12. Nish, Cameron. "Bibliographie des bibliographies relatives à l'histoire économique du Canada français." L'ACTUALITE ECONOMIQUE 40 (July-September 1964): 456-66.

13. _____. "Bibliographie sur l'histoire économique du Canada français." L'ACTUALITE ECONOMIQUE 40 (April-June 1964): 200-209.

14. REVUE D'HISTOIRE DE L'AMERIQUE FRANCAISE. Montréal: L'Institut d'histoire de l'Amérique francaise, 1947-- . Quarterly.

15. Wood, W[illiam] D., et al. CANADIAN GRADUATE THESES 1919-1967: AN ANNOTATED BIBLIOGRAPHY. Kingston, Ontario: Industrial Relations Centre, Queen's University, 1970. xiv, 483 p.

Chapter II

FROM COLONIAL TIMES TO THE PRESENT

While the literature spanning the entire period is substantial, there are notable gaps in a number of topic areas. Many of the references cited were not specifically written as economic history, although major attention is frequently paid in them to one or more important topics in economic history.

II.A. TEXTS AND GENERAL WORKS

The distinction made between texts and general works is based on whether or not the reference is suitable as a comprehensive teaching aid for an undergraduate class in Canadian economic history. Surprisingly few items are available from this instructional point of view.

II.A.i. Texts

The standard text, item 4, remains unrevised since its inception over fifteen years ago, and as a result, lacks the benefit of more recent scholarship during this period. It also tends to emphasize the pre-Confederation period relative to the twentieth century. In 2, the regional dimension of Canadian economic growth is a main theme. Chapters 2, 5, and 6 of item 1 also present a regional outlook, and integrate this with an analytical statement of the staples approach. Though short, chapter 7 of 3 is provocative, and raises some unanswered questions for economic analysis.

II.A.i. Texts

1. Caves, Richard E[arl], and Holton, Richard H. THE CANADIAN ECONOMY; PROSPECT AND RETROSPECT. Harvard Economic Studies, no. 112. Cambridge, Mass.: Harvard University Press, 1961. xxii, 676 p. Diagrams. Bibliography, pp. 647-69.

Colonial Times to Present

2.   Currie, Archibald William. CANADIAN ECONOMIC DEVELOPMENT; FROM THE FRENCH REGIME TO THE PRESENT-DAY CANADA OF TEN PROVINCES. 3d ed. Toronto: Nelson, 1960. viii, 454 p. Bibliography.

3.   Drummond, Ian M[acdonald]. THE CANADIAN ECONOMY, ORGANIZATION AND DEVELOPMENT. Rev. ed. Homewood, Ill.: Irwin, 1972. Bibliographic references.

4.   Easterbrook, W[illiam] T[homas], and Aitken, Hugh G.J. CANADIAN ECONOMIC HISTORY. Toronto: Macmillan of Canada, 1967. 606 p. Illustrations. Chapter bibliographies.

II.A.ii. General Works

Perhaps the most common theme in expositions of Canadian development has been the interplay among Great Britain, the United States, and Canada, and the consequences of this interplay for the rise and fall of the staple export trades of Canada. From this perspective, the emergence of political independence has not been accompanied by economic independence. Though many general Canadian histories tend to exalt the achievement of nationhood, they also note the fact of continuing economic interdependence. In the general histories, items 2, 3, 5, 6, 12, 13, 15, 19, and 20, the authors concentrate on these themes. Creighton and Lower, in particular, in 6 and 12, are sensitive to the viability of a developing Canadian economy. Item 17 is a composite volume including contributions on the political and social, as well as economic, interrelatedness of Canadian-U.S. development. Item 19, though somewhat dated, remains a standard secondary work containing individually authored essays on almost every topic area in economic as well as political and social history. Volume 23 of this series contains a comprehensive index and extensive bibliography, and volume 18 includes essays on a number of topics in pre-1930 economic history. Item 4 also provides individually authored essays on economic and political aspects of Canadian development: see especially parts I, II, III, and VI. Items 7 and 21 provide short essays from different political viewpoints on the general theme of the interplay of British, American, and Canadian development.

Works limited to economic history include items 1, 8, 10, and 11. Chapters on the development of wheat, newsprint, and competition policy are included in 1. A concise application of the staples approach is found in 10, and part 2 of volume II of item II describes the Canadian contribution to the imperial economy. More recently, some of Faucher's writings on Canadian and Quebec economic history are brought together in 8. Through a number of studies differing widely in the time and space they focus upon, 14 presents a picture of the achievements of Canadian business historians.

Given the longstanding importance of resource-intensive exports to Canadian development, and the variety of economic regions within Canada, some references deal systematically with the topic from a regional point of view. In 9, economic aspects of regional development are treated, while 22 includes works by several authors on political and social topics as well, mainly since 1967. A useful account of the development of Canada's boundaries is found in 16. A one-page chart of the principal temporally overlapping themes of economic development is provided by 23.

II.A.ii. General Works

1. Bladen, Vincent Wheeler. AN INTRODUCTION TO POLITICAL ECONOMY. 3d ed., rev. Toronto: University of Toronto Press, 1956. viii, 319 p. Illustrations.

2. Brebner, John Bartlet. CANADA, A MODERN HISTORY. New ed., rev. and enl. by Donald C. Masters. Ann Arbor: University of Michigan Press, 1970. xvii, 570 p. Maps. Bibliography.

3. _____. NORTH ATLANTIC TRIANGLE: THE INTERPLAY OF CANADA, THE UNITED STATES AND GREAT BRITAIN. Toronto: Ryerson Press; New Haven, Conn.: Yale University Press, 1945. xxii, 385 p. Maps. Diagrams. Bibliographic notes, pp. 329-41. New ed. Introduction by D[onald] G[rant] Creighton. Carleton Library, no. 30. Toronto: McClelland & Stewart, 1966. xxviii, 377 p. Bibliography, pp. 337-57.

4. Brown, George Williams, ed. CANADA. Berkeley and Los Angeles: University of California Press, 1950. xviii, 621 p. Illustrations. Maps. Bibliography.

5. Careless, James Maurice Stockford. CANADA: A STORY OF CHALLENGE. 3d ed. Toronto: Macmillan of Canada, 1970. xiii, 444 p. Illustrations. Portraits. Maps.

6. Creighton, Donald Grant. DOMINION OF THE NORTH: A HISTORY OF CANADA. New ed. Toronto: Macmillan of Canada, 1962. ix, 619 p. Maps.

7. _____. TOWARDS THE DISCOVERY OF CANADA: SELECTED ESSAYS. Toronto: Macmillan of Canada, 1972. 315 p. Bibliographic references.

8. Faucher, Albert. HISTOIRE ECONOMIQUE ET UNITE CANADIENNE. Montréal: Fides, 1970. xxix, 296 p.

9. Howland, R.D. SOME REGIONAL ASPECTS OF CANADA'S ECONOMIC DEVELOPMENT. Royal Commission on Canada's Economic Prospects Study.

Colonial Times to Present

Ottawa: Queen's Printer, 1958. 302 p. Maps. Charts. Tables.

10. Innis, Mary Q. AN ECONOMIC HISTORY OF CANADA. New ed. Toronto: Ryerson Press, 1954. ix, 384 p. Illustrations.

11. Knowles, Lilian Charlotte Anne, and Knowles, C.M. THE ECONOMIC DEVELOPMENT OF THE BRITISH OVERSEAS EMPIRE. 3 vols. 2d ed., rev. London: Routledge, 1924-36.

12. Lower, Arthur Reginald Marsden. COLONY TO NATION: A HISTORY OF CANADA. 4th ed. Don Mills, Ontario: Longmans Green, 1964. xlv, 600 p. Maps. Diagrams. Bibliographic footnotes.

13. McInnis, Edgar. CANADA, A POLITICAL AND SOCIAL HISTORY. 3d ed. Toronto: Holt, Rinehart and Winston, 1969. xxii, 761 p. Illustrations. Maps. Bibliography.

14. Macmillan, David S., ed. CANADIAN BUSINESS HISTORY SELECTED STUDIES 1497-1971. Toronto: McClelland & Stewart, 1972. 346 p.

15. Morton, William Lewis. THE KINGDOM OF CANADA; A GENERAL HISTORY FROM EARLIEST TIMES. Toronto: McClelland & Stewart, 1963. 556 p. Maps. Bibliography, pp. 519-23.

16. Nicholson, Norman L. THE BOUNDARIES OF CANADA, ITS PROVINCES AND TERRITORIES. Canada, Department of Mines and Technical Surveys, Geographical Branch, memoir 2. Ottawa: Queen's Printer, 1954. ix, 142 p. Maps. Bibliographic references.

17. Preston, Richard Arthur, ed. THE INFLUENCE OF THE UNITED STATES ON CANADIAN DEVELOPMENT. Durham, N.C.: Duke University Press, 1972. xii, 269 p.

18. Rose, J. Holland, et al., eds. CANADA AND NEWFOUNDLAND. The Cambridge History of the British Empire, vol. 6. Cambridge: At the University Press, 1930. xxi, 939 p. Bibliography, pp. 813-85.

19. Shortt, Adam, and Doughty, Arthur G., eds. CANADA AND ITS PROVINCES, A HISTORY OF THE CANADIAN PEOPLE AND THEIR INSTITUTIONS. 23 vols. Toronto: Publishers' Association of Canada, 1913-17. Illustrations. Portraits. Maps. Facsimiles.

20. Trotter, Reginald George. CANADIAN FEDERATION, ITS ORIGINS AND ACHIEVEMENT: A STUDY IN NATION BUILDING. Toronto: Dent, 1924. 348 p. Illustrations. Bibliography.

21. Underhill, Frank Hawkins. THE IMAGE OF CONFEDERATION. The Massey Lectures, 3d series. Toronto: Canadian Broadcasting Corp., 1964. 84 p. Bibliography, pp. 79-84.

22. Wade, Mason, ed. REGIONALISM IN THE CANADIAN COMMUNITY 1867-1967; CANADIAN HISTORICAL ASSOCIATION CENTENNIAL SEMINARS. Toronto: University of Toronto Press, 1969. x, 300 p. Some essays in French. Bibliographic footnotes.

23. Wolfe, R.I. SPATIAL INTERACTION IN THE ECONOMIC HISTORY OF CANADA, 1800-1867. Toronto: Methuen, 1967. 1 p.

II.A.ii. General Works: The Maritimes

This region contains the territories included in the present-day provinces of Newfoundland, Nova Scotia, New Brunswick, and Prince Edward Island. A single volume, item 29, still remains the classic source. It is the most comprehensive in time and space, and includes relevant statistics. A useful supplement by the same author is 30, containing historical essays on individual topics. A number of the essays included in 27 also bear on economic topics, and 31 provides a general review of the efforts of business historians. Newfoundland entered Confederation only in 1949, and has received separate attention in items 24, 25, 26, and 28. In 24 and 25, annotated documentary impressions of economic change over a long period are given, while 26 is a comprehensive history including statistical materials. A concise coverage is given by 28. See also II.A.i.1, chapter 5 for a concise treatment documented by census materials.

II.A.ii. General Works: The Maritimes

24. Fay, Charles Ryle. CHANNEL ISLANDS AND NEWFOUNDLAND. Cambridge, Engl.: Heffer, 1961. v, 65 p. Sequel to his LIFE AND LABOUR IN NEWFOUNDLAND (item 25).

25. _____. LIFE AND LABOUR IN NEWFOUNDLAND; BASED ON LECTURES DELIVERED AT MEMORIAL UNIVERSITY OF NEWFOUNDLAND. Toronto: University of Toronto Press, 1956. vii, 254 p. Sequel: CHANNEL ISLANDS AND NEWFOUNDLAND (item 24).

26. MacKay, Robert Alexander, ed. NEWFOUNDLAND: ECONOMIC, DIPLOMATIC, AND STRATEGIC STUDIES. Toronto: Oxford University

Press, 1946. 577 p. Illustrations.

27. Rawlyk, G.A., ed. HISTORICAL ESSAYS ON THE ATLANTIC PROVINCES. Carleton Library, no. 35. Toronto: McClelland & Stewart, 1971. 263 p. Bibliography, pp. 260-63.

28. Rothney, Gordon Oliver. NEWFOUNDLAND FROM INTERNATIONAL FISHERY TO CANADIAN PROVINCE. Canadian Historical Association Booklet, no. 10. Ottawa: Canadian Archives, 1959. 27 p. Map. Bibliography on inside of back cover. Rev. ed. NEWFOUNDLAND, A HISTORY. 1964. 28 p.

29. Saunders, Stanley Alexander. "The Economic History of the Maritime Provinces." Royal Commission on Dominion-Provincial Relations. Ottawa: King's Printer, 1939. ii, 148 p. Mimeographed. Also issued in French.

30. _____. STUDIES IN THE ECONOMY OF THE MARITIME PROVINCES. Preface by H[arold] A[dams] Innis. Toronto: Macmillan of Canada, 1939. xii, 266 p.

31. Wilson, Alan. "Maritime Business History: A Reconnaissance of Records, Sources and Prospects." BUSINESS HISTORY REVIEW 47 (Summer 1973): 260-76.

II.A.ii. General Works: Quebec

Under the leadership of Pierre Harvey at the University of Montreal, French Canadian economic historians in recent years have undertaken substantial data gathering in writing the economic history of French Canada. These activities and the materials now available are described in 35. Further commentary on this work is found in 34. The collection of essays in 32 is divided into three parts: the first treats the economic history of French Canada from 1534 to 1965; the second deals with issues in historiography; and the third is a roundup of French Canadian economic thought. The structure of the modern economy of Quebec is described in 36. Chapter 6 of item 36 discusses the historical development of this structure. A useful collection of essays by Pierre Harvey, Maurice Sequin, Norman Taylor, Albert Faucher, and Maurice Lamontagne on the theme of Quebec's industrialization is contained in 33. For a standard, short, but outdated treatment, see also II.A.ii.19, volumes 15 and 16; for Faucher's collected essays on Quebec's economic development, see also II.A.ii.8, part 2.

II.A.ii. General Works: Quebec

32. Comeau, Robert, ed. ECONOMIE QUEBECOISE: LES CAHIERS DE L'UNIVERSITE DU QUEBEC. Montréal: Les Presses de l'Université du Québec, 1969. 495 p. Bibliographic footnotes.

33. Durocher, René, and Linteau, Paul-André, eds. LE "RETARD" DU QUEBEC ET L'INFERIORITE ECONOMIQUE DES CANADIENS-FRANCAIS. Collection d'études d'histoire du Québec, no. 1. Trois-Rivières, Québec: Editions Boréal Express, 1971. 127 p. Bibliography.

34. Harvey, Fernand, and Linteau, Paul-André. "L'Evolution de l'historiographie dans la revue d'histoire de l'amérique française 1947-1972, apercus quantitatifs." REVUE D'HISTOIRE DE L'AMERIQUE FRANCAISE 26 (September 1972): 163-83.

35. Nish, Cameron. RAPPORT SUR LES ACTIVITES DU CENTRE DE RECHERCHE EN HISTOIRE ECONOMIQUE DU CANADA FRANCAIS, 1965-1969. Montréal: Centre de recherche en histoire economique du Canada francais. 94 p.

36. Saint-Germain, Maurice. UNE ECONOMIE A LIBERER, LE QUEBEC ANALYSE DANS SES STRUCTURES ECONOMIQUES. Montréal: Les Presses de l'Université de Montréal, 1973. 471 p. Bibliography, pp. 425-49.

II.A.ii. General Works: Ontario

A comprehensive economic history of Ontario is yet to be written. A short introduction is provided by Innis in 37. The only full treatment is provided by the now dated volumes 17 and 18 of the Shortt and Doughty series, II.A.ii.19, and these do not go beyond World War I.

II.A.ii. General Works: Ontario

37. Innis, Harold Adams. "An Introduction to the Economic History of Ontario from Outpost to Empire." ONTARIO HISTORICAL SOCIETY PAPERS AND RECORDS 30 (1934): 111-23.

II.A.ii. General Works: The West

There is no economic history specifically for the west but some well-documented general histories serve as useful points of departure. For Manitoba and British

Columbia, items 42 and 43 respectively are comprehensive, and cover the entire time span. See also 39 for a history of Manitoba. British Columbia's economic and political interrelations with the United States from colonial times to the 1930s are treated in 38. A comprehensive British Columbian history centered about the salmon industry is provided by 40. For Alberta, see item 41, and for Saskatchewan, 45. The collection of essays in 44 is particularly useful for political topics and protest movements, often economic in origin.

II.A.ii. General Works: The West

38. Howay, Frederic William, et al. BRITISH COLUMBIA AND THE UNITED STATES; THE NORTH PACIFIC SLOPE FROM FUR TRADE TO AVIATION. New York: Russell & Russell, 1970. xv, 408 p. Maps.

39. Jackson, James A. THE CENTENNIAL HISTORY OF MANITOBA. Toronto: McClelland & Stewart, 1970. 270 p. Illustrations.

40. Lyons, Cicely. SALMON, OUR HERITAGE, THE STORY OF A PROVINCE AND AN INDUSTRY. Vancouver, British Columbia: Mitchell Press, 1969. xv, 768 p. Illustrations (some in color). Maps. Bibliography, pp. 749-52.

41. MacGregor, James G. A HISTORY OF ALBERTA. Edmonton, Alberta: Hurtig, 1972. 335 p. Maps. Illustrations.

42. Morton, William Lewis. MANITOBA; A HISTORY. 2d ed. Toronto: University of Toronto Press, 1967. xii, 547 p. Illustrations. Bibliography.

43. Ormsby, Margaret A. BRITISH COLUMBIA: A HISTORY. Rev. ed. Vancouver, British Columbia: Macmillan of Canada, 1971. x, 566 p. Illustrations (some in color). Bibliographic footnotes. Bibliography, pp. 527-35.

44. Swainson, Donald, ed. HISTORICAL ESSAYS ON THE PRAIRIE PROVINCES. Carleton Library, no. 53. Toronto: McClelland & Stewart, 1970. xiii, 312 p. Bibliography, pp. 300-312.

45. Wright, J.F.C. SASKATCHEWAN, THE HISTORY OF A PROVINCE. Toronto: McClelland & Stewart, 1955. xi, 292 p. Illustrations. Bibliography, pp. 282-83.

II.B. STATISTICAL RECORD

Comprehensive statistical sources suffer from a lack of continuity in many series covering long periods of time. Often the decennial census is the only source of published information. The construction of some key economic statistics from primary sources remains an unfinished task. Before 1926, for example, there is still no general agreement on the figures for national income. Pre-World War I data on manufactures are frequently scarce and unorganized. For the colonial period, statistical documentation is thin. Overall, trade statistics are the most continuous and reliable. The most ambitious and complete collection of historical statistics is found in 2. Although some data on colonial production and trade are included in 2, many of the data series start only after World War I. This work represents only the collection under one cover of data series already existing, rather than the construction of new data. The volume is divided into a number of sections (for example, population, lands and forests, agriculture, manufacturing, international trade, banking), each compiled, introduced, and annotated by a subject matter specialist. The terminal date is 1960. In 1, Kerr provides a cartographic picture of early exploration and settlement, and treats political as well as economic development to the mid-twentieth century.

II.B. STATISTICAL RECORD

1. Kerr, D[onald] G.G., ed. A HISTORICAL ATLAS OF CANADA. Toronto: Nelson, 1960. ix, 120 p.

2. Urquhart, M.C., and Buckley, K[enneth] A.H., eds. HISTORICAL STATISTICS OF CANADA. Sponsored by the Canadian Political Science Association and the Social Science Research Council of Canada. Toronto: Macmillan of Canada, 1965. xv, 672 p.

II.C. THESES OF ECONOMIC GROWTH

Interpretations or approaches to Canadian economic history are dominated by the unifying theme of staples. Two of the earliest statements of this approach are found in 18 and 20. More recent consolidations of the same viewpoint are found in 11 below, and part 1 of I.A.4. The staple theme was given its most thorough development by Innis, starting with 15 and with a number of the essays reprinted in 14. A heavy emphasis on technology and communications in much of Innis's later work, as found in 12 and 13, is indicative of that author's search for a more general framework. A similar thrust is evident in 7 and 22. Since the time of Innis, dissatisfaction with staples as a single unifying theme has grown, though no equally persuasive approach has been found. The desire for revision and a new synthesis was heralded by Buckley in 1.

The response to this challenge has taken various forms. Some have searched the writings of Innis for hidden clues and a new point of departure, as in 3, 19, and I.A.7. Others have noted the contrast between the British North American and the United States frontier experiences, as in 2, 17, 23, 24, 25, and 29. Some have defended the staples approach as still fundamentally relevant to Canadian development even at the mid-twentieth century, as in 27. A link between entrepreneurship, the role of the state, and metropolitan influences has been forged and welded to the staples approach, particularly by Easterbrook in 4, 5, 6, and 8. The role of the state is further elaborated by various authors in 16 and by Aitken in II.E.iii.2. The conclusions of leading writers on a number of different issues, including the national policy of the nineteenth century, are compared and contrasted in 21. Quantitative research has so far made little impact on these broad questions of interpretation. However some specification and testing of staple type hypotheses have been undertaken, as in 26 and in IV.D.i.5. The long-swing hypothesis is examined in 10. Finally, 28 is a pioneer attempt to employ the comparative approach.

II.C. THESES OF ECONOMIC GROWTH

1. Buckley, K[enneth A.H.]. "The Role of Staple Industries in Canada's Economic Development." JOURNAL OF ECONOMIC HISTORY 18 (December 1958): 429-50.

2. Cross, Michael Sean, ed. THE FRONTIER THESIS AND THE CANADAS: THE DEBATE ON THE IMPACT OF THE CANADIAN ENVIRONMENT. Issues in Canadian History. Toronto: Copp Clark, 1970. 188 p. Bibliography, pp. 186-88.

3. Easterbrook, W[illiam] T[homas]. "Innis and Economics." CANADIAN JOURNAL OF ECONOMICS AND POLITICAL SCIENCE 19 (August 1953): 291-303.

4. _____. "Long Period Comparative Study: Some Historical Cases." JOURNAL OF ECONOMIC HISTORY 18 (December 1957): 571-95.

5. _____. "Political Economy of Enterprise." CANADIAN JOURNAL OF ECONOMICS AND POLITICAL SCIENCE 14 (August 1949): 322-33.

6. _____. "Possibilities for a Realistic Theory of Entrepreneurship--Climate of Enterprise." AMERICAN ECONOMIC REVIEW 39 (May 1949): 322-35.

7. _____. "Problems in the Relationship of Communications and Economic History." JOURNAL OF ECONOMIC HISTORY 20 (December 1960): 559-65.

8. _____. "Uncertainty and Economic Change." JOURNAL OF ECONOMIC HISTORY 14 (Autumn 1954): 346-60.

9. Fay, C[harles] R[yle]. "The Toronto School of Economic History." ECONOMIC HISTORY 3 (January 1934): 168-71.

10. Harkness, J.P. "A Spectral-Analytic Test of the Long-Swing Hypothesis in Canada." REVIEW OF ECONOMICS AND STATISTICS 50 (November 1968): 429-36.

11. Hartland, P.E. "Factors in Economic Growth in Canada." JOURNAL OF ECONOMIC HISTORY 15 (March 1955): 13-22.

12. Innis, Harold A[dams]. THE BIAS OF COMMUNICATIONS. Toronto: University of Toronto Press, 1951. 226 p. New ed. Introduction by Marshall McLuhan. Canadian University Paperbacks, no. 26. Toronto: University of Toronto Press, 1964. xviii, 226 p. Bibliographic footnotes.

13. _____. EMPIRE AND COMMUNICATIONS. Beit Lectures on Imperial Economic History, 1948. Oxford: Oxford University Press, 1950. 230 p.

14. _____. ESSAYS IN CANADIAN ECONOMIC HISTORY. Toronto: University of Toronto Press, 1956. vi, 418 p.

15. _____. "Significant Factors in Canadian Economic Development." CANADIAN HISTORICAL REVIEW 18 (December 1936): 374-84.

16. _____, ed. ESSAYS IN POLITICAL ECONOMY. Toronto: University of Toronto Press, 1938. xii, 236 p.

17. McDougall, John L[orne]. "The Frontier School of Canadian Historiography." CANADIAN HISTORICAL ASSOCIATION ANNUAL REPORT (1929): 121-25.

18. Mackintosh, W[illiam] A[rchibald]. "Economic Factors in Canadian History." CANADIAN HISTORICAL REVIEW 4 (March 1923): 12-25.

19. _____. "Innis on Canadian Economic Development." JOURNAL OF POLITICAL ECONOMY 61 (June 1953): 185-94.

20. _____. "Some Aspects of a Pioneer Economy." CANADIAN JOURNAL OF ECONOMICS AND POLITICAL SCIENCE 2 (November 1936): 457-63.

Colonial Times to Present

21. MacKirdy, Kenneth A., et al. CHANGING PERSPECTIVES IN CANADIAN HISTORY. SELECTED PROBLEMS. Notre Dame, Ind.: University of Notre Dame, 1967. xxxiii, 373 p. Bibliographic references.

22. McLuhan, M[arshall]. "Effects of the Improvements of Communications Media." JOURNAL OF ECONOMIC HISTORY 20 (December 1960): 566-75.

23. McRae, K.D. "The Structure of Canadian History." In THE FOUNDING OF NEW SOCIETIES: STUDIES IN THE HISTORY OF THE UNITED STATES, LATIN AMERICA, SOUTH AFRICA, CANADA AND AUSTRALIA, edited by Louis Hartz, pp. 219-74. New York: Harcourt and Brace, 1964. Bibliographic references included in notes, pp. 319-30.

24. Sage, Walter Noble. "Some Aspects of the Frontier in Canadian History." CANADIAN HISTORICAL ASSOCIATION ANNUAL REPORT, 1928, pp. 62-72.

25. Stanley, George F[rances] G[ilman]. "Western Canada and the Frontier Thesis." CANADIAN HISTORICAL ASSOCIATION ANNUAL REPORT, 1940, pp. 105-17.

26. Vickery, Edward. "Exports and North American Economic Growth: 'Structuralist' and 'Staple' Models in Historical Perspective." CANADIAN JOURNAL OF ECONOMICS 7 (February 1974): 32-58.

27. Watkins, M[elville] H. "A Staple Theory of Economic Growth." CANADIAN JOURNAL OF ECONOMICS AND POLITICAL SCIENCE 29 (May 1963): 141-58.

28. Young, J.H. "Comparative Economic Development: Canada and the United States." AMERICAN ECONOMIC REVIEW 45 (May 1955): 80-93.

29. Zaslow, M[orris]. "The Frontier Hypothesis in Canadian Historiography." CANADIAN HISTORICAL REVIEW 29 (June 1948): 153-66.

II.D. SECTOR AND INDUSTRIES

As nearly as possible, the classification followed here among primary, secondary, and tertiary activities is based on the degree to which each activity is resource-intensive. Insofar as the story of Canada's development is in part a gradual change in economic structure increasing the importance of secondary relative to primary activities, many of the best works in each category cover a more limited

Colonial Times to Present

span of time than is envisioned in the title of chapter II, "From Colonial Times to the Present." Insofar as many primary activities, like agriculture, have endured, and some secondary activities are of very early origin, however, there are some major works covering long-period change in these areas. The Canadian, or British North American, economy displayed a tendency toward substantial tertiary activities earlier in its growth than many other developing economies, and as a consequence, long-period studies, especially in the field of transportation, have been written.

II.D.i. Sectors and Industries: Primary Industry

The importance of staples in Canadian economic development is the keynote of major works under this heading. Comprehensive accounts of the early staples from colonial times to the present are found (in order of their successive dominance) in 3 and 6 (fish), in 7 and 14 (fur), in 13 and 15 (forest products), in 1, 9, and 12 (agriculture), and in 2, 5, 10, and 11 (mining).

For the earliest staples, fish and fur, 6 and 7 provide minute detail and documentation combined with an interpretation that visualizes these staples to have had a unique formative influence on economic development. Considerable statistical evidence is included in 3, 6, and 7. A concise history of the Hudson's Bay Company is provided by 14, concentrating on the years before 1900.

The development of forest industries in three major geographic areas is treated in 13. Central Canadian activity prior to the development of the pulp and paper industry is dealt with by A.R.M. Lower in the first section; in the second section, W.A. Carrothers traces the growth of British Columbia's lumber and pulp and paper industries into the twentieth century, while the third section by S.A. Saunders treats the development of forest industries in the maritimes. A comprehensive French language treatment of the history of forest industries in Quebec is provided by 15. An excellent statistical record for Canada, Quebec, and Ontario is included. Statistical material is also provided in 13.

A comprehensive history of Canadian agriculture is yet to be written. Some short essays stressing long-period change include 1 and several essays in II.C.14. An introduction to the history of Quebec agriculture is found in 12. For the dairy industry, 9 provides an introductory historical essay by Innis and four additional sections on the state of the industry in the 1930s.

The best overall view of mining history is 11. More concise is 10, addressing the particular roles played by important personalities. A more popularized version is 5. For a good statistical account, see 2.

Interpretive and analytical work in this area is fairly extensive. Among the more general and comprehensive items are 4 and 8. The essays in 8 range over such topics as transportation, iron and steel, the Canadian Pacific Railroad, government ownership, the Canadian North, settlement, and the depression of the 1930s. The conference proceedings recorded in 4 bring to bear a number of analytical points of view including the staples approach and the economics of conservation and property rights.

II.D.i. Sectors and Industries: Primary Industry

1. Burton, F.W. "Wheat in Canadian History." CANADIAN JOURNAL OF ECONOMICS AND POLITICAL SCIENCE 3 (May 1937): 210-17.

2. Canada. Dominion Bureau of Statistics. CHRONOLOGICAL RECORD OF CANADIAN MINING EVENTS FROM 1604 TO 1947 AND HISTORICAL TABLES OF MINERAL PRODUCTION IN CANADA. Ottawa: King's Printer, 1948.

3. Carrothers, W.A. THE BRITISH COLUMBIA FISHERIES. Toronto: University of Toronto Press, 1941. xii, 136 p.

4. Crabbé, Philippe, and Spry, Irene M., eds. NATURAL RESOURCE DEVELOPMENT IN CANADA. Proceedings of University of Ottawa Natural Resource Development Seminar, 1970-71. University of Ottawa Social Science Studies, no. 8. Ottawa: University of Ottawa Press, 1973. xii, 344 p. Bibliographic references.

5. Hoffman, Arnold David. FREE GOLD: THE STORY OF CANADIAN MINING. Illustrations by Irwin D. Hoffman. New York: Rinehart, 1947. 420 p. Illustrations.

6. Innis, Harold Adams. COD FISHERIES: THE HISTORY OF AN INTERNATIONAL ECONOMY. New Haven, Conn.: Yale University Press, 1940. 520 p. Maps. Tables.

7. _____. THE FUR TRADE IN CANADA: AN INTRODUCTION TO CANADIAN ECONOMIC HISTORY. Rev. ed. Toronto: University of Toronto Press, 1956. 463 p. Bibliography, pp. 421-41.

8. _____. PROBLEMS OF STAPLE PRODUCTION IN CANADA. Toronto: Ryerson Press, 1933. 124 p. Illustrations.

9. _____, ed. THE DAIRY INDUSTRY IN CANADA. Toronto: Ryerson Press, 1937. xxxii, 299 p. Bibliographies.

10. Jones, Lawrence F., and Lonn, George. HISTORICAL HIGHLIGHTS OF CANADIAN MINING. Toronto: Pitt, 1973. xiii, 274 p. Bibliography, pp. 272-74.

Colonial Times to Present

11. Le Bourdais, Donat Marc. METALS AND MEN; THE STORY OF CANA-
    DIAN MINING. Toronto: McClelland & Stewart, 1957. 416 p.
    Illustrations (some in color). Portraits. Maps. Map on end paper.

12. Létourneau, Firmin. HISTOIRE DE L'AGRICULTURE (CANADA FRAN-
    CAIS). Québec: Privately published, 1968. 399 p. Bibliographic
    references.

13. Lower, Arthur Reginald Marsden; Carrothers, W.A.; and Saunders,
    S[tanley] A[lexander]. THE NORTH AMERICAN ASSAULT ON THE
    CANADIAN FOREST; A HISTORY OF THE LUMBER TRADE BETWEEN
    CANADA AND THE UNITED STATES; WITH STUDIES OF THE FOREST
    INDUSTRIES IN BRITISH COLUMBIA, and THE FOREST INDUSTRIES IN
    THE MARITIME PROVINCES. Toronto: Ryerson Press, 1938. xxvii,
    377 p. Illustrations. Maps (one folding).

14. MacKay, Douglas. THE HONOURABLE COMPANY: A HISTORY OF
    THE HUDSON'S BAY COMPANY. Maps by R.H.H. Macaulay. Toronto:
    McClelland & Stewart, 1936. 396 p. Illustrations. Bibliography. 2d
    ed., rev. by Alice MacKay. Toronto: McClelland & Stewart, 1949.

15. Minville, Esdras, ed. LA FORET. Montréal: Fides, 1944. 409 p.
    Statistical appendix.

II.D.ii. Sectors and Industries: Secondary Industry

Only fragments of a history of Canadian manufactures have been written. A
short overview is provided in 6. A more detailed account with a Rostovian
flavor, and starting with Confederation, is 7. In item 7, Firestone also includes
national income statistics from 1867, and data on education from 1926. A detailed study of American participation in Canadian industry and vice-versa is
reported in 10, which covers the subject up to the 1930s. Research on the
changing composition of Canadian industry is reported in 9. The best statistical source, not only for Quebec, but for Canada also, is 1.

The histories of a number of individual manufacturing firms have been written.
See, for example, 3, 4, 5, 8, 11, 12, 13, and 14. Some of these, especially 4, 5, 11, and 12, are quite detailed, and include some statistical documentation and analysis. In general, however, there are many gaps and a lack
of uniformity in quality.

In the closely related area of urban history some work is beginning to appear.
For a review of this, see 2.

II.D.ii. Sectors and Industries: Secondary Industry

1. Angers, François Albert, and Parenteau, Roland. STATISTIQUES MANUFACTURIERES DU QUEBEC, 1665-1948. Montréal Ecole des Hautes Etudes Commerciales, Institut d'Economie Appliquée, Etude no. 15. Montréal: Institut de Science Economique. Appliquées, Ecole des Hautes Etudes Commerciales, 1966. 166 p.

2. Armstrong, Frederick H. "Urban History in Canada: Present State and Future Prospects." URBAN HISTORY REVIEW, no. 1 (February 1972), pp. 11-14.

3. Denison, Merrill. BARLEY AND STEAM: THE MOLSON STORY. Toronto: McClelland & Stewart, 1955. xiv, 389 p. Illustrations.

4. _____. HARVEST TRIUMPHANT: THE STORY OF MASSEY-HARRIS. Toronto: McClelland & Stewart, 1948. xii, 351 p. Illustrations.

5. Donald, William John Alexander. THE CANADIAN IRON AND STEEL INDUSTRY: A STUDY IN THE ECONOMIC HISTORY OF A PROTECTED INDUSTRY. Boston: Houghton Mifflin, 1915. 376 p. Illustrations.

6. Easterbrook, W[illiam] T[homas]. "Industrial Development in Canada." In ENCYCLOPEDIA AMERICANA, International ed., vol. 5, pp. 347-53.

7. Firestone, O[tto] J[ack]. INDUSTRY AND EDUCATION: A CENTURY OF CANADIAN DEVELOPMENT. Social Science Studies, no. 5. Ottawa: University of Ottawa Press, 1969. xviii, 295 p. Preface in English and French; summaries in French. Bibliographic footnotes.

8. Kilbourn, William. THE ELEMENTS COMBINED, A HISTORY OF THE STEEL COMPANY OF CANADA. Toronto: Clarke Irwin, 1960. xxii, 335 p. Illustrations in color. Diagrams. Tables in color. Bibliography, pp. 307-14.

9. McInnis, R. Marvin. "Long-Term Changes in Industrial Composition: With Particular Reference to Canada." In PROCEEDINGS OF THE INTERNATIONAL CONGRESS OF ECONOMIC HISTORY, 1970.

10. Marshall, H[ebert], et al. CANADIAN-AMERICAN INDUSTRY: A STUDY IN INTERNATIONAL INVESTMENT. With an excursus on the Canadian balance of payments by Frank A. Knox. New Haven, Conn.: Yale University Press, 1936. 360 p. Illustrations.

Colonial Times to Present

11. Neufeld, Edward Peter. A GLOBAL CORPORATION, A HISTORY OF THE INTERNATIONAL DEVELOPMENT OF MASSEY-FERGUSON LTD. Toronto: University of Toronto Press, 1969. ix, 427 p. Illustrations (some in color). Bibliographic footnotes.

12. Phillips, William Gregory. THE AGRICULTURAL IMPLEMENT INDUSTRY IN CANADA: STUDY IN COMPETITION. Canadian Studies in Economics, no. 7. Toronto: University of Toronto Press, 1956. xi, 208 p. Illustrations. Diagrams. Tables. Bibliographic references included in notes, pp. 165-94.

13. Ritchie, Thomas. CANADA BUILDS 1867-1967. Toronto: University of Toronto Press, 1967. vii, 406 p. Illustrations. Maps. Portraits. Bibliography, pp. 389-97.

14. Stevens, George Roy. OGILVIE IN CANADA--PIONEER MILLERS, 1801-1951. Toronto: Ashton-Potter, 1952. 70 p. Illustrations. Portraits.

II.D.iii. Sectors and Industries: Tertiary Industry

The areas of tertiary industry that have so far received the main attention of economic historians are transportation and banking. This is partly a reflection of the early and long lasting commercial orientation of the economy associated with the staple trades.

Still the most important comprehensive source on transportation development is item 8. For the development of navigation on the Great Lakes, see also 6 and 18. For a definitive history of the Grand Trunk to the formation of the Canadian National Railways after World War I, see 2 and 16. The development of Canada-U.S. rail connections is treated in 17. Most aspects of the transportation story are also covered by selected essays in II.A.ii.19. For interpretative essays discussing transportation problems and the role of transportation in development, see 9, 10, and 11. In 11, such topics as nationalism, financing, rates, and the impact of transportation on agriculture are discussed. The general problem of rate setting and its evolution are concisely treated in 9. The history of another aspect of communications--journalism--is thoroughly documented in 12. For a concise account of the history of Canadian journalism by the same author, see also I.B.2, pages 920-34 for 1957-58, and pages 883-902 for 1959.

Probably the best single history of banking and fiscal development is 13. A useful companion to this is the set of annotated documents provided by 15. For short treatments of the history of banking and currency, see 3, 4, and 5. The history of the oldest and most enduring Canadian bank is exhaustively chronicled in 7. For a comprehensive history of financial intermediation, see 14. For a shorter treatment, see chapter 12 of item 1, or chapter 19 of II.A.i.4.

II.D.iii. Sectors and Industries: Tertiary Industry

1. Bond, David E., and Shearer, Ronald A. THE ECONOMICS OF THE CANADIAN FINANCIAL SYSTEM: THEORY, POLICY AND INSTITUTIONS. Scarborough, Ontario: Prentice-Hall of Canada, 1972. xiv, 633 p. Bibliographic footnotes.

2. Currie, Archibald William. THE GRAND TRUNK RAILWAY OF CANADA. Toronto: University of Toronto Press, 1957. viii, 556 p. Illustrations. Map.

3. Curtis, C[lifford] A[ustin]. "Banking." In ENCYCLOPEDIA OF CANADA, edited by W. Stewart Wallace, vol. 1, pp. 151-64. Toronto: University Associates of Canada, 1935-37.

4. _____. "Currency." In ENCYCLOPEDIA OF CANADA, edited by W. Stewart Wallace, vol. 2, pp. 159-67. Toronto: University Associates of Canada, 1935-37.

5. _____. "Evolution of Canadian Banking." In ANNALS OF THE AMERICAN ACADEMY OF POLITICAL SOCIAL SCIENCE, vol. 253, pp. 115-24.

6. Cuthbertson, George A. FRESHWATER: A HISTORY AND NARRATIVE OF THE GREAT LAKES. Toronto: Macmillan of Canada, 1931. 315 p. Illustrations. Plates (some in color). Bibliography, pp. 305-7.

7. Denison, Merrill. CANADA'S FIRST BANK: A HISTORY OF THE BANK OF MONTREAL. 2 vols. Toronto: McClelland & Stewart, 1966-67. Illustrations (some folding, some in color). Facsimiles. Portraits (some folding, some in color). Bibliography.

8. Glazebrook, George Parkin de Twenebroker. A HISTORY OF TRANSPORTATION IN CANADA. Foreword by H[arold] A[dams] Innis. Toronto: Ryerson Press, 1938. 475 p. Folding maps. New ed. 2 vols. Carleton Library, nos. 11 and 12. Toronto: McClelland & Stewart, 1964. xiv, 191 p.; 276 p. Bibliography.

9. Innis, H[arold] A[dams]. "Memorandum on Transportation." In REPORT OF ROYAL COMMISSION ON TRANSPORTATION, 1951, pp. 294-307. Ottawa: King's Printer, 1951.

10. _____. "Transportation as a Factor in Canadian Economic History." PAPERS AND PROCEEDINGS OF THE CANADIAN POLITICAL SCIENCE ASSOCIATION 3, 1931, pp. 166-84.

Colonial Times to Present

11. _____, ed. ESSAYS IN TRANSPORTATION IN HONOUR OF W.T. JACKMEN. Political Economy Series, no. 11. Toronto: University of Toronto Press, 1941. viii, 165 p.

12. Kesterton, Wilfred N. A HISTORY OF JOURNALISM IN CANADA. Carleton Library, no. 36. Toronto: McClelland & Stewart, 1967. ix, 304 p. Bibliographic references.

13. McIvor, R. Craig. CANADIAN MONETARY, BANKING AND FISCAL DEVELOPMENT. Toronto: Macmillan of Canada, 1958. xix, 263 p. Tables. Bibliography, pp. 253-56.

14. Neufeld, E[dward] P[eter]. THE FINANCIAL SYSTEM OF CANADA, ITS GROWTH AND DEVELOPMENT. Toronto: Macmillan of Canada, 1972. xxi, 645 p. Bibliographic footnotes. Statistical appendix.

15. _____, ed. MONEY AND BANKING IN CANADA. Carleton Library, no. 17. Toronto: McClelland & Stewart, 1964. 369 p.

16. Stevens, George Roy. CANADIAN NATIONAL RAILWAYS. Foreword by Donald [F.] Gordon; introduction by S.W. Fairweather. 2 vols. Toronto: Clarke Irwin, 1960-62. xviii, 514 p.; xii, 547 p. Illustrations. Portraits. Maps. Bibliography.

17. Wilgus, William John. THE RAILWAY INTERRELATIONS OF THE UNITED STATES AND CANADA. New Haven, Conn.: Yale University Press, 1937. xvi, 304 p. Maps. Bibliography, pp. 235-43.

18. Wood, William [D.]. ALL AFLOAT; A CHRONICLE OF CRAFT AND WATERWAYS. Chronicles of Canada, no. 31. Toronto: Gasgow, Brook, 1914. 199 p. Illustrations.

II.E. ECONOMIC ORGANIZATION

Economic activities may be coordinated either privately or publicly. It is useful to divide the topic of economic organization further between industrial organization and the organization of labor. Industrial organization typically refers to the market structure of producers, and labor organization refers to the voluntary unionization of workers. Government coordination involves all aspects of government participation in and regulation of the economy, including the development of property rights.

Colonial Times to Present

II.E.i. Economic Organization: Industrial Organization

A useful analysis relating industrial organization and property rights to various stages in the development of extractive industries is provided in item 1. The spread of the multinational corporation is partially covered in II.D.ii.10. For another account, especially for the period 1870-1914, see chapter 7 of item 2 below.

II.E.i. Economic Organization: Industrial Organization

1. Scott, A[nthony Dalton]. "The Development of Extractive Industries." CANADIAN JOURNAL OF ECONOMICS AND POLITICAL SCIENCE 28 (February 1962): 70-87.

2. Wilkins, Mira. THE EMERGENCE OF MULTINATIONAL ENTERPRISE: AMERICAN BUSINESS ABROAD FROM THE COLONIAL ERA TO 1914. Cambridge, Mass.: Harvard University Press, 1970. xiv, 310 p. Bibliography, pp. 221-52.

II.E.ii. Economic Organization: Labor Organization

The most detailed and complete histories of labor organization so far written are 6 and its predecessor 5. A concise summary of the growth of the labor movement may be found in chapter 1 of 4, or in 2 and 3. International aspects of the union movement are discussed in the first part of 8, and in 7 and 1. See also chapter 22 of II.A.i.4.

II.E.ii. Economic Organization: Labor Organization

1. Abella, Irving Martin. NATIONALISM, COMMUNISM AND CANADIAN LABOUR: THE CIO, THE COMMUNIST PARTY AND THE CANADIAN CONGRESS OF LABOUR 1935-56. Toronto: University of Toronto Press, 1973. vii, 256 p. Bibliography, pp. 243-47.

2. Forsey, Eugene. "History of the Labour Movement in Canada." In CANADA YEARBOOK 1957-58, pp. 795-802. Ottawa: Dominion Bureau of Statistics, 1958.

3. _____. "Insights into Labour History." INDUSTRIAL RELATIONS 20 (July 1965): 445-65.

Colonial Times to Present

4. Jamieson, Stuart [Marshall]. INDUSTRIAL RELATIONS IN CANADA. 2d ed. Toronto: Macmillan of Canada, 1973. 142 p. Bibliography, pp. 143-51.

5. Logan, Harold Amos. THE HISTORY OF TRADE UNION ORGANIZATION IN CANADA. Chicago: University of Chicago Press, 1928. 427 p.

6. _____. TRADE UNIONS IN CANADA: THEIR DEVELOPMENT AND FUNCTIONING. Toronto: Macmillan of Canada, 1948. 639 p. Illustrations.

7. Shotwell, James Thompson, ed. THE ORIGINS OF THE INTERNATIONAL LABOR ORGANIZATION. 2 vols. New York: Columbia University Press, 1934. Vol. 1, History, xxx, 497 p.; vol. 2, Documents, xiii, 592 p. Folding tables.

8. Ware, Norman J., and Logan, H[arold] A[mos]. LABOUR IN CANADIAN-AMERICAN RELATIONS: THE HISTORY OF LABOUR INTERACTION; LABOUR COSTS AND LABOUR STANDARDS. Edited by H[arold] A[dams] Innis. Toronto: Ryerson Press, 1937. 212 p. Illustrations.

II.E.iii. Economic Organization: The Role of Government

For a general introduction to the overall effect of government intervention on Canadian economic development, see items 1, 2, 5, and II.A.i.1, chapter 7. The interpretation given by 1 and 2 is consistent with the nationbuilding theme of historiography. An economic rationale for the nationalistic behavior of governments is given in chapter 1 of item 11, and applied to Canada in chapter 6 of the same source. A related aspect of political behavior is treated in 17. A more diverse and less rigorous interpretation is found among the essays collected together in 10. Aside from these efforts, there are perhaps four main strands of writing in this area: (1) the development of an independent fiscal and commercial policy, (2) the emergence of resource development policies and property rights over resources, (3) the formation of a competition policy, and (4) the evolution of policy toward labor organization.

Fundamental to the emergence of taxing and spending policies is the formation and modification of the constitution, briefly reviewed in 23 and 20. See also I.B.2 for 1942, pages 34-59, and for 1956, pages 101-7. By far the best source on the history of commercial policy is 13, which also attempts to assess the impact of that policy. This account may be supplemented by 3 and 4. The most comprehensive and detailed work on fiscal development, including the tariff, is 18. This also includes a lengthy statistical appendix, concentrating

Colonial Times to Present

on the post-1867 period.

A short introduction to resource policy is provided by 7. Item 16 is a significant and carefully documented landmark in exploring and interpreting the interaction between government and three major resource industries in Ontario. Equally impressive along the same lines, though less interpretive, is 12, for its treatment of Ontario forestland management. In 19, the main emphasis is on economic issues, but a historical account of the development of relevant property rights is also appended. An invaluable study for exposing the persistent pattern of agricultural policy is 8.

Several works deal with regional aspects of government policy. One chapter of 6 relates regional policies to the historical development of resource-intensive staples. Other aspects of policy and regional development are discussed in 15 and 21. For the development of public welfare policies, see 24.

For an overview of the changing state of competition and the development of competition policy see chapter 8 of II.A.ii.1. The history of Combines legislation is reviewed in part 1 of item 22. Part 2 reviews the Combines Reports, and part 3 treats resale price maintenance, patents, and mergers. For the origins and development of patent rights, see 9.

The best treatment of the evolution of labor policy is 26; a more concise summary is chapter 5 of II.E.ii.4.

Finally, in 25 and 14 the evolution of policy towards Indians is described.

II.E.iii. Economic Organization: The Role of Government

1. Aitken, Hugh G.J. "Government and Business in Canada: An Interpretation." BUSINESS HISTORY REVIEW 38 (Spring 1964): 4-21.

2. _____, ed. THE STATE AND ECONOMIC GROWTH. Proceedings of a conference held by Committee on Economic Growth, 11-13 October 1956. New York: Social Science Research Council, 1959. x, 389 p. Bibliographic footnotes.

3. Annett, Douglas Rudyard. BRITISH PREFERENCES IN CANADIAN COMMERCIAL POLICY. Studies in International Affairs, no. 3. Toronto: Ryerson Press, 1948. 188 p. Illustrations.

4. Blake, Gordon. "The Customs Administration in Canadian Historical Development." CANADIAN JOURNAL OF ECONOMICS AND POLITI-

CAL SCIENCE 22 (November 1956): 497-508.

5. Brady, A[lexander]. "Economic Activity of the State in the British Dominions: Some Comments on Comparative Development." CANADIAN JOURNAL OF ECONOMICS AND POLITICAL SCIENCE 5 (August 1939): 300-309.

6. Brewis, Thomas N. REGIONAL ECONOMIC POLICIES IN CANADA. Appendix by T.K. Rymes. Toronto: Macmillan of Canada, 1969. 303 p. Bibliography.

7. Burton, Thomas L. NATURAL RESOURCE POLICY IN CANADA: ISSUES AND PERSPECTIVES. Toronto: McClelland & Stewart, 1972. 174 p. Bibliography, pp. 166-68.

8. Fowke, Vernon Clifford. CANADIAN AGRICULTURAL POLICY, THE HISTORICAL PATTERN. Toronto: University of Toronto Press, 1946. 304 p.

9. Fox, Harold George. MONOPOLIES AND PATENTS; A STUDY OF THE HISTORY AND FUTURE OF PATENT MONOPOLY. Toronto: University of Toronto Press, 1947. xxv, 388 p.

10. Innis, Harold A[dams]. POLITICAL ECONOMY IN THE MODERN STATE. Toronto: Ryerson Press, 1946. 270 p.

11. Johnson, Harry Gordon, ed. ECONOMIC NATIONALISM IN OLD AND NEW STATES. University of Chicago Committee for the Comparative Study of New Nations. Chicago: University of Chicago Press, 1967. xi, 145 p. Bibliographic footnotes.

12. Lambert, Richard Stanton, and Pross, Paul. RENEWING NATURE'S WEALTH; A CENTENNIAL HISTORY OF THE PUBLIC MANAGEMENT OF LANDS, FORESTS AND WILDLIFE IN ONTARIO, 1763-1967. Toronto: Ontario Department of Lands and Forests, 1967. xvi, 630 p. Illustrations (some in color). Maps. Portraits. Notes and references, pp. 557-96. Bibliography, pp. 597-616.

13. McDiarmid, Orville John. COMMERCIAL POLICY IN THE CANADIAN ECONOMY. Cambridge, Mass.: Harvard University Press, 1946. xii, 397 p. Tables. Bibliographic footnotes.

14. MacInnes, T.R.L. "History of Indian Administration in Canada." CANADIAN JOURNAL OF ECONOMICS AND POLITICAL SCIENCE 12 (August 1946): 387-94.

15. Neill, Robin F. "National Policy and Regional Development: A Footnote to the Deutsch Report on Maritime Union." JOURNAL OF CANADIAN STUDIES 9 (May 1974): 12-20.

16. Nelles, H.V. THE POLITICS OF DEVELOPMENT, FORESTS, MINES, AND HYDRO-ELECTRIC POWER IN ONTARIO 1849-1941. Toronto: Macmillan of Canada, 1974. xiii, 514 p. Bibliographic references. Sources notes, pp. 496-98.

17. Paltiel, Khayyan Zev. POLITICAL PARTY FINANCING IN CANADA. Toronto: McGraw-Hill, 1970. xvi, 200 p. Bibliography.

18. Perry, John Harvey. TAXES, TARIFFS, AND SUBSIDIES: A HISTORY OF CANADIAN FISCAL DEVELOPMENT. 2 vols. Toronto: University of Toronto Press, 1955. 763 p. Bibliography.

19. Scott, Anthony Dalton. NATURAL RESOURCES: THE ECONOMICS OF CONSERVATION. Canadian Studies in Economics, no. 3. Toronto: University of Toronto Press, 1955. 184 p. Reprint. Carleton Library, no. 68. Toronto: McClelland & Stewart, 1973. xii, 313 p. Bibliography, pp. 263-300.

20. Scott, F[rank] R. "Constitutional Adaptations to Changing Functions of Government." CANADIAN JOURNAL OF ECONOMICS AND POLITICAL SCIENCE 11 (August 1945): 329-41.

21. Shoyama, T.K. "Public Services and Regional Development in Canada." JOURNAL OF ECONOMIC HISTORY 26 (December 1966): 498-513.

22. Skeoch, L.A., ed. RESTRICTIVE TRADE PRACTICES IN CANADA. Toronto: McClelland & Stewart, 1966. xi, 354 p.

23. Stanley, George Francis Gilman. A SHORT HISTORY OF THE CANADIAN CONSTITUTION. Toronto: Ryerson Press, 1969. ix, 230 p. Bibliographies.

24. Strong, Margaret Kirkpatrick. PUBLIC WELFARE ADMINISTRATION IN CANADA. Montclair, N.J.: Patterson Smith, 1969. xiii, 246 p. Bibliography, pp. 237-41.

25. Upton, L.F.S. "Origins of Canadian Indian Policy." JOURNAL OF CANADIAN STUDIES 8 (November 1973): 51-61.

26. Woods, H.D. LABOUR POLICY IN CANADA. 2d ed. Toronto: Macmillan of Canada, 1972. ix, 377 p. Bibliographic footnotes. 1st ed. published as LABOUR POLICY AND LABOUR ECONOMICS IN CANADA, by H.D. Woods, Sylvia Ostry, and Mahmood A. Zaidi. Vol. 1. Toronto: Macmillan of Canada, 1962.

II.F. TECHNOLOGY, PRODUCTIVITY CHANGE, AND WELFARE

The documentation of changes in welfare is of two kinds: (1) changes in aggregate income or wealth per capita, arising from technological and/or productivity change, and (2) changes in the distribution of gains or losses in this aggregate. No continuous long-period quantitative assessments exist. What is available for shorter time spans is noted in succeeding chapters.

Canada has typically been a heavy borrower of technology. Canadian contributions to technology are described in 1, 2, and 6. All three take a long-period view, and 6 brings together a wide variety of relevant contemporaneous extracts. Some diverse essays in Canadian scientific contributions are included in 7. The impact of climate on the development and adaptation of technology is discussed in 5. Recently, the long-term impact of imported technology on national economic and political life has generated some philosophizing about the political economy of Canadian independence. Items 3, 4, and 8 belong to this literature.

II.F. TECHNOLOGY, PRODUCTIVITY CHANGE, AND WELFARE

1. Brown, John James. IDEAS IN EXILE: A HISTORY OF CANADIAN INVENTION. Toronto: McClelland & Stewart, 1967. xii, 372 p. Illustrations. Portraits. Bibliographic footnotes.

2. _____. THE INVENTORS: GREAT IDEAS IN CANADIAN ENTERPRISE. Canadian Illustrated Library. Toronto: McClelland & Stewart, 1967. 128 p. Illustrations (some in color).

3. Grant, George Parkin. TECHNOLOGY AND EMPIRE. Toronto: House of Ananso, 1969. 143 p.

4. Rotstein, Abraham. THE PRECARIOUS HOMESTEAD: ESSAYS ON ECONOMICS, TECHNOLOGY AND NATIONALISM. Toronto: New Press, 1973. xvi, 331 p. Bibliographies.

5. Scott, Anthony [Dalton]. "Economic Effects of Changing Technology and Population in a Hostile Climate." PROCEEDINGS/AND TRANSACTIONS

OF THE ROYAL SOCIETY OF CANADA, 4th ser. 8 (1970): 61-74.

6. Sinclair, B.; Ball, N.R.; and Petersen, J.O., eds. LET US BE HONEST AND MODEST, TECHNOLOGY AND SOCIETY IN CANADIAN HISTORY. Toronto: Oxford University Press, 1974. xiv, 309 p. Bibliography, pp. 307-9.

7. Tory, H.M., ed. HISTORY OF SCIENCE IN CANADA. Toronto: Ryerson Press, 1939. vi, 152 p.

8. Watkins, M[elville] H. "Technology in Our Past and Present." In A GUIDE TO THE PEACEABLE KINGDOM, edited by W[illiam] Kilbourn, pp. 285-92. Toronto: Macmillan of Canada, 1970.

II.G. RESOURCES

The organization of this section follows the traditional division among land, labor, and capital (physical and human). From a historical point of view, the first of these three is asymmetric with the other two. Land and its contiguous resources, though depletable and in some cases reproducible, are relatively fixed, and have a history only of discovery and use, whereas population and capital are typically in some degree mobile, and grow or decline partly as a consequence of the attractive pull of the relatively fixed endowments and of the extent of our technical knowledge of these endowments. It seems appropriate, therefore, from a long-run point of view, to include under land quite recent assessments of its endowment even though this was only known imperfectly in the past. The discovery of the endowment has not usually been a matter for separate treatment, but instead is integrated with an exposition of the growth of primary industries based upon these endowments.

II.G.i. Resources: Land and Its Endowment

The best single atlas to display resource endowments and other economic characteristics is 3. A thorough discussion of these features is provided in 1, 2, 4, and 6. For economic implications, see especially 2 and 4. The notion that Canadian economic development has been substantially determined by geographic influences is particularly evident in the work of writers of the Laurentian School, for example, in item 5. For a fully fledged geographical interpretation, see the essays contained in 7. A brief systematic statistical assessment of land and natural resources is provided in chapter 5 of item 8. See also volume 9 of II.A.ii.19.

II.G.i. Resources: Land and Its Endowment

1. Atwood, Wallace Walter. THE PHYSIOGRAPHIC PROVINCES OF NORTH AMERICA. Boston: Ginn, 1940. 535 p. Illustrations.

2. Camu, P., et al. ECONOMIC GEOGRAPHY OF CANADA. Toronto: Macmillan of Canada, 1964. xvi, 393 p. Illustrations. Maps. Tables. Bibliography, pp. 375-81.

3. Canada. Department of Energy, Mines and Resources. THE NATIONAL ATLAS OF CANADA. 4th ed. Toronto: Macmillan of Canada, 1974. 254 p.

4. Currie, Archibald William. ECONOMIC GEOGRAPHY OF CANADA. Toronto: Macmillan of Canada, 1945. 455 p. Illustrations.

5. Lower, A[rthur] R[eginald] M[arsden]. "Geographical Determinants in Canadian History." In ESSAYS IN CANADIAN HISTORY PRESENTED TO GEORGE MACKINNON WRONG FOR HIS EIGHTIETH BIRTHDAY, edited by Ralph Flenley, pp. 229-52. Toronto: Macmillan of Canada, 1939. Bibliographic footnotes.

6. Robinson, John Lewis. RESOURCES OF THE CANADIAN SHIELD. Toronto: Methuen, 1969. viii, 136 p. Illustrations. Maps. Bibliographic footnotes. Bibliography, pp. 129-32.

7. Warkentin, John, ed. CANADA, A GEOGRAPHICAL INTERPRETATION. Toronto: Methuen, 1967. xvi, 608 p.

8. Wilson, George W., et al. CANADA: AN APPRAISAL OF ITS NEEDS AND RESOURCES. New York: Twentieth Century Fund; University of Toronto Press, 1965. lxx, 453 p. Bibliographic footnotes.

II.G.ii. Resources: Population

Most work on population has one or more of the decennial censuses as its foundation and point of departure. The most detailed and complete account of this source of information up to 1931 is 2. The most complete demographic study of the growth of Canadian population is 13. For a more concise account, see 14, and II.G.i.8, chapter 6. Further analyses are provided in 17 and 18.

The contribution of immigration to Canadian population is relatively large in comparison with the history of most modern industrial countries. A comprehensive account is provided in 12. The story of early settlement associated with the emergence of the nineteenth- and early twentieth-century staples is told in 15 and 16. Population exchange between Canada and the United States is documented in 3, 9, and 22, and an economic analysis of some of these migrations is provided in 8, 21, and 23. Analyses of the relation between immigration and economic growth are made in 20, 4, and 1.

Internal migrations also mark Canadian population history and are documented and analyzed in 7 and 19.

Long-run changes in the labor force are treated in 5 and 6.

Two specialized studies by Henripin, 10 and 11, treat French Canada and fertility respectively.

II.G.ii. Resources: Population

1. Buckley, Kenneth [A.H.]. "Working Paper on Population, Labour Force and Economic Growth." Banff Business Policies Conference on Canadian Economic Survival, vol. 2. Banff, Alberta: Banff School of Advanced Management, and the Universities of Alberta, British Columbia, Manitoba, and Saskatchewan, 1963. 103 p. Mimeographed.

2. Canada. Dominion Bureau of Statistics. SUMMARY. SEVENTH CENSUS OF CANADA, 1931. Vol. 1. Ottawa: King's Printer, 1936. 1,520 p.

3. Coats, Robert Hamilton, and MacLean, M.C. THE AMERICAN BORN IN CANADA; A STATISTICAL INTERPRETATION. Toronto: Ryerson Press, 1943. xviii, 176 p. Illustrations. 2 folding maps.

4. Corbett, D.C. "Immigration and Economic Development." CANADIAN JOURNAL OF ECONOMICS AND POLITICAL SCIENCE 27 (August 1951): 360-68.

5. Denton, Frank T. THE GROWTH OF MANPOWER IN CANADA. 1961 Census Monograph, Labour Force Studies Series. Ottawa: Dominion Bureau of Statistics, 1970. xi, 85 p.

6. Denton, Frank T., and Ostry, S[ylvia]. HISTORICAL ESTIMATES OF THE CANADIAN LABOUR FORCE. Ottawa: Dominion Bureau of Statistics, 1967. viii, 49 p.

7. George, M.V. INTERNAL MIGRATION IN CANADA, A DEMOGRAPHIC ANALYSIS. 1961 Census Monograph. Ottawa: Dominion Bureau of Statistics, 1970. xv, 249 p. Bibliography, pp. 245-49.

8. Green, Alan G., et al. ECONOMICS OF IMMIGRATION. Canadian Perspectives in Economics, no. E-3. Toronto: Collier-Macmillan, 1973. 12 p.

9. Hansen, Marcus Lee. THE MINGLING OF THE CANADIAN AND AMERICAN PEOPLES. Toronto: Ryerson Press, 1940. xviii, 274 p. Maps (1 folding). Bibliographic footnotes.

10. Henripin, J[acques]. "From Acceptance of Nature to Control: The Demography of the French Canadians." CANADIAN JOURNAL OF ECONOMICS AND POLITICAL SCIENCE 23 (February 1957): 9-19.

11. _____. TRENDS AND FACTORS OF FERTILITY IN CANADA. 1961 Census Monograph. Ottawa: Dominion Bureau of Statistics, 1972. xxiii, 421 p.

12. Kalbach, Warren E. THE IMPACT OF IMMIGRATION ON CANADA'S POPULATION. 1961 Census Monograph. Ottawa: Dominion Bureau of Statistics, 1970. xxxiv, 465 p. Illustrations. Maps.

13. Kalbach, Warren E., and McVey, Wayne W. THE DEMOGRAPHIC BASIS OF CANADIAN SOCIETY. Toronto: McGraw-Hill, 1971. 354 p. Illustrations. Maps. Bibliographic references.

14. Keyfitz, Nathan. "The Growth of the Canadian Population." POPULATION STUDIES 4 (June 1950): 47-63.

15. Lower, Arthur Reginald Marsden, and Innis, H[arold] A[dams]. SETTLEMENT AND THE FOREST FRONTIER OF EASTERN CANADA: SETTLEMENT AND THE MINING FRONTIER. Canadian Frontiers of Settlement, edited by William Archibald Mackintosh and W.L.G. Joerg, vol. 9. Toronto: Macmillan of Canada, 1936. 424 p. Illustrations.

16. Mackintosh, William Archibald. PRAIRIE SETTLEMENT: THE GEOGRAPHIC SETTING. Canadian Frontiers of Settlement, edited by William Archibald Mackintosh and W.L.G. Joerg, vol. 1. Toronto: Macmillan of Canada, 1934. 242 p. Illustrations.

17. MacLean, M.C. ANALYSIS OF STAGES IN THE GROWTH OF POPULATION IN CANADA. Ottawa: King's Printer, 1935. 53 p.

18. Ryder, N.B. "Components of Canadian Population Growth." POPULATION INDEX 20 (April 1954): 71-80.

19. Stone, Leroy O. MIGRATION IN CANADA, SOME REGIONAL ASPECTS. 1961 Census Monograph. Ottawa: Dominion Bureau of Statistics, 1969. 407 p. Bibliography, pp. 395-407.

20. Thomas, Brinley. MIGRATION AND ECONOMIC GROWTH; A STUDY OF GREAT BRITAIN AND THE ATLANTIC COMMUNITY. 2d ed. Cambridge: At the University Press, 1973. xxxi, 498 p. Illustrations. Bibliography, pp. 473-87.

21. Timlin, Mabel Frances. DOES CANADA NEED MORE PEOPLE? Toronto: Oxford University Press, 1951. 143 p.

22. Truesdell, Leon Edgar. THE CANADIAN BORN IN THE UNITED STATES; AN ANALYSIS OF THE STATISTICS OF THE CANADIAN ELEMENT IN THE POPULATION OF THE U.S.; 1850-1930. New Haven, Conn.: Yale University Press, 1943. xvi, 263 p. Illustrations.

23. Vedder, R.K., and Gallaway, L.E. "Settlement Patterns of Canadian Emigrants to the United States, 1850-1960." CANADIAN JOURNAL OF ECONOMICS 3 (August 1970): 476-86.

II.G.iii. Resources: Capital Formation

Long-period change in this area has not been well researched. For an introduction, see II.G.i.8, chapter 7. In 3, it is the accumulation of private fortunes rather than the stock of social capital that is reported. To the extent that real capital formation was promoted by the inflow of foreign capital, the story is partly documented in II.E.i.2, and the contribution of long-term U.S. capital is recorded and discussed in 1 below. Long-period human capital formation has not been estimated. The development of the educational system is documented and analyzed in 2 and 4.

II.G.iii. Resources: Capital Formation

1. Aitken, Hugh G.J. AMERICAN CAPITAL AND CANADIAN RESOURCES. Cambridge, Mass.: Harvard University Press, 1962. xii, 217 p. Diagrams. Tables. Bibliography, pp. 203-12.

2. Lawr, Douglas A., and Gidney, Robert D., eds. EDUCATING CANADIANS: A DOCUMENTARY HISTORY OF PUBLIC EDUCATION. Toronto: Van Nostrand Reinhold, 1973. 284 p. Reading list, pp. 268-74.

3. Myers, Gustavas. HISTORY OF CANADIAN WEALTH. 1914. Reprint. New York: Argosy-Antiquarian, 1968. vi, 337 p. Bibliographic references.

4. Wilson, John Donald, et al., eds. CANADIAN EDUCATION: A HISTORY. Scarborough, Ontario: Prentice-Hall, 1970. xiv, 528 p. Illustrations. Portraits. Bibliographic references.

Chapter III
THE COLONIAL PERIOD TO 1867

The colonial period extends from the time of earliest settlement associated with the establishment of dry fisheries, through the period of English-French rivalry prior to 1763, to the formation of Canadian Confederation in 1867. Taken as a whole, the period has been quite well researched and documented, particularly from the point of view of the Laurentian School. Even the more general works tend to be dominated by writing that falls within the domain of economic history, since the process of colonization itself was largely inseparable from economic considerations.

III.A. GENERAL WORKS

General works that are specialized to the colonial period tend also to be specialized by region since colonial economies were typically regional economies dominated by one or more staple productions. Regional development before Confederation is systematically treated in item 1. In addition, a number of the works listed under II.A.ii. devoted their early chapters to the colonial period. See especially II.A.ii.18 and II.A.ii.19.

III.A. GENERAL WORKS

1. Creighton, Donald Grant. BRITISH NORTH AMERICA AT CONFEDERATION. Royal Commission on Dominion-Provincial Relations, Appendix 2. Ottawa: King's Printer, 1939. 104 p. Tables.

III.A.i. General Works: The Maritimes

The early discovery and exploration of North America is well summarized in 2. Early colonialization efforts are treated in 1, while eighteenth- and nineteenth-century developments are summarized in the well-documented works 6 and 7. See also 9 for the pre-Confederation years. For New Brunswick, see 8. In addition, II.A.ii.29 and 30 are indispensable. The importance of naval de-

Colonial Period to 1867

fense considerations to the progress of the maritimes is emphasized in 4, and the parting of the ways with other American colonies is discussed in 5. For several useful, short essays, see chapters 2, 4, 5, 7, 8, 10, 14, and 17 in II.A.ii.18.

III.A.i. General Works: The Maritimes

2. Brebner, John Bartlet. THE EXPLORERS OF NORTH AMERICA, 1492-1806. New York: World Publishing Co., 1964. 431 p. Bibliography.

3. _____. NEW ENGLAND'S OUTPOST: ACADIA BEFORE THE CONQUEST OF CANADA. Columbia University Faculty of Political Science Studies in History, Economics and Public Law, no. 293. New York: Columbia University Press, 1927. 291 p. Map.

4. Graham, Gerald S[andford]. EMPIRE OF THE NORTH ATLANTIC: THE MARITIME STRUGGLE FOR NORTH AMERICA. 2d ed. Toronto: University of Toronto Press, 1958. xvii, 338 p. Bibliographic footnotes.

5. Kerr, Wilfred Brenton. THE MARITIME PROVINCES OF BRITISH NORTH AMERICA AND THE AMERICAN REVOLUTION. Sackville, New Brunswick: Busy East Press, 1941. 172 p. Works cited, pp. 125-31. Footnotes and references, pp. 132-58.

6. MacNutt, William Stewart. THE ATLANTIC PROVINCES, THE EMERGENCE OF COLONIAL SOCIETY 1712-1857. Canadian Centenary Series, edited by W[illiam] L[ewis] Morton and D[onald] G[rant] Creighton, vol. 9. Toronto: McClelland & Stewart, 1965. xii, 305 p. Illustrations. Maps. Portraits. Bibliography, pp. 290-96.

7. _____. THE MAKING OF THE MARITIME PROVINCES 1713-1784. Canadian Historical Association Booklet, no. 4. Ottawa: Canadian Archives, 1970. 20 p. Map. Bibliographic note.

8. _____. NEW BRUNSWICK; A HISTORY: 1784-1867. Toronto: Macmillan of Canada, 1963. 496 p. Illustrations.

9. Whitelaw, William Menzies. THE MARITIMES AND CANADA BEFORE CONFEDERATION. Introduction by P[eter] B. Waite. Toronto: Oxford University Press, 1966. xx, 347 p. Maps. Bibliography, pp. 285-308.

Colonial Period to 1867

III.A.ii. General Works: The Canadas

Prior to the British victory in 1759, the St. Lawrence-Great Lakes region was central to the domain of New France. Following 1759, until 1791, the region was included within the old province of Quebec that extended over most of the territory earlier penetrated by the French. From 1791 to 1840 the region was divided between Upper Canada or Canada West, and Lower Canada or Canada East. These two territories, corresponding to the more settled parts of present-day Ontario and Quebec, were combined into a single United Province of Canada between 1840 and 1867. In 1867 Ontario and Quebec were created. See II.A.ii.16 for a review of these territory changes.

The history of New France has been extensively researched. Still one of the best general histories is 32. More recent efforts along similar lines include the sequence of items 30 and 15, both from the Canadian Centenary series. A somewhat more topical arrangement including a section on the economy is provided by 31. Seven essays on various political, social, and economic topics make up 18. See also chapters 3 and 4 in II.A.ii.18 for brief accounts of the old French regime and its struggle with the British.

The economic history of New France is probably best treated in 19, which also includes substantial statistical material. A supplement useful for statistical material is 29, which extends the story to 1867. More specialized and interpretive items are 14 and 20. The notion that unique institutional and social factors played a role in French Canadian economic development is a theme that emerges in writings on the colonial period. See, for example, 17, 20, and 22. For a fairly exhaustive inventory of archival materials, see 23 and 24.

For the period following 1760, one of the best general histories is still 10. A parallel comprehensive economic history is provided by 25 and the interpretive essay 26. A classic example of the Laurentian School that covers the same period is 13. For the history of Upper Canada prior to the 1840 union, the best single source is 12. Item 16 is a useful comment on the extent of the market at this time. See also chapters 6-10 in II.A.ii.18.

The history of the union of the Canadas for two and one-half decades before Confederation is given a thorough treatment in the sequence of 11 and 21, volumes in the Canadian Centenary series. An older, but still useful general source on this period is 28. See also chapters 11-15 in II.A.ii.18 for brief but authoritative accounts of important political developments in British North America in this period. For an introduction to the development of class consciousness associated with the rise of Canadian business in the period, see 27.

Colonial Period to 1867

III.A.ii. General Works: The Canadas

10. Burt, Alfred LeRoy. THE OLD PROVINCE OF QUEBEC. 1933. Reprint. New York: Russell & Russell, 1970. xiii, 511 p. Illustrations. Maps. Plans. Portraits. Bibliographic references. New ed. Introduction by Hilda Neatby. 2 vols. Carleton Library, nos. 37 (1760-78) and 38 (1778-91). Toronto: McClelland & Stewart.

11. Careless, James Maurice Stockford. THE UNION OF THE CANADAS; THE GROWTH OF CANADIAN INSTITUTIONS 1841-57. Canadian Centenary Series, edited by W[illiam] L[ewis] Morton and D[onald] G[rant] Creighton, vol. 10. Toronto: McClelland & Stewart, 1967. xii, 256 p. Illustrations. Facsimiles. Maps. Portraits. Bibliography, pp. 241-47.

12. Craig, Gerald Marquis. UPPER CANADA, THE FORMATIVE YEARS 1784-1841. Canadian Centenary Series, edited by W[illiam] L[ewis] Morton and D[onald] G[rant] Creighton, vol. 7. Toronto: McClelland & Stewart, 1963. xiv, 315 p. Illustrations. Portraits. Bibliography, pp. 299-310.

13. Creighton, Donald Grant. THE COMMERCIAL EMPIRE OF THE ST. LAWRENCE, 1760-1850. Toronto: Ryerson Press, 1937. 441 p. Illustrations.

14. Delage, D. "Les structures économiques de le Nouvelle-France et de la Nouvelle York." L'ACTUALITE ECONOMIQUE 46 (April-June 1970): 67-118.

15. Eccles, William John. CANADA UNDER LOUIS XIV, 1663-1701. Canadian Centenary Series, edited by W[illiam] L[ewis] Morton and D[onald] G[rant] Creighton, vol. 3. Toronto: McClelland & Stewart, 1964. xii, 275 p. Illustrations. Portraits. Maps. Facsimiles. Bibliography, pp. 263-67.

16. Fowke, V[ernon] C[lifford]. "The Myth of the Self-Sufficient Canadian Pioneer." PROCEEDINGS AND TRANSACTIONS OF THE ROYAL SOCIETY OF CANADA, 3d ser. 56, sec. 2 (June 1962): 23-37.

17. Frégault, Guy. CANADIAN SOCIETY IN THE FRENCH REGIME. Canadian Historical Association Booklet, no. 3. Ottawa: Canadian Archives, 1971. 16 p.

18. _____. LE XVIIIe SIECLE CANADIEN. Montréal: Editions HMH, 1970. 387 p. Bibliography.

19. Hamelin, Jean. ECONOMIE ET SOCIETE EN NOUVELLE-FRANCE. Les Cahiers de l'Institut d'Histoire, l'Université Laval, no. 3. Québec: Les Presses de l'Université Laval, 1961. 137 p. Maps. Diagrams. Tables.

20. Harris, R[ichard] C[olebrook]. "Of Poverty and Helplessness in Petite-Nation." CANADIAN HISTORICAL REVIEW 52 (March 1971): 23-50.

21. Morton, William Lewis. THE CRITICAL YEARS; THE UNION OF BRITISH NORTH AMERICA 1857-1873. Canadian Centenary Series, edited by W[illiam] L[ewis] Morton and D[onald] G[rant] Creighton, vol. 12. Toronto: McClelland & Stewart, 1964. xii, 322 p. Illustrations. Maps. Portraits. Bibliography, pp. 305-14.

22. Nish, Cameron. LES BOURGEOIS--GENTILSHOMMES DE LA NOUVELLE-FRANCE 1729-1748. Montréal: Fides, 1968. xxxix, 202 p. Bibliography, pp. xxiii-xxxix.

23. _____. "Documents relatifs à l'histoire économique du régime francais." L'ACTUALITE ECONOMIQUE 40 (October-December 1964): 630-66.

24. _____. "Inventaire des documents relatifs à l'histoire économique du Canada français." L'ACTUALITE ECONOMIQUE 43 (April-June 1967): 146-97; (July-September 1967): 374-411; (October-December 1967): 585-613; (January-March 1968): 789-808; 44 (April-June 1968): 176-215; (July-September 1968): 349-97; (October-December 1968): 571-617; (January-March 1969): 785-827; 45 (April-June 1969): 152-204; (July-September 1969): 356-98; (October-December 1969): 581-635; (January-March 1970): 837-89; 46 (July-September 1971): 373-415; (October-December 1971): 561-606.

25. Ouellet, F. HISTOIRE ECONOMIQUE ET SOCIALE DU QUEBEC 1760-1850: STRUCTURES ET CONJUNCTURE. Histoire économique et sociale du Canada français. Montréal: Fides, 1966. xxxii, 639 p. Diagrams (some folding). Map. Bibliography, pp. xix-xxxii.

26. Paquet, G[illes], and Wallot, J[ean-] P[ierre]. "Canada 1760-1850, anamorphoses et perspective." In ECONOMIE QUEBECOISE, edited by R[obert] Comeau, pp. 255-300. Les Cahiers de l'Université du Québec. Sillery: Les Presses de l'Université du Québec, 1969.

27. Ryerson, Stanley Brehaut. UNEQUAL UNION; CONFEDERATION AND THE ROOTS OF CONFLICT IN THE CANADAS, 1815-1873. Toronto: Progress Books, 1968. 477 p. Illustrations. Maps. Reference notes, pp. 447-63.

Colonial Period to 1867

28. Skelton, Oscar Douglas. THE LIFE AND TIMES OF SIR ALEXANDER TILLOCK GALT. Toronto: Oxford University Press, 1920. 586 p. Illustrations. New ed. Edited and introduced by Guy MacLean. Carleton Library, no. 26. Toronto: McClelland & Stewart, 1966. xviii, 293 p.

29. Trudel, Marcel. ATLAS HISTORIQUE DU CANADA FRANCAIS DES ORIGINES A 1867. Quebec: Les Presses de l'Université Laval, 1961. 93 maps (some folding).

30. _____. THE BEGINNINGS OF NEW FRANCE, 1524-1663. Translated by Patricia Claxton. Canadian Centenary Series, edited by W[illiam] L[ewis] Morton and D[onald] G[rant] Creighton, vol. 2. Toronto: McClelland & Stewart, 1973. xii, 323 p. Illustrations. Bibliography, pp. 308-12.

31. _____. INTRODUCTION TO NEW FRANCE. Translated by Patricia Claxton. Toronto: Holt, Rinehart and Winston, 1968. xxix, 300 p. Illustrations. Facsimiles. Maps. Bibliography.

32. Wrong, George MacKinnon. THE RISE AND FALL OF NEW FRANCE. 2 vols. New York: Macmillan, 1928. 925 p. Maps (1 folding). "Authorities" at end of each volume.

III.A.iii. General Works: The West

Except for scattered trading posts, colonization efforts in the west were limited prior to 1867 to settlements at Red River, the lower mainland of what later became British Columbia, and Vancouver Island. The most detailed and comprehensive history is item 34 which covers the entire geographic area to the Pacific. For an account of the Red River settlement, see 36, and II.A.ii.42. For a definitive account of the implications of the progress of settlement on the native peoples of the west, see 37. The early history of settlement in the far west is treated in II.A.ii.43, and in 33 below. The attitudes of all these settlers and the forces that pulled them into Confederation are briefly treated in 35 below, and in III.A.1. See also chapter 19 in II.A.ii.18 for a very brief account of western expansion up to 1880.

III.A.iii. General Works: The West

33. Bancroft, Hubert Howe. HISTORY OF BRITISH COLUMBIA 1792-1887. San Francisco: The History Co., 1887. 792 p. Maps (1 folding).

34. Morton, Arthur S. A HISTORY OF THE CANADIAN WEST TO 1870-71.

Colonial Period to 1867

    2d ed. Toronto: University of Toronto Press, 1973. xxviii, 1,039 p. Map. Bibliographic notes, pp. 933-94.

35. Morton, William Lewis. THE WEST AND CONFEDERATION 1857-71. Canadian Historical Association Booklet, no. 9. Ottawa: Canadian Archives, 1958. 19 p. Bibliography on inside of back cover.

36. Pritchett, John Perry. THE RED RIVER VALLEY, 1811-1849: A Regional Study. New Haven, Conn.: Yale University Press, 1942. 295 p. Maps.

37. Stanley, George F[rancis] G[ilman]. THE BIRTH OF WESTERN CANADA, A HISTORY OF THE RIEL REBELLIONS. Toronto: University of Toronto Press, 1960. xii, 475 p. Maps. Illustrations. Bibliographic references. Bibliographic note, pp. 408-9.

III.B. STATISTICAL RECORD

Except for statistics of population and agricultural production, II.B.2 contains no data for the colonial period. A useful picture of early Canadian statistical compilations is presented in 2. The colonial censuses, summarized in 1 and 7, are by far the best overall statistical documentation. Quite detailed trade statistics for the 1850s and 1860s are contained in 7. Some additional data are provided in 3 and 4, although 3, especially, is largely narrative. The documents collected in 5 and 6 are drawn mainly from archival sources, and are organized by topics similar to those chosen for this bibliography. Much of the material is qualitative, but statistical evidence is also included.

III.B. STATISTICAL RECORD

1. Canada. Department of Agriculture. CENSUS OF CANADA 1870-71. Censuses of Canada 1665-1871, vol. 4. Ottawa: I.B. Taylor, 1876. 422 p.

2. Coats, Robert Hamilton. "Beginnings in Canadian Statistics." CANADIAN HISTORICAL REVIEW 27 (June 1946): 109-30.

3. Gourlay, Robert Fleming. STATISTICAL ACCOUNT OF UPPER CANADA, COMPILED WITH A VIEW TO A GRAND SYSTEM OF EMIGRATION. London: Simpkin and Marshall, 1822. New ed., abridged. Introduction by S.R. Mealing. Carleton Library, no. 75. Toronto: McClelland & Stewart, 1974. 395 p. Maps. Bibliography, p. 19.

4. Hind, Henry Youle, et al. EIGHTY YEARS' PROGRESS IN BRITISH

Colonial Period to 1867

NORTH AMERICA. Showing the wonderful development of its natural resources . . . giving in historical form the vast improvements made in agriculture, commerce and trade, modes of travel and transportation, mining and educational interests, etc., with a large amount of statistical information, from the best and latest authorities. Toronto: Stebbins, 1863. 776 p. Illustrations. Frontispiece. Plates.

5. Innis, Harold Adams, ed. SELECT DOCUMENTS IN CANADIAN ECONOMIC HISTORY, 1497-1783. Toronto: University of Toronto Press, 1929. xxxiv, 581 p.

6. Innis, Harold A[dams], and Lower, A[rthur] R[eginald] M[arsden], eds. SELECT DOCUMENTS IN CANADIAN ECONOMIC HISTORY, 1783-1885. Toronto: University of Toronto Press, 1933. viii, 846 p.

7. THE YEARBOOK AND ALMANAC OF CANADA. An annual statistical abstract for the Dominion and a Record of Legislation and of Public Men in British North America. Montreal and Ottawa: MacLean, Roger, and Co., 1867 and 1868.

III.C. THESES OF ECONOMIC GROWTH

The varieties of interpretation that have been applied to colonial economic growth are outlined in the introduction and documented in section II.C. The staples approach is virtually without rival as a unifying theme of Colonial economic growth. See especially 1, 4, 15, 20, and 27 under II.C. The only real debate here relates to the influence of the frontier vis-a-vis metropolitan centers. For this, see items 2, 4, 24, 25, and 29, all under II.C. For an interpretation of Lower Canada at the start of the nineteenth century, see 2 below. For a review of the economic and social historiography of New France, see item 1.

III.C. THESES OF ECONOMIC GROWTH

1. Blain, Jean. "Economie et société en Nouvelle-France: Le Cheminement historiographique dans la première moitié du XXe siècle." REVUE D'HISTOIRE DE L'AMERIQUE FRANCAISE 26 (June 1972): 3-32.

2. Paquet, Gilles, and Wallot, Jean-Pierre. "Le Bas-Canada au début du XIXe siècle: Une Hypothèse." REVUE D'HISTOIRE DE L'AMERIQUE FRANCAISE 25, (June 1971): 39-61.

Colonial Period to 1867

III.D. SECTORS AND INDUSTRIES

The principal economic activities prior to Confederation were primary resource-intensive productions, and the addition of social overhead capital in the transportation sector. Consequently, the literature in these areas is quite extensive, while the relatively undeveloped manufacturing activities have received less scholarly attention.

III.D.i. Sectors and Industries: Primary Industry

In the colonial period prior to 1867, the main staple trades were, in chronological order, fish, fur, timber, and wheat. The most important source for history of fish trade is II.D.i.6. For an account of the early Newfoundland fishery see 8 below, II.A.ii.26, and II.A.ii.14, pages 7-26. Perhaps no staple trade has been more extensively researched than the early fur trade. In addition to II.D.i.7, items 17 and 22 below are comprehensive; items 18 and 22 are definitive on the activities of the Hudson's Bay Company, and 25 summarizes a thesis on the reconstruction of the St. Lawrence fur trade after 1763. See also item 7 for the French period. To supplement II.D.i.13 on the timber trade, see items 9, 10, and 11 below, which are also by Lower. The latter two items by Lower provide good statistical documentation. The origins of the timber trade in the demands of the British navy are described in items 1 and 3. Works on colonial agriculture include 2, a short essay on Quebec before 1760; several specialized essays, 5, 12, and 14, on early French Canada after 1760; and 23, a substantial account of post-1760 Quebec agriculture. For Ontario, 6 remains the only standard work. Some works, such as 4, 13, 15, 19, 20, and 24, are directed at documenting and summarizing the commercial and international aspects of the early staple trades. See also II.A.ii.14, pages 27-43, for an account of commerce in New France. Statistics are included in 20 and 24. For general accounts of these trades and their role in economic development, see 16 and 3.

III.D.i. Sectors and Industries: Primary Industry

1. Albion, Robert Greenhalgh. FORESTS AND SEA POWER: THE TIMBER PROBLEM OF THE ROYAL NAVY, 1652-1862. Harvard Economic Studies, vol. 29. Cambridge, Mass.: Harvard University Press, 1926. 485 p. Illustrations. Bibliography.

2. Burton, F.W. "The Wheat Supply of New France." PROCEEDINGS AND TRANSACTIONS. Royal Society of Canada, 3d ser. 30, sec. 2 (May 1936): 137-50.

3. Calvin, Delano Dester. A SAGA OF THE ST. LAWRENCE; TIMBER AND SHIPPING THROUGH THREE GENERATIONS. Toronto: Ryerson Press,

1945. x, 176 p. Illustrations. 2 facsimiles. Plates.

4. Farnie, D.A. "The Commercial Empire of the Atlantic 1607-1783." ECONOMIC HISTORY REVIEW. 2d ser. 15, no. 2 (1962): 205-18.

5. Hamelin, J[ean], and Ouellet, F. "Le Mouvement des prix agricoles dans la Province de Québec: 1760-1851." In FRANCE ET CANADA FRANCAIS DU XVIe AU XXe SIECLE, edited by Claude Galarmeau and Elzéar Lavoie, pp. 35-48. Les Cahiers de l'Institute d'Histoire, l'Université Laval, no. 7. Québec: Les Presses de l'Université Laval, 1966. Bibliographic footnotes.

6. Jones, Robert Leslie. HISTORY OF AGRICULTURE IN ONTARIO 1613-1880. University of Toronto Studies in History and Economics, vol. 11. Toronto: University of Toronto Press, 1946. xvi, 420 p. Bibliography, pp. 361-90.

7. LeBlaut, Robert. "Le commerce compliqué des fourruers Canadiennes au début du XVIIe siècle. REVUE D'HISTOIRE DE L'AMERIQUE FRANCAISE 26 (June 1972): 53-66.

8. Lounsbury, Ralph Greenbe. THE BRITISH FISHERY AT NEWFOUNDLAND, 1634-1763. Yale Historical Publications, Miscellany no. 27. New Haven, Conn.: Yale University Press, 1934. 398 p. Illustrations.

9. Lower, A[rthur] R[eginald] M[arsden]. "The Forest in New France, A Sketch of Lumbering in Canada before the English Conquest." CANADIAN HISTORICAL ASSOCIATION ANNUAL REPORT, 1928, pp. 78-90.

10. _____. GREAT BRITAIN'S WOODYARD, BRITISH AMERICA AND THE TIMBER TRADE 1763-1867. Montreal: McGill-Queen's University Press, 1973. xiv, 271 p. Illustrations. Bibliographic references.

11. _____. "The Trade in Square Timber." University of Toronto Studies in History and Economics, VI, pp. 40-61. Toronto: University of Toronto Press, 1933. Maps. Diagrams.

12. Ouellet, F., and Hamelin, J[ean]. "La Crise agricole dans le Bas-Canada, 1802-37." RAPPORT ANNUAL DE LA SOCIETE HISTORIQUE DU CANADA, 1962, pp. 17-33.

13. Paquet, G[illes], and Wallot, J[ean-] P[ierre]. "Aperçu sur le commerce international et les prix domestiques dans le Bas-Canada 1793-1813." REVUE D'HISTOIRE DE L'AMERIQUE FRANCAISE 21 (December 1967): 447-73.

Colonial Period to 1867

14. _____. "Crise agricole et tensions socioethniques dans le Bas-Canada, 1802-1812: Elements pour une reinterpretation." REVUE D'HISTOIRE DE L'AMERIQUE FRANCAISE 26 (September 1972): 185-237.

15. _____. "International Circumstances of Lower Canada 1786-1810: Prolegomenon." CANADIAN HISTORICAL REVIEW 53 (December 1972): 371-401.

16. Parker, Keith Alfred. THE STAPLE INDUSTRIES AND ECONOMIC DEVELOPMENT, CANADA 1841-1867. Ph.D. dissertation, University of Maryland, 1966. Ann Arbor, Mich.: University Microfilms, 1966. iv, 316 p.

17. Phillips, Paul Chrisler. THE FUR TRADE. 2 vols. Norman: Oklahoma University Press, 1961. xxvi, 686 p.; viii, 696 p. Illustrations. Portraits. Maps. Bibliography, vol. 2, pp. 577-656.

18. Ray, Arthur I. INDIANS IN THE FUR TRADE: THEIR ROLE AS HUNTERS, TRAPPERS AND MIDDLEMEN IN THE LANDS SOUTHWEST OF HUDSON BAY 1660-1870. Toronto: University of Toronto Press, 1974. xii, 249 p. Maps. Bibliography, pp. 232-42.

19. Reid, Allana G. "General Trade between Quebec and France during the French Regime." CANADIAN HISTORICAL REVIEW 34 (March 1953): 18-32.

20. _____. "Intercolonial Trade during the French Regime." CANADIAN HISTORICAL REVIEW 32 (September 1951): 236-51.

21. Rich, Edwin Ernest. THE FUR TRADE AND THE NORTHWEST TO 1857. Canadian Centenary Series, edited by W[illiam] L[ewis] Morton and D[onald] G[rant] Creighton, vol. 11. Toronto: McClelland & Stewart, 1967. xii, 336 p. Illustrations. Maps. Portraits. Bibliography, pp. 311-25.

22. _____. THE HISTORY OF THE HUDSON'S BAY COMPANY 1670-1870. 2 vols. London: Hudson's Bay Record Society, 1958-59. Vol. 1, 1670-1763, 687 p.; vol. 2, 1763-1870, 974 p. Portraits (some in color). Maps (some folding, on lining papers). Bibliographies.

23. Seguin, Maurice. LA "NATIONAL CANADIENNE" ET L'AGRICULTURE 1760-1850: ESSAI D'HISTOIRE ECONOMIQUE. Trois-Rivières, Québec: Editions Boreal Express, 1970. 279 p. Illustrations. Maps (some in color, some folding). Bibliography, pp. 7-16.

24. Shepherd, J[ames] F. "Commodity Exports from the British North American Colonies to Overseas Areas 1768-1772: Magnitudes and Patterns of Trade." EXPLORATIONS IN ECONOMIC HISTORY 8 (Fall 1970): 5-76.

25. Stevens, Wayne Edson. THE NORTHWEST FUR TRADE 1763-1800. Studies in the Social Sciences, vol. 14, no. 3. Urbana: University of Illinois, 1928. Bibliography, pp. 187-97.

III.D.ii. Sectors and Industries: Secondary Industry

In the colonial period, most manufacturing was limited to small-scale craft production for strictly local markets. The significant exceptions were the milling of forest and agricultural products, mainly in the Canadas: see II.D.i.13 and II.D.ii.14. The general state of manufacturing by the 1850s is described by Firestone in IV.B.7. The earliest craft activities present in the economy of New France are treated in item 2 below. Later developments in Ontario are briefly described in 3. Hat making in relation to the fur trade is discussed in 1.

III.D.ii. Sectors and Industries: Secondary Industry

1. Crean, J.F. "Hats and the Fur Trade." CANADIAN JOURNAL OF ECONOMICS AND POLITICAL SCIENCE 28 (August 1962): 373-86.

2. Fauteux, Joseph Noel. ESSAI SUR L'INDUSTRIE AU CANADA SOUS LE REGIME FRANCAIS. 2 vols. Québec: LS-A Proulx, 1927. xx, 572 p. Bibliographic footnotes.

3. Innis M[ary] Q. "The Industrial Development of Ontario 1783-1820." ONTARIO HISTORICAL SOCIETY PAPERS AND RECORDS 32, 1937, pp. 104-13.

III.D.iii. Sectors and Industries: Tertiary Industry

In the field of transportation, the rise of wooden shipbuilding in the Maritimes and at Quebec dominate the first half of the nineteenth century. The story of this important industry is discussed in the context of maritime development in items 29 and 30 from II.A.ii. For greater detail on shipbuilding, see II.D.iii.8, and 12 and 15 below. The passing of shipbuilding as a major Quebec industry is documented in 4. The last two decades before Confederation witnessed the completion of extensive water and rail improvements in the St. Lawrence region. Again, for general reference on the history of transportation, consult II.D.iii.8. For contemporary accounts of the development and significance of the canal system in the St. Lawrence-Great Lakes area, see 8 and 10. Definitive studies of two canals, the Welland and the Rideau, are provided by 1 and 11, respectively. For railroads, II.D.iii.8, supplemented by II.D.iii.2, probably provides the best coverage. An older and less detailed overview is supplied in 13, and a contemporary interpretive view is given by 9. See also volume 10 of II.A.ii.19 for railroad history. The impact of railroad developments on Canadian-American relations is explored in 7 as well as II.D.iii.17. Finally, for the history of the post office, see 14.

The other major area of tertiary activity, banking, is treated in 2 and 6. Pre-1867 developments are also described in 13, 14, and 15 of II.D.iii. For methods of financial intermediation to facilitate the transfer of land, see the thorough treatment in 3.

III.D.iii. Sectors and Industries: Tertiary Industry

1. Aitken, Hugh G.J. THE WELLAND CANAL COMPANY: A STUDY IN CANADIAN ENTERPRISE. Studies in Entrepreneurial History. Cambridge, Mass.: Harvard University Press, 1954. ix, 178 p. Diagrams. Illustrations. Maps. Bibliographic references included in notes, pp. 149-68.

2. Breckenridge, Roeliff Morton. CANADIAN BANKING SYSTEM 1817-1890. American Economic Association Monograph, vol. 10, nos. 1-3. New York: Macmillan, 1895. 476 p. Folding table. Folding chart. Bibliography, pp. 471-76.

3. Drummond, William Malcolm. "Financing of Land Purchase in Canada." Toronto: Privately published, n.d. 470 p. Mimeographed.

4. Faucher, A[lbert]. "The Decline of Shipbuilding at Quebec in the Nineteenth Century." CANADIAN JOURNAL OF ECONOMICS AND POLITICAL SCIENCE 33 (May 1957): 195-215.

5. Guillet, Edwin Clarence. THE STORY OF CANADIAN ROADS. Toronto: University of Toronto Press, 1966. 246 p. Illustrations. Maps. Bibliography, pp. 235-41.

6. Hammond, Bray. "Banking in Canada before Confederation, 1792-1867." In his BANKS AND POLITICS IN AMERICA FROM THE REVOLUTION TO THE CIVIL WAR, chap. 20, pp. 631-70. Princeton, N.J.: Princeton University Press, 1957. Bibliography, pp. 747-60.

7. Irwin, Leonard Bertrain. PACIFIC RAILWAYS AND NATIONALISM IN THE CANADIAN-AMERICAN NORTHWEST, 1845-1873. New York:

Colonial Period to 1867

Greenwood Press, 1968. xii, 246 p. Bibliography.

8. Keefer, Thomas Coltrin. THE CANALS OF CANADA, THEIR PROSPECTS AND INFLUENCE. Toronto: A.H. Armor and Co., 1850. 111 p.

9. _____. PHILOSOPHY OF RAILROADS AND OTHER ESSAYS. Edited, with an introduction by H.V. Nelles. Toronto: University of Toronto Press, 1972. lxiii, 185 p. Map. Bibliographic references.

10. Kingsford, William. THE CANADIAN CANALS: THEIR HISTORY AND COST; WITH AN INQUIRY INTO THE POLICY NECESSARY TO ADVANCE THE WELL-BEING OF THE PROVINCE. Toronto: Rollo, 1865. 191 p.

11. Legget, Robert Ferguson. RIDEAU WATERWAY. Rev. ed. Toronto: University of Toronto Press, 1972. xiv, 249 p. Illustrations. Maps. Bibliography, pp. 223-25.

12. Parker, John P. SAILS OF THE MARITIMES; THE STORY OF THE THREE- AND FOUR-MASTED CARGO SCHOONERS OF ATLANTIC CANADA, 1859-1929. Halifax, Nova Scota: Maritime Museum of Canada, 1961. 226 p. Folding frontispiece. Plates. Portraits. Map. Diagrams (part folding). Alphabetical list of the three- and four-masted Canadian-built schooners, pp. 199-218.

13. Skelton, Oscar Douglas. THE RAILWAY BUILDERS, A CHRONICLE OF OVERLAND HIGHWAYS. Chronicles of Canada, no. 32. Toronto: Glasgow, Brook and Co., 1916. 254 p. Illustrations.

14. Smith, William. HISTORY OF THE POST OFFICE IN BRITISH NORTH AMERICA 1639-1870. Cambridge: At the University Press, 1920. ix, 356 p. Bibliographic footnotes.

15. Wallace, Frederick William. WOODEN SHIPS AND IRON MEN; THE STORY OF THE SQUARE-RIGGED MERCHANT MARINE OF BRITISH NORTH AMERICA, THE SHIPS, THEIR BUILDERS AND OWNERS, AND THE MEN WHO SAILED THEM. London: Hodder and Stoughton, 1924. xviii, 337 p. Plates. Illustrated with photographs and drawings.

III.E. ECONOMIC ORGANIZATION

Industrial and labor organization tend to be overshadowed in the colonial period by the direct government participation in, and regulation of, economic affairs. Government policies relating to colonization, commerce, resource use, and social

Colonial Period to 1867

capital formation have received the attention of most writers. For the colonial period, industrial organization is interpreted to mean the state of competition in the staple trades. Voluntary labor organization is of only minor significance before the 1850s.

III.E.i Economic Organization: Industrial Organization

Items 6 and 7 of II.D.i. explore the interplay of competition and monopoly in the early fisheries and in the fur trade, respectively. The story of the early French companies is told in 1 below. The organization of later fur trading companies such as the Hudson's Bay Company and the Northwest Company is described in II.D.i.14 and in 2 below, respectively. For a discussion of similar issues in the Pacific northwest, see 3. The early appearance of agricultural societies is recorded in 5, while the voluntary organization of an early board of trade is treated in 4.

III.E.i. Economic Organization: Industrial Organization

1. Biggar, Henry Percival. THE EARLY TRADING COMPANIES OF NEW FRANCE; A CONTRIBUTION TO THE HISTORY OF COMMERCE AND DISCOVERY IN NORTH AMERICA. Toronto: University of Toronto Library, 1901. Reprint. New York: Argonaut Press, 1965. xii, 308 p. Bibliographic references.

2. Davidson, Gordon Charles. THE NORTH WEST COMPANY. University of California Publications in History, vol. 7. Berkeley and Los Angeles: University of California Press, 1918. Reprint. New York: Russell & Russell, 1967. xi, 349 p. 5 folding maps (including frontispiece).

3. Elliott, G.R. "Frontiers and Forms of Enterprise: The Case of the North Pacific 1785-1825." CANADIAN JOURNAL OF ECONOMICS AND POLITICAL SCIENCE 24 (May 1958): 251-61.

4. McCalla, D. "The Commercial Policies of the Toronto Board of Trade 1850-1860." CANADIAN HISTORICAL REVIEW 50 (March 1969): 51-67.

5. Talman, J.J. "Agricultural Societies of Upper Canada." ONTARIO HISTORICAL SOCIETY PAPERS AND RECORDS 27 (1931): 545-52.

Colonial Period to 1867

III.E.ii. Economic Organization: Labor Organization

The history of labor organization before 1867 has not received separate treatment. The early chapters of 5, 6, and 7 in II.E.ii provide the only available systematic account. See also section 5 of item 1 below, and chapter 22 of II.A.i.4.

III.E.ii. Economic Organization: Labor Organization

1. Cross, Michael S[ean], ed. THE WORKINGMAN IN THE NINETEENTH CENTURY. Toronto: Oxford University Press, 1974. 316 p. Bibliographic note, pp. 313-16.

III.E.iii. Economic Organization: The Role of Government

The rigidity of French mercantilism was exemplified by the detailed state regulations accompanying seigneurialism and its colonizing purpose. For an introduction to the seigneurial system, see 35. A more complete study is provided by Munro in 26 and the accompanying documents in 27. A revisionist interpretation of the impact of seigneurialism on agricultural development is presented in 16. For a general view of the raison d'etre of New France, see 22.

The English mercantilist approach is developed in 19 with respect to the fisheries, in 21 with respect to the fur trade, and more generally in 22. English colonial policy toward the settlement of Upper Canada is exhaustively treated in the well-documented item 13. A special aspect of land policy, the setting aside of clergy reserves, is discussed in 38 and 39.

Government intervention in the late eighteenth and early nineteenth centuries, particularly with respect to trade, was partly determined by the evolution of colonial political power. The early financial administration of Quebec following 1760 is described in 5, while a subsequent episode in the evolution of this administration is discussed in 29 and 30. The development of the franchise is recorded in 12. Political groupings that have economic consequences are explored in 1, 8, and 10. The emergence of a government bureaucracy following the 1840 union of the Canadas is described in detail in 17, and the attending financial problems are discussed in 11. Early social welfare legislation in Ontario is discussed fully in 34.

With respect to commercial policy, early British attitudes are elaborated in 14 and 15. See also 21 regarding British attitudes. The emergence of an independent commercial policy is discussed in II.E.iii.13 and in 36 below. Belonging to this same development is the repeal of the Navigation Acts discussed in 6 and 36. An example of early Canadian commercial policy is described in 18. A considerable literature has developed on the Reciprocity Treaty, 1854-66. A general background is provided by 2. Among the first analyses of the treaty and its impact are 24 and 25, followed by a regional study, 33. The treaty period has more recently been subjected to economic analysis in the revisionist interpretations of 28 and 3. A relevant technical note pertinent to the data used in these analyses is item 4.

The development of property rights over the resources that formed the basis of the early staple trades has also been studied: see, for example, II.E.iii.19. In addition, for the fur staple, the view expressed in 32 is challenged in 23, and a general approach using the economics of property rights is outlined in 9. The development of timber rights and forestland leases is recorded in 37 and further discussed in II.E.iii.12 and II.D.i.15. Aside from the work on seigneurialism already noted, land tenure developments in Upper and Lower Canada are discussed in 31.

III.E.iii. Economic Organization: The Role of Government

1. Aitken, Hugh G.J. "The Family Compact and the Welland Canal Company." CANADIAN JOURNAL OF ECONOMICS AND POLITICAL SCIENCE 18 (February 1952): 63-76.

2. Allin, Celphas Daniel, and Jones, George M. ANNEXATION, PREFERENTIAL TRADE AND RECIPROCITY. AN OUTLINE OF THE CANADIAN ANNEXATION MOVEMENT OF 1849-50, WITH SPECIAL REFERENCE TO THE QUESTIONS OF PREFERENTIAL TRADE AND RECIPROCITY. Toronto: Musson, 1912. Reprint. Westport, Conn.: Greenwood Press, 1971. x, 398 p. Bibliographic references.

3. Ankli, Robert. "The Reciprocity Treaty of 1834." CANADIAN JOURNAL OF ECONOMICS 4 (February 1971): 1-20.

4. Armstrong, F[rederick] H. "Ports of Entry and Collectors of Customs in Upper Canada." INLAND SEAS 26 (Summer1970): 137-244.

5. Balls, H.R. "Quebec 1763-1774: The Financial Administration." CANADIAN HISTORICAL REVIEW 41 (September 1960): 203-14.

6. Brown, G[eorge] W[illiams]. "The Opening of the St. Lawrence to American Shipping." CANADIAN HISTORICAL REVIEW 7 (March 1926): 4-12.

Colonial Period to 1867

7. Cooper, J.I. "Some Early French Canadian Advocacy of Protection 1871-03." CANADIAN JOURNAL OF ECONOMICS AND POLITICAL SCIENCE 3 (November 1937): 530-40.

8. Creighton, D[onald] G[rant]. "The Commercial Class in Canadian Politics 1792-1840." PAPERS AND PROCEEDINGS OF THE CANADIAN POLITICAL SCIENCE ASSOCIATION 5 (May 1933): 43-61.

9. Demsetz, Harold. "Toward a Theory of Property Rights." AMERICAN ECONOMIC REVIEW 57 (May 1967): 347-59.

10. Earl, David W.L., ed. THE FAMILY COMPACT: ARISTOCRACY OR OLIGARCHY? Issues in Canadian History. Toronto: Copp Clark, 1967. vi, 153 p. Bibliography.

11. Faucher, A[lbert]. "Some Aspects of Financial Difficulties of the Province of Canada." CANADIAN JOURNAL OF ECONOMICS AND POLITICAL SCIENCE 26 (November 1960): 617-24.

12. Garner, John [F.]. THE FRANCHISE AND POLITICS IN BRITISH NORTH AMERICA 1755-1867. Canadian Studies in History and Government, no. 13. Toronto: University of Toronto Press, 1969. 258 p. Bibliography included in notes, pp. 217-53.

13. Gates, Lillian Frances. LAND POLICIES OF UPPER CANADA. Canadian Studies in History and Government, no. 9. Toronto: University of Toronto Press, 1968. 378 p. Bibliography, pp. 355-66. Bibliographic references included in notes, pp. 311-52.

14. Graham, Gerald Sandford. BRITISH POLICY AND CANADA 1774-1791, A STUDY IN 18TH CENTURY TRADE POLICY. 1930. Reprint. Westport, Conn.: Greenwood Press, 1974. xi, 161 p. Bibliography, pp. 141-56.

15. _____. SEA POWER AND BRITISH NORTH AMERICA 1783-1820; A STUDY IN BRITISH COLONIAL POLICY. Cambridge, Mass.: Harvard University Press, 1941. xii, 294 p. Tables. Diagrams. Maps. Bibliographic footnotes. Bibliographic note, pp. 291-94.

16. Harris, Richard Colebrook. THE SEIGNEURIAL SYSTEM IN EARLY CANADA. Madison: University of Wisconsin Press, 1966. xvi, 247 p. Illustrations. Maps. Bibliography, pp. 231-39.

17. Hodgetts, J.E. PIONEER PUBLIC SERVICE. Canadian Government Series, no. 7. Toronto: University of Toronto Press, 1956. xii, 292 p. Charts (1 folding). Tables.

Colonial Period to 1867

18. Jones, R[obert] L[eslie]. "The Canadian Agricultural Tariff of 1843." CANADIAN JOURNAL OF ECONOMICS AND POLITICAL SCIENCE 7 (November 1941): 528-37.

19. Judah, Charles Burnett, Jr. ENGLISH COLONIAL POLICY AND THE NORTH AMERICAN FISHERY INDUSTRY 1498-1713. Urbana: University of Illinois, 1933. 7 p. Abstract of "The North American Fisheries and British Policy to 1713," Ph.D. dissertation, University of Illinois, 1933. 183 p. Bibliography, pp. 177-80.

20. Knorr, Klaus Eugen. BRITISH COLONIAL THEORIES, 1570-1850. Foreword by Harold [Adams] Innis. Toronto: University of Toronto Press, 1944. xix, 429 p. Index of names, books, and periodicals, pp. 415-23. Bibliographic footnotes.

21. Lawson, Murray E. FUR: A STUDY IN ENGLISH MERCANTILISM 1700-1775. Foreword by Harold A[dams] Innis. University of Toronto Studies in History and Economics, no. 9. Toronto: University of Toronto Press, 1943. xxiii, 140 p. Bibliography and essay on source material, pp. 73-85.

22. Macdonald, L.R. "France and New France: The Internal Contradictions." CANADIAN HISTORICAL REVIEW 52 (June 1971): 121-43.

23. McManus, John C. "An Economic Analysis of Indian Behaviour in the North American Fur Trade." JOURNAL OF ECONOMIC HISTORY 32 (March 1972): 36-53.

24. Masters, Donald Campbell. RECIPROCITY 1846-1911. Canadian Historical Association Booklet, no. 12. Ottawa: Canadian Archives, 1962. 20 p. Bibliography on inside of back cover.

25. _____. THE RECIPROCITY TREATY OF 1854; ITS HISTORY, ITS RELATION TO BRITISH COLONIAL AND FOREIGN POLICY AND TO THE DEVELOPMENT OF CANADIAN FISCAL AUTONOMY. London: Longmans Green, 1937. xxiv, 267 p. Reprint. Carleton Library, no. 9. Toronto: McClelland & Stewart, 1963. xvi, 191 p. Bibliography, p. 191.

26. Munro, William Bennett. THE SEIGNEURIAL SYSTEM IN CANADA: A STUDY IN FRENCH COLONIAL POLICY. Harvard Historical Studies, no. 13. New York: Longmans Green, 1907. xiii, 296 p. Bibliographic appendix, pp. 253-65. Alphabetical list of printed materials, pp. 267-75.

27. _____, ed. DOCUMENTS RELATING TO THE SEIGNEURIAL TENURE SYSTEM IN CANADA 1598-1854. Historical introduction and explanatory notes by W[illiam] B[ennett] Munro. Toronto: Champlain Society, 1908. cxxiii, 380 p.

28. Officer, L[awrence H.], and Smith, L. "The Canadian-American Reciprocity Treaty 1855-1866." JOURNAL OF ECONOMIC HISTORY 28 (December 1968): 598-623.

29. Paquet, G[illes], and Wallot, J[ean-] P[ierre]. "La Liste civile du Bas-Canada 1794-1812: Un Essai d'économie historique." REVUE D'HISTOIRE DE L'AMERIQUE FRANCAISE 23 (September 1969): 209-31; (December 1969): 361-92; 24 (September 1970): 251-86.

30. _____. PATRONAGE ET POUVOIR DANS LE BAS CANADA 1794-1812. Québec: Les presses de l'Université du Québec, 1973. 185 p.

31. Phillips, Paul [Chrisler]. "Land Tenure and Development in Upper and Lower Canada." JOURNAL OF CANADIAN STUDIES 9 (May 1974): 35-45.

32. Rich, E[dwin] E[rnest]. "Trade Habits and Economic Motivation among the Indians of North America." CANADIAN JOURNAL OF ECONOMICS AND POLITICAL SCIENCE 24 (February 1960): 35-53.

33. Saunders, S[tanley] A[lexander]. "The Reciprocity Treaty of 1854: A Regional Study." CANADIAN JOURNAL OF ECONOMICS AND POLITICAL SCIENCE 2 (February 1936): 41-53.

34. Splane, Richard B. SOCIAL WELFARE IN ONTARIO, 1791-1893; A STUDY OF PUBLIC WELFARE ADMINISTRATION. Toronto: University of Toronto Press, 1965. 305 p. Bibliography, pp. 296-300.

35. Trudel, Marcel. THE SEIGNEURIAL REGIME. Canadian Historical Association Booklet, no. 6. Ottawa: Canadian Archives, 1971. 21 p.

36. Tucker, G.N. CANADIAN COMMERCIAL REVOLUTION 1845-1851. New Haven, Conn.: Yale University Press, 1936. New ed. Introduction by Hugh G.J. Aitken. Carleton Library, no. 19. Toronto: McClelland & Stewart, 1964. xvi, 180 p.

37. White, Aubrey. "A History of Crown Timber Regulations from the Date

of the French Occupation to the Present Time. In REPORT OF THE DEPARTMENT OF LANDS AND FORESTS, pp. 148-284. 2d ed. Toronto: Ontario Department of Lands and Forests, 1907.

38. Wilson, A[lan]. "The Clergy Reserves: Economical Mischiefs or Sectarian Issue?" CANADIAN HISTORICAL REVIEW 42 (December 1961): 281-99.

39. _____. THE CLERGY RESERVES OF UPPER CANADA. Canadian Historical Association Booklet, no. 23. Ottawa: Canadian Archives, 1969. 22 p.

III.F. TECHNOLOGY, PRODUCTIVITY CHANGE, AND WELFARE

The main sources of productivity change in the colonial period were associated with trade and shipping. In addition to II.F.1, an economic analysis of some of these changes pertinent to all North American staple exporters is provided in 1 and 2 below. Little work has been done on the assessment of colonial wealth or income per capita for British North America excluding the thirteen colonies; see, however, IV.B.7 for the 1850s. Although no measures of income distribution exist for the colonial period, divisions of interest based on specific economic function were clearly recognized, as in III.E.iii.8.

III.F. TECHNOLOGY, PRODUCTIVITY CHANGE, AND WELFARE

1. North, Douglass C. "Sources of Productivity Change in Ocean Shipping, 1500-1850." JOURNAL OF POLITICAL ECONOMY 76 (September-October 1968): 953-70.

2. Walton, Gary M., and Shepherd, James F. SHIPPING, MARITIME TRADE, AND ECONOMIC DEVELOPMENT OF COLONIAL NORTH AMERICA. Cambridge: At the University Press, 1972. ix, 255 p. Illustrations. Bibliography, pp. 246-52.

III.G. RESOURCES

In the colonial period, the main research has been to document and interpret the growth of population, particularly the growth resulting from immigration. Capital formation has received little study except for the role played by capital imports, especially in railroad construction.

Colonial Period to 1867

III.G.i. Resources: Land and Its Endowments

For land and resource endowments, see II.G.i. For a study of the relationships between man and land before 1867, see 1 below.

III.G.i. Resources: Land and Its Endowments

1. Harris, R[ichard] Cole[brook], and Warkentin, John. CANADA BEFORE CONFEDERATION, A STUDY IN HISTORICAL GEOGRAPHY. Historical Geography of North America Series, edited by Andrew H. Clark. New York: Oxford University Press, 1974. x, 338 p. Chapter bibliographies.

III.G.ii. Resources: Population

The problems of studying population growth in New France are described in 8. Some attempts to reconstruct this growth are reported in 2 and 3. The record of English immigration to British North America has been extensively documented and discussed. For a short recent summary, see 5. Longer definitive works are 6 and its antecedent 4. An older detailed treatment that also includes a discussion of imperial policy is 10. Some early nineteenth century issues are raised in 1 and 9. The beginnings of settlement at Red River are described in 11, and in the more recent 7.

III.G.ii. Resources: Population

1. Ashton, E.J. "Soldier Land Settlement in Canada." QUARTERLY JOURNAL OF ECONOMICS 39 (May 1925): 488-98.

2. Beauroy, J. "Regards sur la colonisation en Nouvelle France." LA REVUE DE L'UNIVERSITE DE MONCTON, 3e armee, no. 3 (September 1970): 129-40.

3. Charbonneau, Hubert, and Lavoie, Yolande. "Introduction à la reconstitution de la population du Canada au XVIIe siècle, Etude critique des sources de la période 1665-1668." REVUE D'HISTOIRE DE L'AMERIQUE FRANCAISE 24 (March 1971): 485-571.

4. Cowan, Helen I. BRITISH EMIGRATION TO BRITISH NORTH AMERICA, 1783-1837. Studies in History and Economics, vol. 4, no. 2. Toronto: University of Toronto Press, 1928. 275 p. Bibliography, pp. 254-64.

Colonial Period to 1867

5. _____. BRITISH IMMIGRATION BEFORE CONFEDERATION. Canadian Historical Association Booklet, no. 22. Ottawa: Canadian Archives, 1968. 24 p. Diagrams. Map. Bibliography, p. 22.

6. _____. BRITISH IMMIGRATION TO BRITISH NORTH AMERICA; THE FIRST HUNDRED YEARS. Rev. ed. Toronto: University of Toronto Press, 1961. xi, 321 p. Illustrations. Map. Tables. Bibliography.

7. Gray, John Morgan. LORD SELKIRK OF RED RIVER. Toronto: Macmilli n of Canada, 1963. xvii, 388 p. Illustrations. Bibliographic notes.

8. Légaré, Jacques, et al. "The Early Canadian Population: Problems in Automatic Record Linkage." CANADIAN HISTORICAL REVIEW 53 (December 1972): 427-42.

9. Lower, A[rthur] R[eginald] M[arsden]. "Immigration and Settlement in Canada, 1812-20." CANADIAN HISTORICAL REVIEW 3 (March 1933): 37-47.

10. MacDonald, Norman. CANADA, 1763-1841: IMMIGRATION AND SETTLEMENT: THE ADMINISTRATION OF THE IMPERIAL LAND REGULATIONS. London: Longmans Green, 1939. xii, 577 p. Folding map. Bibliography, pp. 531-59.

11. Martin, Chester Bailey. LORD SELKIRK'S WORK IN CANADA. Oxford Historical and Library Studies, vol. 7. Oxford: Clarendon Press, 1916. 240 p. Maps. Bibliographic note, pp. 8-14.

III.G.iii. Resources: Capital Formation

Colonial capital formation is a neglected topic in the literature. There has been some controversy about the relative scarcity of capital at the mid-nineteenth century in British North America, as reflected in the exchange of ideas contained in 1, 3, and 4. That substantial imports of capital from Great Britain went into colonial railroads, however, is incontestable, and is recorded in chapter 7 of item 2.

III.G.iii. Resources: Capital Formation

1. Aitken, Hugh G.J. "A Note on the Capital Resources of Upper Canada." CANADIAN JOURNAL OF ECONOMICS AND POLITICAL SCIENCE 18 (November 1952): 525-32.

Colonial Period to 1867

2. Jenks, Leland Hamilton. THE MIGRATION OF BRITISH CAPITAL TO 1875. New York: Nelson, 1927. 442 p. Bibliographic notes, pp. 337-415.

3. Pentland, H[arry] C[lare]. "Further Observations on Canadian Development." CANADIAN JOURNAL OF ECONOMICS AND POLITICAL SCIENCE 19 (August 1953): 403-10.

4. _____. "The Role of Capital in Canadian Economic Development Before 1875." CANADIAN JOURNAL OF ECONOMICS AND POLITICAL SCIENCE 16 (November 1950): 457-74.

Chapter IV
CONFEDERATION (1867) TO 1920

In this early national period, the original Confederation of Nova Scotia, New Brunswick, and Upper and Lower Canada, henceforward Ontario and Quebec, is enlarged by the addition of Manitoba in 1870, British Columbia in 1871, Prince Edward Island in 1873, and Saskatchewan and Alberta in 1905. These new provinces, however, represented little by way of territorial extension since the western provinces were originally created and subsequently expanded out of Rupert's Land, a major part of the territory formerly attached to the Hudson's Bay Company and purchased by the new Dominion in 1869. The carving up into new provinces of this territory, already under direct Dominion jurisdiction, occurred following the spread of settlement westward. The period is dominated by transcontinental railroad construction and the emergence of wheat as the main export staple. Perhaps because of better statistical documentation, this period has attracted considerable quantitative and analytical attention from economists, as well as voluminous writing by general historians.

IV.A. GENERAL WORKS

Many of the works listed under II.A.ii devote space to the post-1867 period; see especially 2, 4, 6, 18, 19, and 22 of II.A.ii. Most of the works listed below begin at 1867 or later. The most general are 5 and 7. From an economic history standpoint, 9, though old, is still superlative, supplemented by the additional commentary and documentation of 4. See also II.A.ii.19, volume 9, which covers this period. For a series of essays on economic development from 1867 to 1921, see chapters 25-28 of II.A.ii.18. For a recent treatment of the controversial "depression" period before 1900, see item 10 below. Concentrating on the emergence and significance of wheat, particularly after 1900, are 1 and 2. In 3, editorial essays accompany a representative cross section of a wide range of documents pertinent to staple development in four major areas: wheat, minerals, pulp and paper, and hydroelectricity. In 6, an entire issue of THE ANNALS is devoted to the achievements and twentieth-century trends of the Canadian economy to World War II. Many leading scholars contribute in their respective areas. Topics include natural resources, government and politics, industry and labor, finance and trade, and social and cultural features. Finally, the emergence of the north as an economic region is recorded in 11. For a briefer introduction to this aspect of Canadian development, see chapter 12 of II.A.i.2. For an interpretive and quantitative essay from a regional perspective, see 8.

IV.A. GENERAL WORKS

1. Britnell, George Edwin. THE WHEAT ECONOMY. Toronto: University of Toronto Press, 1939. xvi, 259 p. Maps. Bibliographic footnotes.

2. Brown, Robert Craig, and Cook, Ramsey. CANADA 1896-1921: A NATION TRANSFORMED. Canadian Centenary Series, edited by W[illiam] L[ewis] Morton and D[onald] G[rant] Creighton, vol. 14. Toronto: McClelland & Stewart, 1974. xiv, 412 p. Illustrations. Bibliography, pp. 339-44.

3. Burley, Kevin H., ed. THE DEVELOPMENT OF CANADA'S STAPLES 1867-1939. A DOCUMENTARY COLLECTION. Carleton Library, no. 56. Toronto: McClelland & Stewart, 1971. xvi, 376 p. Bibliographies.

4. Canada. Royal Commission on Dominion-Provincial Relations. REPORT OF THE ROYAL COMMISSION ON DOMINION-PROVINCIAL RELATIONS: BOOK I. CANADA 1867-1939; BOOK II. RECOMMENDATIONS; BOOK III. DOCUMENTATION. 3 vols. 1940. Reprint (3 vols. in 1). Ottawa: Queen's Printer, 1954. 223 p. Charts. Tables. BOOK I. CANADA 1867-1939. Abridged ed. Introduction by Donald V. Smiley. Carleton Library, no. 5. Toronto: McClelland & Stewart, 1963. 228 p. Tables.

5. Careless, J[ames] M[aurice] S[tockford], and Brown, Robert Craig. THE CANADIANS 1867-1967. Toronto: Macmillan of Canada, 1967. xix, 856 p.

6. Coats, Robert Hamilton, ed. "Features of Present-Day Canada." ANNALS OF THE AMERICAN ACADEMY OF POLITICAL AND SOCIAL SCIENCE 253 (September 1947): 1-201. Bibliography, pp. 200-201.

7. Creighton, Donald Grant. CANADA'S FIRST CENTURY 1867-1967. Toronto: Macmillan of Canada, 1970. 372 p. Illustrations.

8. Green, Alan G. "Regional Aspects of Canada's Economic Growth, 1890-1929." CANADIAN JOURNAL OF ECONOMICS AND POLITICAL SCIENCE 33 (May 1967): 232-45.

Confederation to 1920

9. Mackintosh, William Archibald. THE ECONOMIC BACKGROUND OF DOMINION PROVINCIAL RELATIONS. Royal Commission on Dominion-Provincial Relations, Appendix 3. Ottawa: King's Printer, 1939. 102 p. New ed. Edited with an introduction by J[ohn] H[arkness] Dales. Carleton Library, no. 13. Toronto: McClelland & Stewart, 1964. 191 p.

10. Waite, Peter B. CANADA 1874-1896, ARDUOUS DESTINY. Canadian Centenary Series, edited by W[illiam] L[ewis] Morton and D[onald] G[rant] Creighton, vol. 12. Toronto: McClelland & Stewart, 1971. 340 p. Illustrations. Map. Bibliographic footnotes. Bibliography, pp. 318-29.

11. Zaslow, Morris. THE OPENING OF THE CANADIAN NORTH 1870-1914. Canadian Centenary Series, edited by W[illaim] L[ewis] Morton and D[onald] G[rant] Creighton, vol. 16. Toronto: McClelland & Stewart, 1971. xii, 339 p. Illustrations. Bibliographic essay, pp. 300-321.

IV.A.i. General Works: The Maritimes

The story of this region's late nineteenth century eclipse by the technology of iron and steam is nowhere better told than in 29 and 30 of II.A.ii. See also 15 below, and chapter 27 of II.A.ii.18, by C.R. Fay. A good statistical treatment of maritime progress since 1867 is provided by 12 below. For a general account of the fisheries, see 14. For Newfoundland, which remained outside Confederation till 1949, there is little to substitute for II.A.ii.26. For a good short treatment, see chapter 28 of II.A.ii.18, by C.A. Harris. For a recent and well-documented account, see 13 below. For an older general treatment of maritime development as a whole, see volume 14 of II.A.ii.19.

IV.A.i. General Works: The Maritimes

12. Canada. Dominion Bureau of Statistics. MARITIME PROVINCES IN THEIR RELATION TO THE NATIONAL ECONOMY OF CANADA; A STATISTICAL STUDY OF THEIR SOCIAL AND ECONOMIC CONDITION SINCE CONFEDERATION. Ottawa: King's Printer, 1934. 133 p.

13. Chadwick, St. John. NEWFOUNDLAND, ISLAND INTO PROVINCE. Cambridge: At the University Press, 1967. xiv, 268 p. Bibliographic references.

14. Grant, Ruth Fulton. THE CANADIAN ATLANTIC FISHERY. Editorial preface by H[arold] A[dams] Innis. Toronto: Ryerson Press, 1934. xxiii, 147 p.

15. Saunders, S[tanley] A[lexander]. THE ECONOMIC WELFARE OF THE MARITIME PROVINCES. Acadia University, Economic Publications, no. 1. Wolfville, Nova Scotia: Acadia University Press, 1932. 160 p. Notes and references, pp. 145-60.

IV.A.ii. General Works: Quebec

The economic development of Quebec in this period has received two comprehensive treatments--in 18 (summarized in 17), and in 20. Both are carefully documented, and include quantitative evidence. A useful cartographic presentation is provided by 19. In 20, the issue of what role the Church played in economic change in this period is raised explicitly, an issue that continues to be alive in recent work on a subsequent period. In item 16, another essay bearing on this issue, Quebec development is placed in a North American context. For an older but still useful treatment, see the essays contained in volumes 15 and 16 of II.A.ii.19.

IV.A.ii. General Works: Quebec

16. Faucher, Albert. QUEBEC EN AMERIQUE AU XIXe SIECLE; ESSAI SUR LES CARACTERES ECONOMIQUES DE LA LAURENTIC. Montréal: Fides, 1973. xvi, 247 p. Illustrations. Bibliographic references.

17. Hamelin, Jean, and Roby, Y[ves]. "L'Evolution économique et sociale de Québec, 1851-96." RECHERCHES SOCIOGRAPHIQUES 10 (May/December 1969): 157-269.

18. _____. HISTOIRE ECONOMIQUE DU QUEBEC 1851-1896. Montréal: Fides, 1971. xxv, 436 p. Tables.

19. Letarte, Jacques. ATLAS D'HISTOIRE ECONOMIQUE ET SOCIALE DU QUEBEC 1851-1901. Montréal: Fides, 1971. 44 maps.

20. Ryan, William F. THE CLERGY AND ECONOMIC GROWTH IN QUEBEC 1896-1914. Québec: Les Presses de l'Université Laval, 1966. 348 p. Map. Bibliography.

IV.A.iii. General Works: Ontario

A comprehensive economic history of Ontario has so far not been undertaken. Short essays on the major topics, however, are available in volumes 17 and 18 of II.A.ii.19, written at the outset of World War I. A classic and well-documented study covering some economic aspects of the period is 22. More recently, two essay collections, 23 and 24, have appeared. Part III of item

23 includes essays on early oil, hydro, tourism, and agricultural development, as well as the Innis introductory essay cited in II.A.ii.37. Chapter 4 of item 21 contains a useful bibliography of a wide variety of items under an economic history heading.

IV.A.iii. General Works: Ontario

21. French, Goldwin S., and Oliver, Peter N. ONTARIO SINCE 1867, A BIBLIOGRAPHY. Ontario Historical Studies Series. Toronto: Queen's Printer; Ontario Ministry of Colleges and Universities, 1973. 330 p.

22. Landon, Fred. WESTERN ONTARIO AND THE AMERICAN FRONTIER. Toronto: Ryerson Press, 1941. xvi, 305 p. Maps. Bibliography, pp. 285-93.

23. Stevenson, Hugh A., and Armstrong, F[rederick] H., eds. ASPECTS OF NINETEENTH CENTURY ONTARIO: ESSAYS PRESENTED TO JAMES J. TALMAN. Toronto: University of Toronto Press, 1974. xiii, 355 p. Maps. Bibliographies.

24. Zaslow, Morris, ed. PROFILES OF A PROVINCE, STUDIES IN THE HISTORY OF ONTARIO. A collection of essays commissioned by the Ontario Historical Society to commemorate the centennial of Ontario. Toronto: Ontario Historical Society, 1967. xiii, 233 p.

IV.A.iv. General Works: The West

For a short introduction to western settlement, see chapters 22 and 23 of II.A.ii.18. Older but still useful are the essays in volumes 19 and 20 of II.A.ii.19. For the prairies, see 41, 42, and 45, in II.A.ii and the statistical source, 26, listed below. For British Columbia, volumes 21 and 22 of II.A.ii.19, together with the later chapters of II.A.ii.38, remain useful. See also 25, 27, and 29 below. Although mainly political, 29 often touches upon topics of economic importance. For some comparative views of western prairie developments, see 28 and 30.

IV.A.iv. General Works: The West

25. British Columbia. Economic Council. STATISTICS OF INDUSTRY IN BRITISH COLUMBIA 1871-1934. Victoria, British Columbia: King's Printer, 1935. 314 p.

26. Canada. Dominion Bureau of Statistics. THE PRAIRIE PROVINCES IN THEIR RELATION TO THE NATIONAL ECONOMY OF CANADA: A

Confederation to 1920

STATISTICAL STUDY OF THEIR SOCIAL AND ECONOMIC CONDITION IN THE TWENTIETH CENTURY. Ottawa: King's Printer, 1934. vi, 153 p.

27. Carrothers, W.A. "The Barter Terms of Trade between British Columbia and Eastern Canada." CANADIAN JOURNAL OF ECONOMICS AND POLITICAL SCIENCE 1 (November 1935): 568-77.

28. MacKirdy, K[enneth] A. "Conflict of Loyalties: The Problem of Assimilating the Far Wests into Canadian and Australian Federations." CANADIAN HISTORICAL REVIEW 32 (December 1951): 337-55.

29. Robin, Martin. THE RUSH FOR SPOILS, THE COMPANY PROVINCE 1871-1933. Toronto: McClelland & Stewart, 1972. 318 p. Bibliography, pp. 308-11. Bibliographic footnotes.

30. Sharp, Paul Fredrick. WHOOP-UP COUNTRY: THE CANADIAN-AMERICAN WEST 1865-85. Minneapolis: University of Minnesota Press, 1955. 347 p. Illustrations. Bibliography.

IV.B. STATISTICAL RECORD

Although the data is more abundant and better organized for this period than for the preceding one, it is still scanty apart from the decennial censuses and the trade statistics. The best single source is II.B.2. Somewhat more detailed, though drawn from virtually the same raw sources, are the later issues of III.B.7, followed by 2 and 3 listed below. For Quebec, see 9. Of special interest, though controversial, are the national income compilations of O.J. Firestone contained in 6. See also the critical commentary on these provided in 1. For a short account of pre-1900 Canadian development, also controversial and by the same author, see 7. Pre-1930 statistics have been collected together in 5 for the area of banking and in 10 for trade and commerce. A useful volume of price statistics is provided by 4. In addition to the foregoing, many of the items listed in other special topic sections below contain substantial statistical material. Numerous Federal Royal Commissions over the years frequently developed statistical documentation not elsewhere published. A complete index of these is provided by 8.

IV.B. STATISTICAL RECORD

1. Buckley, Kenneth A.H. "Review of O.J. Firestone, CANADA'S ECONOMIC DEVELOPMENT, 1867-1953." AMERICAN ECONOMIC REVIEW 39 (June 1959): 431-33.

2. Canada. Department of Agriculture. STATISTICAL ABSTRACT AND RECORD. Ottawa: MacLean, Roger, 1885-1904. Annual.

3. Canada. Department of Trade and Commerce. THE CANADA YEAR BOOK. 2d ser. Ottawa: King's Printer, 1905-- . Annual.

4. Coats, Robert Hamilton. WHOLESALE PRICES IN CANADA 1890-1909. Canada, Department of Labour Special Report. Ottawa: King's Printer, 1910. xiii, 509 p.

5. Curtis, Clifford Austin. STATISTICS OF BANKING. Statistical Contributions to Canadian Economic History, vol. 1. Toronto: Macmillan of Canada, 1931. xii, 93 p. Tables. Diagrams.

6. Firestone, Otto Jack. CANADA'S ECONOMIC DEVELOPMENT, 1867-1953 WITH SPECIAL REFERENCE TO CHANGES IN THE COUNTRY'S NATIONAL PRODUCT AND NATIONAL WEALTH. Preface by Simon Kuznets. International Association for Research in Income and Wealth Series, no. 7. London: Bowes and Bowes, 1958. xxvi, 384 p. Tables (some folding).

7. _____. "Development of Canada's Economy, 1850-1900." In TRENDS IN THE AMERICAN ECONOMY IN THE NINETEENTH CENTURY, pp. 217-52. National Bureau of Economic Research Studies in Income and Wealth, vol. 24. Princeton, N.J.: Princeton University Press, 1960.

8. Henderson, George Fletcher. FEDERAL ROYAL COMMISSIONS IN CANADA 1867-1966. Toronto: University of Toronto Press, 1967. xiii, 212 p. Bibliography, pp. 185-86.

9. STATISTICAL YEARBOOK OF THE PROVINCE OF QUEBEC. Quebec: King's Printer, 1914-- . Annual.

10. Taylor, Kenneth Wiffin, and Mitchell, H. STATISTICS OF TRADE; STATISTICS OF PRICES. Statistical Contributions to Canadian History, vol. 2. Toronto: Macmillan of Canada, 1931. 93 p. Tables. Diagrams.

IV.C. THESES OF ECONOMIC GROWTH

There have been at least two major sources of debate over the interpretation of Canadian economic growth in this period. The first relates to the presence or absence of discontinuity in the growth process. A leading spokesman for discontinuity is Rostow. His argument is developed in item 6, especially chapter

4. For a contrary view, see 1, and chapter 16 in item 7. A second controversy is over the contribution to Canadian economic growth made by the early twentieth century wheat boom. The arguments that have been advanced here are summarized in 2. A third area of revisionism has focused on the role of nineteenth-century national policies. In item 4 Fowke presents a comparative view, while in 3 Dales questions what positive contribution, if any, these policies have made to economic growth. In part 1 of a general study, 5, Goodwin describes the development of Canadian economic thought and policy in the century before World War I.

IV.C. THESES OF ECONOMIC GROWTH

1. Bertram, Gordon W. "Economic Growth and Canadian Industry, 1870-1915: The Staple Model and the Take-off Hypothesis." CANADIAN JOURNAL OF ECONOMICS AND POLITICAL SCIENCE 29 (May 1963): 162-84.

2. Caves, Richard Earl. "Export-Led Growth and the New Economic History." In TRADE, BALANCE OF PAYMENTS AND GROWTH, edited by Jagdish N. Bhagwati et al., pp. 403-42. Amsterdam: North-Holland, 1971. Bibliography, pp. 439-42.

3. Dales, John Harkness. "Some Historical and Theoretical Comments on Canada's National Policies." QUEEN'S QUARTERLY 71 (Autumn 1964): 297-316.

4. Fowke, Vernon Clifford. "National Policy and Western Development in North America." JOURNAL OF ECONOMIC HISTORY 14 (December 1956): 461-79.

5. Goodwin, Craufurd D.W. CANADIAN ECONOMIC THOUGHT; THE POLITICAL ECONOMY OF A DEVELOPING NATION, 1814-1914. Duke University, Commonwealth Studies Center, publication no. 15. Durham, N.C.: Duke University Press, 1961. xvi, 214 p. Diagrams. Bibliographic footnotes.

6. Rostow, Walt W. THE STAGES OF ECONOMIC GROWTH, A NON-COMMUNIST MANIFESTO. 2d ed. Cambridge: At the University Press, 1971. xix, 253 p.

7. _____, ed. THE ECONOMICS OF TAKE-OFF INTO SUSTAINED GROWTH. Proceedings of a conference held by the International Economic Association, ca. 1961. London: Macmillan and Co., 1968. xxvi, 481 p. Tables. Diagrams. Bibliographic footnotes.

Confederation to 1920

IV.D. SECTORS AND INDUSTRIES

Under the impetus of the wheat boom, considerable expansion and diversification in the Canadian economy took place. By 1920, the value of secondary production exceeded that of primary production. At the same time, railroad mileage expanded rapidly with two new transcontinentals before World War I. The literature reflects the attention paid to all of these developments.

IV.D.i. Sectors and Industries: Primary Industry

Although forest products continued to be major Canadian staple exports almost to the end of the nineteenth century, by the mid-1890s primary attention had turned to wheat, the leading staple export thereafter to World War I. The forest industry in the late nineteenth century is well covered in II.D.i.13 and II.D.i.15. A further account with statistical documentation is provided in 8.

The development of wheat growing on the Canadian prairie, and of wheat exports is treated concisely in chapter 6 of II.A.ii.1. Fuller accounts are provided by 3, 4, 14, and 18. The international setting of Canadian wheat growing is explored in items 23, 17, and 15. Item 15 also provides an economic and statistical analysis of the world wheat market. The best sources of statistical materials are compiled under the auspices of the Stanford Food Research Institute, as in 1 and 28.

Trade and balance of payment adjustments during the wheat boom have been extensively researched. The underlying statistical work is found in 9 and 10. Key analytical studies are 27 and a major interpretive revision, 26; see also 16 and 11. Several related works, 25, 24, 19, 22, and 20, deal with the overseas trade of Great Britain, Canada's most important trading partner for wheat and cattle. Trade in agricultural goods with the United States is treated in 12.

The significance of wheat for early twentieth century Canadian economic growth has recently been explored with the aid of economic and quantitative analysis in 5, sparking the exchange in 6 and 7. Extensions of the analysis have led to the revisions contained in 2 and IV.C.2.

For eastern agricultural development, III.D.i.6 covers part of the Ontario story, and 13 below extends this briefly to 1919. For Quebec, see II.D.i.12, and for the maritimes, see items 29 and 30 in II.A.ii.

Finally, the early petroleum story is treated in 21. For mining in general, see, II.D.i.11.

Confederation to 1920

IV.D.i. Sectors and Industries: Primary Industry

1. Bennett, M.D. "World Wheat Crops 1885-1932, New Series with Areas and Yields by Countries." WHEAT STUDIES 9 (April 1933): 239-74.

2. Bertram, Gordon W. "The Relevance of the Wheat Boom in Canadian Economic Growth." CANADIAN JOURNAL OF ECONOMICS 6 (November 1973): 545-66.

3. Bracken, John. CROP PRODUCTION IN WESTERN CANADA. Winnipeg, Manitoba: Grain Growers' Guide, 1920. xxvi, 423 p. Statistical appendix.

4. Buller, Arthur Henry Reginald. ESSAYS ON WHEAT, INCLUDING THE DISCOVERY AND INTRODUCTION OF MARQUIS WHEAT, THE EARLY HISTORY OF WHEAT GROWING IN MANITOBA, WHEAT IN WESTERN CANADA, ETC. New York: Macmillan, 1919. xv, 339 p. Frontispiece portrait. Illustrations. Plates.

5. Chambers, E.J., and Gordon, D[onald] F. "Primary Products and Economic Growth: An Empirical Measurement." JOURNAL OF POLITICAL ECONOMY 74 (August 1966): 315-22.

6. _____. "Primary Products and Economic Growth: A Rejoinder." JOURNAL OF POLITICAL ECONOMY 75 (December 1967): 881-85.

7. Dales, John Harkness, et al. "Primary Products and Economic Growth: A Comment." JOURNAL OF POLITICAL ECONOMY 75 (December 1967): 876-80.

8. Defebaugh, James Elliot. HISTORY OF THE LUMBER INDUSTRY IN AMERICA. Vol. 1, chaps. 1-25. 2d ed. Chicago: American Lumberman, 1906.

9. Firestone, O[tto] J[ack]. "Canada's External Trade and Net Foreign Balance 1851-1900." In TRENDS IN THE AMERICAN ECONOMY IN THE NINETEENTH CENTURY, pp. 757-71. National Bureau of Economic Research Studies in Income and Wealth, vol. 24. Princeton, N.J.: Princeton University Press, 1960.

10. Hartland, P. [E.]. "Canadian Balance of Payments since 1868." In TRENDS IN THE AMERICAN ECONOMY IN THE NINETEENTH CENTURY, pp. 717-55. National Bureau of Economic Research Studies in Income and Wealth, vol. 24. Princeton, N.J.: Princeton University Press, 1960.

Confederation to 1920

11. Ingram, J.C. "Growth in Capacity and Canada's Balance of Payments." AMERICAN ECONOMIC REVIEW 48 (March 1957): 93-104.

12. Innis, Harold Adams, and Jacobsen, M.W. "Agriculture and Canadian-American Trade." Sixth conference of the Institute of Pacific Relations. CANADIAN PAPERS 3 (August 1936): 1-17.

13. Lawr, D[ouglas] A. "The Development of Ontario Farming, 1870-1919: Patterns of Growth and Change." ONTARIO HISTORY 44 (December 1972): 239-51.

14. MacGibbon, Duncan Alexander. THE CANADIAN GRAIN TRADE. Toronto: Macmillan of Canada, 1932. xiv, 503 p. Frontispiece. Illustrations. Plates.

15. Malenbaum, Wilfred. THE WORLD WHEAT ECONOMY 1885-1939. Cambridge, Mass.: Harvard University Press, 1953. xiv, 262 p. Illustrations. Map. Bibliography.

16. Meier, Gerald M. "Economic Development and the Transfer Mechanism: Canada 1895-1913." CANADIAN JOURNAL OF ECONOMICS AND POLITICAL SCIENCE 19 (February 1953): 1-19.

17. Mitchell, H. "Notes on Prices of Agricultural Commodities in the United States and Canada 1850-1934." CANADIAN JOURNAL OF ECONOMICS AND POLITICAL SCIENCE 1 (May 1935): 269-79.

18. Murchie, Robert Welch, et al. AGRICULTURAL PROGRESS ON THE PRAIRIE FRONTIER. Toronto: Macmillan of Canada, 1936. xii, 344 p. Illustrations. Diagrams.

19. Olson, Marcus, and Harris, Curtis C. "Free Trade in 'Corn': A Statistical Study of the Prices and Production of Wheat in Great Britain from 1873-1914." QUARTERLY JOURNAL OF ECONOMICS 73 (February 1959): 145-68.

20. Perren, Richard. "The North American Beef and Cattle Trade with Great Britain, 1870-1914." ECONOMIC HISTORY REVIEW, 2d ser. 24 (August 1971): 430-44.

21. Ross, Victor Harold. PETROLEUM IN CANADA. Toronto: Southam Press, 1917. 109 p. Illustrations.

22. Rutherford, John Gunion. THE CATTLE TRADE OF WESTERN CANADA. Ottawa: King's Printer, 1909. 23 p.

23. Rutter, William Pickering. WHEAT-GROWING IN CANADA, THE UNITED STATES AND ARGENTINA. London: Adam and Charles Black, 1911. x, 315 p.

24. Saul, Samuel Berrick. "British Trade with the Empire: I. Canada." In STUDIES IN BRITISH OVERSEAS TRADE 1870-1914, pp. 169-87. Liverpool: Liverpool University Press, 1960. Bibliographic footnotes.

25. Schlote, Werner. BRITISH OVERSEAS TRADE FROM 1700 TO THE 1930'S. Oxford: Blackwell, 1952. xvi, 181 p. Illustrations.

26. Stovel, John A. CANADA IN THE WORLD ECONOMY. Harvard Economic Studies, no. 108. Cambridge, Mass.: Harvard University Press, 1959. xiii, 364 p. Diagrams. Bibliography, pp. 347-58.

27. Viner, Jacob. CANADA'S BALANCE OF INTERNATIONAL INDEBTEDNESS, 1900-1913. Introduction by H[arry] C. Eastman. Carleton Library, no. 86. Toronto: McClelland & Stewart, 1975. xvi, 312 p. Bibliography, pp. 309-12.

28. Wright, C.P., and Davis, J[ohn] S. "Canada as a Producer and Exporter of Wheat." WHEAT STUDIES 1 (July 1925): 217-86.

IV.D.ii. Sectors and Industries: Secondary Industry

The development of the manufacturing sector and the associated urbanization in central Canada in this period have been carefully examined. A short overview of manufacturing development is provided in II.A.ii.18, section III, chapter 25, or by IV.B.7. In addition to the pioneering analysis of census data undertaken in IV.C.1, the statistical documentation has been reworked in 4, 10, and 11, listed below. There are also the industry studies noted under II.D.ii. See, in addition, 7 below, for the early history of Canada's leading industry in this period, and other specialized studies, 2, 5, and 16. See also pages 467-75 of I.B.2 for 1952-53.

Connections with urban development have been examined by both geographers and economists, as well as sociologists and general historians. Geographers have contributed 8 and 17 which include considerable statistical detail and interpretation. For an economist's approach, see 3 and 6. A good historical section is included in 15, the work of a sociologist. For an explicitly sociological essay, see 1. Probably the most complete statistical effort is the census monograph, 19. The two largest centers of manufacturing, Toronto and Montreal,

Confederation to 1920

have been examined in a number of studies. Representative are 9 for Toronto and 14 for Montreal, and their rivalry is discussed in 13. For the rise of a company town, typical of mining operations in the shield, see 18.

IV.D.ii. Sectors and Industries: Secondary Industry

1. Acheson, T[homas] W[illiam]. "Changing Social Origins of the Canadian Industrial Elite, 1880-1910." BUSINESS HISTORY REVIEW 47 (Summer 1973): 189-217.

2. Brady, Alexander. "The Ontario Hydro-Electric Power Commission." CANADIAN JOURNAL OF ECONOMICS AND POLITICAL SCIENCE 2 (August 1936): 331-53.

3. Chambers, E.J., and Bertram, G[ordon] W. "Urbanization and Manufacturing in Central Canada 1870-90." In CANADIAN POLITICAL SCIENCE ASSOCIATION CONFERENCE PAPERS ON STATISTICS, 1964, edited by S[ylvia] Ostry and T.K. Rymes, pp. 225-58. Toronto: University of Toronto Press, 1964.

4. Dales, John H[arkness]. "Estimates of Canadian Manufacturing Output by Markets 1870-1915." In CANADIAN POLITICAL SCIENCE ASSOCIATION CONFERENCE PAPERS ON STATISTICS, 1962-63, edited by J[acques] Henripin and A. Asimakopulos, pp. 61-92. Toronto: University of Toronto Press, 1964.

5. _____. HYDROELECTRICITY AND INDUSTRIAL DEVELOPMENT: QUEBEC 1898-1940. Cambridge, Mass.: Harvard University Press, 1957. xii, 269 p. Illustrations. Maps. Bibliography.

6. Faucher, A[lbert], and Lamontagne, M[aurice]. "History of Industrial Development." In ESSAYS ON CONTEMPORARY QUEBEC, edited by J.C. Falardeau, pp. 23-37. Québec: Les Presses de L'Université Laval, 1953. Tables. Bibliographic footnotes.

7. Forsey, E[ugene]. "The Pulp and Paper Industry." CANADIAN JOURNAL OF ECONOMICS AND POLITICAL SCIENCE 1 (August 1935): 501-9.

8. Gilmour, James M. SPATIAL EVOLUTION OF MANUFACTURING, SOUTHERN ONTARIO 1851-1891. Toronto: University of Toronto Press, 1972. xvi, 214 p.

9. Glazebrook, G[eorge] P[arkin] de T[wenebroker]. THE STORY OF TORONTO. Toronto: University of Toronto Press, 1971. xi, 310 p. Illustrations. Bibliographic footnotes. Bibliography, pp. 295-301

10. McDougall, Duncan M. "Canadian Manufactured Commodity Output, 1870-1915." CANADIAN JOURNAL OF ECONOMICS 4 (February 1971): 21-36.

11. _____. "The Domestic Availability of Manufactured Commodity Output, Canada, 1870-1915." CANADIAN JOURNAL OF ECONOMICS 6 (May 1973): 189-206.

12. Masters, Donald Campbell. THE RISE OF TORONTO 1850-1890. Toronto: University of Toronto Press, 1947. xi, 299 p. Maps. Bibliographic footnotes.

13. _____. "Toronto vs. Montreal, The Struggle for Financial Hegemony 1860-1875." CANADIAN HISTORICAL REVIEW 22 (June 1941): 133-46.

14. Minville, Esdras, ed. MONTREAL ECONOMIQUE. Montreal: Fides, 1943. 430 p.

15. Nader, George A. THEORETICAL, HISTORICAL AND PLANNING PERSPECTIVES. Cities of Canada, vol. 1. Toronto: Macmillan of Canada, 1975. xi, 404 p. Bibliography, pp. 371-88.

16. Reid, D.J. THE DEVELOPMENT OF THE FRASER RIVER SALMON CANNING INDUSTRY 1885-1913. Vancouver, British Columbia: Department of the Environment, 1973.

17. Spelt, Jacob. URBAN DEVELOPMENT IN SOUTH CENTRAL ONTARIO. Carleton Library, no. 57. Toronto: McClelland & Stewart, 1972. 296 p.

18. Stetler, Gilbert. "The Origins of a Company Town, Sudbury in the Nineteenth Century." LAURENTIAN UNIVERSITY REVIEW 3 (February 1971): 3-37.

19. Stone, Leroy O. URBAN DEVELOPMENT IN CANADA. 1961 Census Monograph. Ottawa: Dominion Bureau of Statistics, 1967. xxi, 293 p. Tables. Folding map. Bibliography, pp. 283-93.

IV.D.iii. Sectors and Industries: Tertiary Industry

The development of the transportation system, particularly with the construction of transcontinental railroads, and the extension of branch banking, dominate the writing on changes in the tertiary sector in this period.

Confederation to 1920

The standard comprehensive work on transportation development is II.D.iii.8. Somewhat older, but still useful for this period, is volume 10 of II.A.ii.19. For water transportation, see also II.D.iii.18; 12 and 15 of III.D.iii; and 5. below. For railroads, in addition to III.D.iii.13 and items 2, 16, and 17 of II.D.iii, considerable published research has been undertaken on the Canadian Pacific Railroad, the first Canadian transcontinental. For a short recent introduction, see 13. Still useful is 12, the first detailed study to be made. A more stylish treatment is provided by 11, and more recently by 1 and 2. Quantitative evaluations of the private rate of return to the C.P.R. include 10 and 14. See also the short discussions in 9, and especially the introduction to the recent reprint of 12, discussing issues of historiography. A useful record of all Canadian railroad construction before World War I is 4. A brief account of Canada's second transcontinental, the Canadian Northern and Grand Trunk Pacific, is provided in 15. This road together with a third, the National Transcontinental, became part of the government-owned Canadian National Railroad system formed in 1922. For this story, see 2 and 16 of II.D.iii. A concise account of the post office since 1867 is given in 6.

For the evolution of the banking system and of the capital market, see again 13, 14, and 15 of II.D.iii. A much older but reliable nineteenth-century history of Canadian banking is 3; see also III.D.iii.2. Detailed histories up to 1920 of two of the chartered banks are supplied in 16 and 18. The appearance of nonbank financial intermediaries was well under way by 1900. See, for example, 19 for mortgage lending, and 7 for life insurance. The evolution of sources of farm credit is treated in 8.

IV.D.iii. Sectors and Industries: Tertiary Industry

1. Berton, Pierre. THE LAST SPIKE; THE GREAT RAILWAY, 1881-1885. Toronto: McClelland & Stewart, 1971. 478 p. Illustrations. Maps. Bibliography, pp. 451-61. Sequel to THE NATIONAL DREAM, item 2.

2. _____. THE NATIONAL DREAM; THE GREAT RAILWAY, 1871-1881. Toronto: McClelland & Stewart, 1970. xiii, 439 p. Maps. Bibliography, pp. 415-23.

3. Breckenridge, Roeliff Morton. THE HISTORY OF BANKING IN CANADA. Publications of the National Monetary Commission, vol. 9, no. 1. Washington: Government Printing Office, 1910. vi, 308 p. 6 folding tables.

4. Butlin, Noel G. FINDING LIST OF CANADIAN RAILWAY COMPANIES BEFORE 1915. Washington, D.C.: Library of the Bureau of Railway Economics, Association of American Railroads, 1953. 31 p.

5. Croil, James. STEAM NAVIGATION, AND ITS RELATION TO THE

Confederation to 1920

      COMMERCE OF CANADA AND THE UNITED STATES. Toronto: W. Briggs, 1898. xiv, 381 p. Frontispiece. Illustrations. Portraits. Plates.

6. Currie, Archibald William. "The Post Office Since 1867." CANADIAN JOURNAL OF ECONOMICS AND POLITICAL SCIENCE 24 (May 1958): 241-50.

7. Drummond, Ian Macdonald. "Life Insurance Companies and the Capital Market 1890-1914." CANADIAN JOURNAL OF ECONOMICS AND POLITICAL SCIENCE 28 (May 1962): 204-24.

8. Easterbrook, William Thomas. FARM CREDIT IN CANADA. Toronto: University of Toronto Press, 1938. viii, 260 p.

9. George, Peter J. GOVERNMENT INTERVENTION, RAILWAYS AND CANADIAN ECONOMIC DEVELOPMENT: THE CASE OF THE C.P.R. Canadian Perspectives in Economics. Toronto: Collier-Macmillan, 1973. 8 p.

10. _____. "Rates of Return in Railway Investment and Implications for Government Subsidization of the Canadian Pacific Railway: Some Preliminary Results." CANADIAN JOURNAL OF ECONOMICS 1 (November 1968): 740-62.

11. Gibbon, John Murray. THE ROMANTIC HISTORY OF THE CANADIAN PACIFIC: THE NORTHWEST PASSAGE OF TODAY. New York: Tudor Publishing Co., 1937. 423 p. Illustrations. Plates. Maps. Bibliography.

12. Innis, Harold A[dams]. HISTORY OF THE CANADIAN PACIFIC RAILWAY. London: King and Son, 1923. viii, 365 p. Reprint. Introduction by Peter George. Toronto: University of Toronto Press, 1971. xxii, 365 p.

13. McDougall, John Lorne. CANADIAN PACIFIC, A BRIEF HISTORY. Montreal: McGill University Press, 1968. xi, 200 p.

14. Mercer, Lloyd J. "Rates of Return and Government Subsidization of the Canadian Pacific Railway: An Alternative View." CANADIAN JOURNAL OF ECONOMICS 6 (August 1973): 428-37.

15. Regehr, T.D. "The Canadian Northern Railway: The West's Own Product." CANADIAN HISTORICAL REVIEW 51 (June 1970): 177-87.

16. Ross, Victor [Harold]. A HISTORY OF THE CANADIAN BANK OF COMMERCE, WITH AN ACCOUNT OF THE OTHER BANKS THAT NOW FORM PART OF ITS ORGANIZATION. 3 vols. Toronto: Oxford University Press, 1920. xvi, 515 p.; xiii, 595 p.; xv, 576 p. Footnotes. Plates. Portraits. Facsimiles.

17. Savage, Rosemary Lorna. "American Concern over Canadian Railway Competition in the Northwest, 1885-1890." CANADIAN HISTORICAL ASSOCIATION ANNUAL REPORT, 1942, pp. 82-93

18. Skelton, Oscar Douglas, and the Dominion Bank. FIFTY YEARS OF BANKING SERVICE, 1871-1921. Toronto: Toronto Dominion Bank, 1922. 227 p. Plates. Portraits.

19. Stevens, George Roy. THE CANADA PERMANENT STORY, 1855-1955. Toronto: Canada Permanent Mortgage Corp., 1955. 60 pages of illustrations. Portraits.

IV.E. ECONOMIC ORGANIZATION

The role of the state in coordinating economic activity continues to be important in this period. Voluntary organizations among farmers, workers, and industrialists appear more marked than earlier, partly to enlist government support for their interests. These developments accompany the achievement of substantial prairie settlement before 1920, and increasing urbanization and concentration of industry in central Canada.

IV.E.i. Economic Organization: Industrial Organization

The voluntary organization of both farmers and manufacturers is included here. One of the earliest works dealing with farmer organization is 9. The cooperative movement among western farmers is given a detailed treatment in 2, 3, 4, and 5. For the movement in Ontario, see 8. A comparative view of Canadian and American western farm protest is presented in 7. Within industry, a tendency toward concentration and association among manufacturers is described in 1. For the establishment of American branch plants, see II.D.ii.10, II.E.i.2, and 6 below.

IV.E.i. Economic Organization: Industrial Organization

1. Clark, Samuel Delbert. THE CANADIAN MANUFACTURERS' ASSOCIATION; A STUDY IN COLLECTIVE BARGAINING AND POLITICAL PRESSURE. Toronto: University of Toronto Press, 1939. xiii, 107 p.

Confederation to 1920

2. Colquette, R.D. THE FIRST FIFTY YEARS, A HISTORY OF THE UNITED GRAIN GROWERS LIMITED. Winnipeg, Manitoba: The Public Press, 1957. viii, 309 p.

3. Mackintosh, William Archibald. AGRICULTURAL CO-OPERATION IN WESTERN CANADA. Toronto: Ryerson Press, 1924. viii, 173 p. Bibliography, pp. 160-65.

4. _____. THE CANADIAN WHEAT POOLS. Kingston, Ontario: Jackson Press, 1925. 28 p.

5. Patton, Harold S. GRAIN GROWERS' CO-OPERATION IN WESTERN CANADA. Cambridge, Mass.: Harvard University Press, 1928. xix, 471 p. Sources and references, pp. 449-60.

6. Radosh, Ronald. "American Manufacturers, Canadian Reciprocity and the Origins of the Branch Factory System." BULLETIN OF THE CANADIAN ASSOCIATION FOR AMERICAN STUDIES 3 (Spring-Summer 1967): 19-54.

7. Sharp, Paul F[redrick]. THE AGRARIAN REVOLT IN WESTERN CANADA, A SURVEY SHOWING AMERICAN PARALLELS. Minneapolis: University of Minnesota Press, 1948. ix, 204 p. Bibliography, pp. 193-98.

8. Staples, Meville H., ed. THE CHALLENGE OF AGRICULTURE, THE STORY OF THE UNITED FARMERS OF ONTARIO. Toronto: Morang, 1921. 197 p.

9. Wood, L.A. HISTORY OF FARMERS' MOVEMENTS IN CANADA. Toronto: Ryerson Press, 1924. 372 p.

IV.E.ii. Economic Organization: Labor Organization

The main sources for the growth of the labor movement in this period remain 5, 6, and 7 of II.E.ii. Some aspects of the movement in Quebec are dealt with briefly in 1 and 4 below, and the contribution of the Knights of Labor is reviewed in 6. An excellent short essay on the development of the labor market is supplied by 8. A fairly exhaustive history of industrial disputes is provided by 5, and some aspects of the Winnipeg General Strike are treated in 2, 3, and 7. For the political adventures of Canadian labor in this period, see 9. See also II.A.i.4, chapter 22.

Confederation to 1920

IV.E.ii. Economic Organization: Labor
Organization

1. Babcock, Robert H. "Samuel Gompers and the French Canadian Worker 1900-1914." AMERICAN REVIEW OF CANADIAN STUDIES 3 (Autumn 1973): 47-66.

2. Balawyder, A. THE WINNIPEG GENERAL STRIKE. Vancouver, British Columbia: Copp Clark, 1967. 49 p. Bibliography, p. 49.

3. Bercuson, David J. "The Winnipeg General Strike, Collective Bargaining and the One Big Union Issue." CANADIAN HISTORICAL REVIEW 51 (June 1970): 164-76.

4. Espessat, Hélène; Hardy, Jean-Pierre; and Ruddell, Thierry. "Le monde du travail du Québec au XVIIIe et au XIXe siècles: Historiographie et état de la question." REVUE D'HISTOIRE DE L'AMERIQUE FRANCAISE 25 (March 1972): 499-539.

5. Jamieson, Stuart Marshall. TIMES OF TROUBLE: LABOUR UNREST AND INDUSTRIAL CONFLICT IN CANADA 1900-1966. Task Force on Labour Relations Study, no. 22. Ottawa: Queen's Printer, 1971. xii, 524 p. Resume in French. Bibliographic references.

6. Kennedy, Douglas Ross. THE KNIGHTS OF LABOUR IN CANADA. London, Ontario: University of Western Ontario, 1956. 127 p. Portraits. Tables. Bibliography, pp. 125-27.

7. Masters, D[onald] C[ampbell]. THE WINNIPEG GENERAL STRIKE. Social-Credit in Alberta; Its Background and Development, no. 2. Toronto: University of Toronto Press, 1950. xv, 159 p. Illustrations.

8. Pentland, Harry Clare. "The Development of the Capitalistic Labour Market in Canada." CANADIAN JOURNAL OF ECONOMICS AND POLITICAL SCIENCE 28 (May 1962): 204-24.

9. Robin, Martin. RADICAL POLITICS AND CANADIAN LABOUR 1880-1930. Kingston, Ontario: Industrial Relations Centre, Queen's University, 1968. xi, 321 p. Bibliography, pp. 295-301.

IV.E.iii. Economic Organization: The Role of
Government

As under III.E.iii, the literature can be divided into four fairly well-defined areas: (1) commercial policy; (2) settlement, railroad, and resource policies; (3) competition policy; and (4) labor policy. A general essay, by way of introduction, is provided by 33, and an overview of the history of changing government activities is given by 13 and 14. Fiscal development is well treated by II.E.iii.18, which can be supplemented by 5 and 27 below for the post-1867 period. For a discussion of alternative interpretations of the growth of government activities in Canada, see 6 and 36. Most government activities in the late nineteenth and early twentieth centuries are related to the major themes of national policy: the promotion of western development and a second transcontinental economy within North America. Accordingly, the most important writings are dominated by this theme. See, for example, the important full-scale works of Fowke, 20, and Brown, 10.

The most comprehensive treatment of commercial policy is still probably II.E.iii.13. Older and less well documented are studies 24 and 34. The role of British preferences in Canadian policy is discussed in 2, and the renewed issue of reciprocal trade with the United States is reviewed in 19. The special interests of the newsprint industry are discussed in 37. Item 12 deals with the tariff lobby. A recent reexamination of the impact of tariffs on the west is 30; for another view, see 42. On the issue of the tariff and industrialization, see II.E.iii.13, and 1 and 40 below.

For settlement policy, 28 reviews the Dominion's land grant legislation and its impact. The related subsidies made to railroads are treated in detail in 21 and 25; see also 18. The ending of seigneurial tenure in Quebec is discussed in 39, and immigration policy at the turn of the century is treated in 38.

Natural resource policy is intimately bound up with settlement arrangements. For the effect of the constitution on resource disposal, see 23. Other specialized works on resource property right development include III.E.iii.37 for forest lands in Ontario; items 3, 29, and 43 below, and II.E.iii.16 for Ontario forests, mines, and hydroelectricity; II.D.i.15 for Quebec forests; and II.D.i.13 for British Columbia forests; see also 11. For additional background on public hydroelectricity in Ontario, see 26, 7, and a comprehensive history, 16.

The development of Canadian competition policy is contrasted to that of the United States in 9. An older, but thorough and indispensible study of policy in this area is 35. A more recent and briefer treatment dealing with restrictive trade practices is II.E.iii.22. For a short introduction, see chapter 8 in II.A.ii.1, and 8 below by the same author. The background of incorporation legislation is well recorded in 15, and the proliferation over time of government corporations is noted in 4.

In the area of labor policy, the best single source is II.E.iii.26. For the political activities of labor, the nineteenth century is discussed in 31, 32, and 41. The story is carried into the twentieth century in IV.E.ii.9. One aspect of conscription is discussed in 44.

IV.E.iii. Economic Organization: The Role of
Government

1. Acheson, Thomas William. "The National Policy and the Industrialization of the Maritimes 1880-1910." ACADIENSIS 1 (Spring 1972): 3-28.

2. Annett, Douglas R[udyard]. BRITISH PREFERENCE IN CANADIAN COMMERCIAL POLICY. Studies in International Affairs, no. 3. Toronto: Ryerson Press, 1948. 188 p. Illustrations.

3. Armstrong, C., and Nelles, H.V. "Private Property in Peril: Ontario Businessmen and the Federal System, 1898-1911." In ENTERPRISE AND NATIONAL DEVELOPMENT; ESSAYS IN CANADIAN BUSINESS AND ECONOMIC HISTORY, edited by Glenn Porter and Robert D. Cuff, pp. 20-38. Toronto: Hakkert, 1973. Bibliographic references. Reprinted from BUSINESS HISTORY REVIEW 47 (Summer 1973): 20-38.

4. Ashley, Charles Allan, and Smails, R[eginald] G[eorge] H[ampden]. CANADIAN CROWN CORPORATIONS; SOME ASPECTS OF THEIR ADMINISTRATION AND CONTROL. Toronto: Macmillan of Canada, 1965. x, 360 p. Bibliography.

5. Bates, Stewart. FINANCIAL HISTORY OF CANADIAN GOVERNMENTS. Ottawa: King's Printer, 1939. 309 p. Diagrams. French edition. Ottawa: King's Printer, 1939.

6. Bird, Richard M. THE GROWTH OF GOVERNMENT OF SPENDING IN CANADA. Toronto: Canadian Tax Foundation, 1970. Bibliography.

7. Biss, Irene M. "Contracts of Hydro-Electric Power Commission of Ontario." ECONOMIC JOURNAL 46 (September 1936): 549-54.

8. Bladen, Vincent Wheeler. "A Note on the Reports of Public Investigations into Combines in Canada 1888-1932." CONTRIBUTIONS TO CANADIAN ECONOMICS 5, 1932, pp. 61-76.

9. Bliss, John William Michael. "Another Anti-Trust Tradition: Canadian Anti-Combines Policy 1889-1910." In ENTERPRISE AND NATIONAL DEVELOPMENT; ESSAYS IN CANADIAN BUSINESS AND ECONOMIC HISTORY, edited by Glenn Porter and Robert D. Cuff, pp. 39-50. Toronto: Hakkert, 1973. Bibliographic references. Reprinted from BUSINESS HISTORY REVIEW 47 (Summer 1973): 39-50.

10. Brown, Robert Craig. CANADA'S NATIONAL POLICY, 1883-1900. Princeton, N.J.: Princeton University Press, 1964. xi, 436 p.

Illustrations. Map. Bibliography.

11. _____. "The Doctrine of Usefulness: Natural Resource and National Park Policy in Canada, 1887-1914." In THE CANADIAN NATIONAL PARKS: TO-DAY AND TO-MORROW, edited by J.G. Nelson and R.C. Scace, vol. 1, pp. 94-110. Calgary, Alberta: University of Calgary, 1969.

12. Clark, Samuel Delbert. "The Canadian Manufacturers' Association and the Tariff." CANADIAN JOURNAL OF ECONOMICS AND POLITICAL SCIENCE 5 (February 1939): 19-39.

13. Corry, J[ames] A[lexander]. "The Expansion of Government Activities in Canada, 1914-1920." CANADIAN HISTORICAL ASSOCIATION ANNUAL REPORT, 1940, pp. 63-73.

14. _____. "The Growth of Government Activities since Confederation." Royal Commission on Dominion-Provincial Relations Study. Ottawa: King's Printer, 1939. 174 p. Mimeographed.

15. Currie, Archibald William. "The First Dominion Companies Act." CANADIAN JOURNAL OF ECONOMICS AND POLITICAL SCIENCE 28 (August 1962): 387-404.

16. Denison, Merrill. THE PEOPLE'S POWER, THE HISTORY OF ONTARIO HYDRO. Toronto: McClelland & Stewart, 1960. viii, 295 p. Illustrations. Portraits. Folding maps. Facsimiles.

17. Deutsch, J.J. "War Finance and the Canadian Economy 1914-1920." CANADIAN JOURNAL OF ECONOMICS AND POLITICAL SCIENCE 6 (November 1940): 525-42.

18. Dougall, Herbert Edward. "Taxation of Railways in Canada: Development and Present Status." JOURNAL OF LAND AND PUBLIC UTILITY ECONOMICS 5 (August 1929): 260-74.

19. Ellis, Lewis Ethan. RECIPROCITY 1911; A STUDY IN CANADIAN-AMERICAN RELATIONS. New Haven, Conn.: Yale University Press, 1939. x, 207 p. Bibliography.

20. Fowke, Vernon Clifford. THE NATIONAL POLICY AND THE WHEAT ECONOMY. Social Credit in Alberta; Its Background and Development, no. 7. Toronto: University of Toronto Press, 1957. viii, 312 p. Illustrations. Tables. Bibliography, pp. 299-302. Bibliographic footnotes.

21. Hedges, James Blaine. THE FEDERAL RAILWAY LAND SUBSIDY POLICY OF CANADA. Cambridge, Mass.: Harvard University Press, 1934. viii, 151 p. Bibliography.

22. Knox, F[rank] A. "Canadian War Finance and the Balance of Payments 1914-18." CANADIAN JOURNAL OF ECONOMICS AND POLITICAL SCIENCE 6 (May 1940): 226-57.

23. La Forest, Gerard V. NATURAL RESOURCES AND PUBLIC PROPERTY UNDER THE CANADIAN CONSTITUTION. Toronto: University of Toronto Press, 1969. xiv, 230 p. Bibliographic footnotes.

24. McLean, Simon James. THE TARIFF HISTORY OF CANADA. Toronto: Warwick Brothers and Rutter, printers, 1895. 53 p.

25. Martin, C[hester Bailey]. "Our 'Kingdom for a Horse,' the Railway Land Grant System in Western Canada." CANADIAN HISTORICAL ASSOCIATION ANNUAL REPORT, 1934, pp. 73-79.

26. Mavor, James. NIAGARA IN POLITICS, A CRITICAL ACCOUNT OF THE HYDRO-ELECTRIC POWER COMMISSION. New York: Dutton, 1925. vi, 255 p.

27. Maxwell, James Ackley. FEDERAL SUBSIDIES TO THE PROVINCIAL GOVERNMENTS IN CANADA. Harvard Economic Studies, vol. 56. Cambridge, Mass.: Harvard University Press, 1937. xi, 284 p. Bibliography, pp. 257-65.

28. Morton, Arthur S., and Martin, Chester [Bailey]. HISTORY OF PRAIRIE SETTLEMENT AND "DOMINION LANDS" POLICY. Canadian Frontiers of Settlement, edited by William Archibald Mackintosh and W.L.G. Joerg, vol. 2. Toronto: Macmillan of Canada, 1938. xviii, 571 p. Frontispiece. Illustrations. Maps. Diagrams.

29. Nelles, H.V. "Empire Ontario: The Problems of Resource Development." In OLIVER MOWAT'S ONTARIO, edited by Donald Swainson, pp. 189-210. Toronto: Macmillan of Canada, 1972.

30. Norrie, K.H. "Agricultural Implement Tariffs, the National Policy, and Income Distribution in the Wheat Economy." CANADIAN JOURNAL OF ECONOMICS 7 (August 1974): 449-62.

31. Ostry, Bernard. "Conservatives, Liberals, and Labour in the 1880's." CANADIAN JOURNAL OF ECONOMICS AND POLITICAL SCIENCE 27 (May 1961): 141-61.

Confederation to 1920

32. _____. "Conservatives, Liberals, and Labour in the 1870's." CANADIAN HISTORICAL REVIEW 41 (June 1960): 93-127.

33. Plumptre, Arthur Fitzwalter Wynne. "The Nature of Political and Economic Development in the British Dominions." CANADIAN JOURNAL OF ECONOMICS AND POLITICAL SCIENCE 3 (November 1937): 489-507.

34. Porritt, Edward. SIXTY YEARS OF PROTECTION IN CANADA, 1846-1907; WHERE INDUSTRY LEANS ON THE POLITICIAN. London: Macmillan and Co., 1908. xii, 478 p.

35. Reynolds, Lloyd G. THE CONTROL OF COMPETITION IN CANADA. Harvard Economic Studies in Monopoly and Competition, no. 2. Cambridge, Mass.: Harvard University Press, 1940. xiv, 324 p. Tables. Diagrams. Bibliography, pp. 312-18.

36. Rosenfeld, Barry D. "The Displacement Effects in the Growth of Canadian Government Expenditures." PUBLIC FINANCE 27-28 (1973): 301-14.

37. Southworth, Constant. "The American-Canadian Newsprint Paper Industry and the Tariff." JOURNAL OF POLITICAL ECONOMY 30 (October 1922): 681-97.

38. Timlin, Mabel Frances. "Canada's Immigration Policy 1896-1910." CANADIAN JOURNAL OF ECONOMICS AND POLITICAL SCIENCE 26 (November 1960): 517-32.

39. Wallot, Jean-Pierre. "Le Régime seigneurial et son abolition au Canada." CANADIAN HISTORICAL REVIEW 50 (December 1969): 367-93.

40. Watkins, Melville H. "The 'American System' and Canada's National Policy." BULLETIN OF THE CANADIAN ASSOCIATION FOR AMERICAN STUDIES 2 (Winter 1967): 26-45.

41. Watt, F.W. "National Policy, the Workingman and Proletarian Ideas in Victorian Canada." CANADIAN HISTORICAL REVIEW 40 (March 1959): 1-26.

42. Westcott, F.J. "An Approach to the Problem of Tariff Burdens on Western Canada." CANADIAN JOURNAL OF ECONOMICS AND POLITICAL SCIENCE 4 (May 1938): 209-18.

43. Wilkes, George C. "Ground Rent for Provincial Forest Land in Ontario." CANADIAN JOURNAL OF ECONOMICS AND POLITICAL SCIENCE 22 (February 1956): 63-72.

44. Young, W.R. "Conscription, Rural Depopulation and the Farmers of Ontario 1917-1919." CANADIAN HISTORICAL REVIEW 53 (September 1972): 289-320.

IV.F. TECHNOLOGY, PRODUCTIVITY CHANGE, AND WELFARE

For the history of Canadian contributions to technology in this period, see II.F.1 and II.F.6. For a general discussion of the implications of technological change, see 7. Estimates of income per capita are contained in IV.B.6, and regional estimates are available in IV.A.8 and in items 2, 3, and 5 of V.C.v. See also 2, 5, 6, and 7 in IV.D.i, and IV.C.2. Limited data on productivity change are contained in chapter 8 of II.G.i.8. Increased efficiency attributable to falling ocean freight rates were especially significant for Canadian wheat exports: see 8 below. The available evidence on changing real wages is summarized in 9. Some documentation on the welfare of particular economic classes can be found in 6 for agriculture, in 3 for industrial workers, and in 1 for business leaders. The instability of economic growth is carefully documented in 2, 4, and 5; the cyclical analysis employed by the National Bureau of Economic Research in the United States is applied to Canadian business cycle behavior.

IV.F. TECHNOLOGY, PRODUCTIVITY CHANGE, AND WELFARE

1. Bliss, John William Michael. A LIVING PROFIT: STUDIES IN THE SOCIAL HISTORY OF CANADIAN BUSINESS 1883-1911. Toronto: McClelland & Stewart, 1974. 160 p. Illustrations.

2. Chambers, E.J. "Late Nineteenth Century Business Cycles in Canada." CANADIAN JOURNAL OF ECONOMICS AND POLITICAL SCIENCE 30 (August 1964): 391-412.

3. Copp, John Terry. ANATOMY OF POVERTY: THE CONDITION OF THE WORKING CLASS IN MONTREAL, 1897-1929. Toronto: McClelland & Stewart, 1974. 192 p. Illustrations. Bibliography.

4. Hay, Keith A.J. "Early Twentieth Century Business Cycles in Canada." CANADIAN JOURNAL OF ECONOMICS AND POLITICAL SCIENCE 32 (August 1966): 354-65.

5. _____. "Money and Cycles in Post-Confederation Canada." JOURNAL OF POLITICAL ECONOMY 75 (June 1967): 263-71.

6. Hope, E.C. "Agriculture's Share of the National Income." CANADIAN JOURNAL OF ECONOMICS AND POLITICAL SCIENCE 9 (August 1943): 384-93.

7. Jecchinis, Chris. "Technological Change and Socio-Economic Development in North America: Problems and Prospects." LAKEHEAD UNIVERSITY REVIEW 6 (Fall/Winter 1973): 138-71.

8. North, Douglass C. "Ocean Freight Rates and Economic Development 1750-1913." JOURNAL OF ECONOMIC HISTORY 28 (December 1958): 537-55.

9. Ostry, Sylvia, and Zaidi, Mahmood A. LABOUR ECONOMICS IN CANADA. 2d ed. Toronto: Macmillan of Canada, 1973. 354 p. Bibliographic footnotes. 1st ed. published as LABOUR POLICY AND LABOUR ECONOMICS IN CANADA by H.D. Woods, Sylvia Ostry, and Mahmood A. Zaidi, vol. 2. Toronto: Macmillan of Canada, 1962.

IV.G. RESOURCES

As in III.G., the main topic is the arrival of new immigrants and, in the time period now under review, their settlement in the prairie west. Substantial capital formation also accompanied the growth in population.

IV.G.i. Resources: Land and Its Endowments

The most useful single source is the statistical treatment given in chapter 5 of II.G.i.8. For additional references to land resources, see the other items listed in II.G.i. For a review of the forest resources of British Columbia, see 1.

IV.G.i. Resources: Land and Its Endowments

1. Whitford, H.N., and Craig, Roland D. FORESTS OF BRITISH COLUMBIA. Commission of Conservation Canada, Committee on Forests. Ottawa: King's Printer, 1918. 409 p. Tables.

IV.G.ii. Resources: Population

Many of the references contained in II.G.ii are also useful for the post-1867 period. In addition, for the history of French Canadian population, see 14. For immigration and settlement, see in particular 9, 12, 15, 16, and 23 from II.G.ii. In addition, a comprehensive study of nineteenth-century immigration to Canada is 15 below. Reworking of the census data has led to some modifications of the view presented in II.G.ii.14, as seen in 21 and 16 below. For migration from Great Britain and the accompanying flow of investment, see 22. For studies of migration between Canada and the United States, see also 1, 2, 10, 20, and 27. An additional source on early prairie settlement is 6. Peace River settlement is recorded in 7. For an overall view see 5 and 26.

For internal migration, in addition to 7 and 19 from II.G.ii, an overview is presented in 29 below. The interpretation of these migrations is controversial. See, for example, 25, followed by the critique in 18. Another view is expressed in 24 and criticized in 19. See also II.G.ii.1, and the estimates made by the same author in 4 below. Other interpretive essays include 3 and 12. For French Canadian attitudes, see 23.

Settlers acquired prairie land not only directly from the government, but also from the Hudson's Bay Company and from railroads. These land disposal operations are documented in 9 and 13 respectively. For an overall view, including statistics, of western Canadian settlement, see 8.

For the growth of the labor force, see 5 and 6 of II.G.ii. A further analysis is provided in 11 and 17 below.

For the discussion of the appropriate population size, see 28 below, and II.G.ii.21.

IV.G.ii. Resources: Population

1. Bicha, Karel Denis. THE AMERICAN FARMER AND THE CANADIAN WEST, 1896-1914. Kansas City: Coronado Press, 1968. 173 p. Bibliographic footnotes.

2. _____. "The Plains Farmer and The Prairie Province Frontier 1897-1914." JOURNAL OF ECONOMIC HISTORY 25 (June 1965): 263-70.

3. Breen, David H. "The Canadian Prairie West and the 'Harmonious' Settlement Interpretation." AGRICULTURAL HISTORY 47 (January 1973): 63-75.

4. Buckley, Kenneth [A.H.]. "Historical Estimates of Internal Migration in Canada." In CANADIAN POLITICAL SCIENCE ASSOCIATION CONFERENCE PAPERS ON STATISTICS 1960, edited by E.F. Beach and J.C. Weldon, pp. 1-37. Toronto: University of Toronto Press, 1962.

Confederation to 1920

5. Coats, [Robert] H[amilton]. "Canada." In INTERNATIONAL MIGRATIONS, edited by Walter F. Willcox; vol. 1, STATISTICS, pp. 357-70; vol. 2, INTERPRETATIONS, pp. 123-42. New York: National Bureau of Economic Research, 1931. Reprinted as vols. 7 and 8 of DEMOGRAPHIC MONOGRAPHS, edited by Richard A. Easterlin, M. Perlman, and Dorothy Swaine Thomas, eds. New York: Gordon and Breach, Science Publishers, 1969.

6. Dawson, Carl Addington. PIONEERING IN THE PRAIRIE PROVINCES: THE SOCIAL SIDE OF THE SETTLEMENT PROCESS. Canadian Frontiers of Settlement, edited by William Archibald Mackintosh and W.L.G. Joerg, vol. 8. Toronto : Macmillan of Canada, 1940. xi, 388 p. Illustrations.

7. _____. THE SETTLEMENT OF THE PEACE RIVER COUNTRY: A STUDY OF A PIONEER AREA. Canadian Frontiers of Settlement, edited by William Archibald Mackintosh and W.L.G. Joerg, vol. 6. Toronto: Macmillan of Canada, 1934. xii, 284 p. Illustrations. Maps.

8. England, Robert. THE COLONIZATION OF WESTERN CANADA: A STUDY OF CONTEMPORARY LAND SETTLEMENT 1896-1934. London: King and Son, 1936. 341 p. Illustrations. Maps. Bibliography, pp. 323-31.

9. Galbraith, John A[lexander] "Land Policies of the Hudson's Bay Co. 1870-1913." CANADIAN HISTORICAL REVIEW 32 (March 1931): 1-21.

10. Gold, N.L. "Net Emigration from the United States to Canada: 1909-1931." JOURNAL OF THE AMERICAN STATISTICAL ASSOCIATION 29 (September 1934): 282-87.

11. Haythorne, George V., and Marsh, Leonard C. LAND AND LABOUR, A SOCIAL SURVEY OF AGRICULTURE AND FARM LABOUR MARKET IN CENTRAL CANADA. Toronto: Oxford University Press, 1941. xxviii, 568 p. Statistical appendices, pp. 519-54.

12. Heaton, Herbert. "Other Wests Than Ours." THE TASKS OF ECONOMIC HISTORY, supp. no. 6 to JOURNAL OF ECONOMIC HISTORY, 1946, pp. 50-62.

13. Hedges, James Blaine. BUILDING THE CANADIAN WEST; THE LAND AND COLONIZATION POLICIES OF THE CANADIAN PACIFIC RAILWAY. New York: Macmillan, 1939. vii, 422 p. Maps. Bibliographic note, pp. 411-12.

Confederation to 1920

14. Langlois, Georges. HISTOIRE DE LA POPULATION CANADIENNE-FRANCAISE. 2d ed. Documents historiques. Montréal: Editions Albert Lévesque, 1935. 309 p. Bibliography, pp. 269-87.

15. MacDonald, Norman. CANADA: IMMIGRATION AND COLONIZATION 1841-1903. Toronto: Macmillan of Canada, 1966. xi, 381 p. Illustrations. Maps. Facsimiles. Tables. Bibliography.

16. McDougall, Duncan M. "Immigration into Canada, 1851-1920." CANADIAN JOURNAL OF ECONOMICS AND POLITICAL SCIENCE 27 (May 1961): 162-75.

17. McInnis, R. M[arvin]. "Long-Run Changes in the Industrial Structure of the Canadian Work Force." CANADIAN JOURNAL OF ECONOMICS 4 (August 1971): 353-61.

18. Norrie, K.H. "Economic Opportunity and the Westward Migration of Canadians during the Late Nineteenth Century: A Comment." CANADIAN JOURNAL OF ECONOMICS 7 (February 1974): 132-35.

19. _____. "The Rate of Settlement of the Canadian Prairies, 1870-1911." JOURNAL OF ECONOMIC HISTORY 35 (June 1975): 410-27.

20. Paquet, Gilles. "L'Emigration des Canadiens Français vers la Nouvelle-Angleterre 1870-1910: Prises de vue quantitative." RECHERCHES SOCIOGRAPHIQUES 5 (September-December 1964): 319-70.

21. Pickett, J. "An Evaluation of Estimates of Immigration into Canada in the Late Nineteenth Century." CANADIAN JOURNAL OF ECONOMICS AND POLITICAL SCIENCE 31 (November 1965): 499-508.

22. Richardson, Harry Ward. "British Emigration and Overseas Investment 1870-1914." ECONOMIC HISTORY REVIEW, 2d ser. 25 (February 1972): 99-113.

23. Silver, A.I. "French Canada and the Prairie Frontier, 1870-1890." CANADIAN HISTORICAL REVIEW 50 (March 1969): 11-36.

24. Stabler, Jack C. "Factors Affecting the Development of a New Region: The Canadian Great Plains, 1870-1897." ANNALS OF REGIONAL SCIENCE 7 (June 1973): 75-87.

25. Studness, C.M. "Economic Opportunity and the Westward Migration of Canadians during the Late Nineteenth Century." CANADIAN JOURNAL OF ECONOMICS AND POLITICAL SCIENCE 30 (November 1964): 570-84.

26. Timlin, Mabel [Frances]. "Canada." In ECONOMICS OF INTERNATIONAL MIGRATION, edited by Brinley Thomas, pp. 146-62. London: Macmillan and Co., 1958.

27. Vicero, Ralph D. "Sources statistiques pour l'étude de l'immigration et du peuplement Canadien-Français en Nouvelle-Angleterre au cours du XIXe siècle." RECHERCHES SOCIOGRAPHIQUES 12 (September-December 1971): 361-72.

28. Waines, W.J. "Prairie Population Possibilities." Royal Commission on Dominion-Provincial Relations. Ottawa: King's Printer, 1939. Mimeographed.

29. Wilson, Roland. "Migration Movements in Canada, 1868-1925." CANADIAN HISTORICAL REVIEW 13 (June 1932): 157-82.

IV.G.iii. Resources: Capital Formation

The key contribution here is the painstakingly detailed and pioneering quantitative study of Buckley in 2, and the shorter account in 1. The contribution of foreign capital, particularly British, was substantial; see 6, and the older study 3, partly devoted to Canada. For the inflow of American capital, see II.G.iii.1. An inflow of French capital into Quebec is documented in 5. Two specialized studies on residential and human capital formation are provided in 4 and 7. For a short general treatment, see chapter 7 in II.G.i.8.

IV.G.iii. Resources: Capital Formation

1. Buckley, Kenneth [A.H.]. "Capital Formation in Canada." In PROBLEMS OF CAPITAL FORMATION, pp. 91-145. National Bureau of Economic Research Studies in Income and Wealth, vol. 19. Princeton, N.J.: Princeton University Press, 1957.

2. _____. CAPITAL FORMATION IN CANADA 1896-1930. Toronto: University of Toronto Press, 1955. x, 163 p.

3. Cairncross, Alexander Kirkland. "Investment in Canada, 1900-13." In his HOME AND FOREIGN INVESTMENT, 1870-1913; STUDIES IN CAPITAL ACCUMULATION, pp. 37-64. Cambridge: At the University Press, 1953

4. Pickett, J. "Residential Capital Formation in Canada, 1871-1921." CANADIAN JOURNAL OF ECONOMICS AND POLITICAL SCIENCE 29 (February 1963): 40-58.

5. Quinn, Magella. "Les Capitaux français et le Québec 1855-1900." REVUE D'HISTOIRE DE L'AMERIQUE FRANCAISE 24 (March 1971): 527-66.

6. Simon, M. "New British Investments in Canada, 1865-1914. CANADIAN JOURNAL OF ECONOMICS 3 (May 1970): 238-54.

7. Stamp, Robert M. "Technical Education, the National Policy, and Federal Provincial Relations in Canadian Education, 1899-1919." CANADIAN HISTORICAL REVIEW 52 (December 1971): 404-23.

Chapter V

FROM 1920 TO THE PRESENT

In this period the Confederation expanded to its present membership with the inclusion of Newfoundland in 1949. This new province also incorporates Labrador, formerly part of Quebec. A transformation that may loosely be described as industrialization probably belongs most clearly to the post-1920 years when the relative importance of manufacturing by almost any measure surpassed that of agriculture. These years also include the second twentieth-century burst of rapid economic growth, the post-World War II period. Many of the writings dealing with this final period provide more analysis, and are richer in statistical documentation, than those treating earlier time periods. This is partly the result of the availability of better statistics, and partly because many investigators focusing on the recent past are analytically trained, particularly in economics.

V.A. GENERAL WORKS

Several of the general works listed under II.A.ii, notably 2, 5, 6, 12, 13, and 15, carry the story into the post-World War II period. The major theme of writers since the 1920s and 1930s has been the importance of the international setting of the Canadian economy with respect both to world war and to international markets and trade. For studies dealing with the economy in wartime and the transition to peace, see 9, 13, and 14. Cooperation in resource use and competition in trade between Canada and the United States during World War II are discussed in 9. In 13, essay 3 by H.A. Innis discusses economic trends, and essay 4 by V.W. Bladen deals with population problems and policies. A good short overall view of recent economic development is provided by 18.

The interrelations of the Canadian economy and the international economy are treated in 5, 6, 8, and 10. Three essays, one giving a historical perspective, one an international perspective, and another a policies perspective, are contained in 6. A number of essays in 8 treat international commodity and capital flows, especially with the United States. A statistical study of the relation between trade and economic growth prior to World War II is presented in

19. Probably no aspect of external economic relations has received more attention than Canadian-American economic relations. For a short introduction to this topic, see 7. The best and most comprehensive treatment is 2. It includes statistically documented sections on business cycle transmission, nonresident ownership, commercial relations, trade unions, and comparative economic growth. In 1, another series of essays, acknowledged specialists discuss U.S. influence on Canadian economic structure, economic policy, the Quebec economy, capital formation, and labor. See also II.A.ii.17 for more recent, further social science essays on the American impact on Canadian development.

For a brief review of the main features of the post-World War II Canadian economy, with occasional glimpses into their historical origins, see 12 and 16. Essays on population, nationalism, the economy, industrial structure, federalism, and welfare policy are included in 12. A critical economic review of recent Canadian economic policies and attitudes is contained in 11. For a quantitative assessment of the rate and pattern of Canadian economic growth in this period, see 3 and 4. For a regional perspective, see II.A.ii.9, and for recent development in the north, see 15.

V.A. GENERAL WORKS

1. Aitken, Hugh G.J., et al. THE AMERICAN ECONOMIC IMPACT ON CANADA. Durham, N.C.: Duke University Press, 1959. xviii, 176 p. Diagram. Tables. Bibliographic footnotes.

2. Brecher, Irving, and Reisman, S.S. CANADA-UNITED STATES ECONOMIC RELATIONS. Royal Commission on Canada's Economic Prospects Study. Ottawa: Queen's Printer, 1957. 344 p. Tables. Bibliographic footnotes.

3. Economic Council of Canada. FIFTH ANNUAL REVIEW: THE CHALLENGE OF GROWTH AND CHANGE. Ottawa: Queen's Printer, 1968. 205 p. Tables. Diagrams.

4. _____. SEVENTH ANNUAL REVIEW: PATTERNS OF GROWTH. Ottawa: Queen's Printer, 1970. 100 p. Tables. Diagrams.

5. English, Harry Edward. TRANSATLANTIC ECONOMIC COMMUNITY: CANADIAN PERSPECTIVES. Canada in the Atlantic Economy Series, no. 2. Published for the Private Planning Association of Canada. Toronto: University of Toronto Press, 1968. 70 p. Bibliographic footnotes.

6. _____, ed. CANADA AND THE NEW INTERNATIONAL ECONOMY: THREE ESSAYS. Published for Carleton University. Toronto: University of Toronto Press, 1961. 75 p.

1920 to Present

7. Gibson, James Douglas. "The Changing Influence of the U.S. on the Canadian Economy." CANADIAN JOURNAL OF ECONOMICS AND POLITICAL SCIENCE 22 (November 1956): 421-36.

8. _____, ed. CANADA'S ECONOMY IN A CHANGING WORLD. Toronto: Macmillan of Canada, 1948. xiii, 380 p. Illustrations. Statistical appendix. Bibliography, pp. 364-73.

9. James, Robert Warren. WARTIME ECONOMIC CO-OPERATION; A STUDY OF RELATIONS BETWEEN CANADA AND THE UNITED STATES. Toronto: Ryerson Press, 1949. xiii, 415 p. Bibliography.

10. Johnson, Harry G[ordon]. CANADA IN A CHANGING WORLD ECONOMY. Alan B. Plaunt Memorial Lectures. Published for Carleton University. Toronto: University of Toronto Press, 1962. 62 p.

11. _____. THE CANADIAN QUANDARY: ECONOMIC PROBLEMS AND POLICIES. Toronto: McGraw-Hill, 1963. xx, 352 p. Bibliographic footnotes.

12. Leach, Richard H., ed. CONTEMPORARY CANADA. Durham, N.C.: Duke University Press, 1968. xii, 328 p. Illustrations. Bibliographic footnotes.

13. Martin, Chester Bailey, ed. CANADA IN PEACE AND WAR; EIGHT STUDIES IN NATIONAL TRENDS SINCE 1914. London: Oxford University Press, 1941. 244 p.

14. Plumptre, A[rthur] F[itzwalter] W[ynne]. MOBILIZING CANADA'S RESOURCES FOR WAR. Toronto: Macmillan of Canada, 1941. xiii, 306 p. Statistical appendix, pp. 275-99.

15. Rea, K[enneth] J. THE POLITICAL ECONOMY OF THE CANADIAN NORTH. Toronto: University of Toronto Press, 1968. 453 p. Map. Tables. Bibliographic footnotes.

16. Raynauld, A[ndré]. THE CANADIAN ECONOMIC SYSTEM. Translated from the French by C.M. Ross. Toronto: Macmillan of Canada, 1967. 440 p. Chapter bibliographies.

17. Slater, David W. WORLD TRADE AND ECONOMIC GROWTH: TRENDS AND PROSPECTS WITH APPLICATIONS TO CANADA. Canada in the Atlantic Economy Series, no. 1. Published for the Private Planning Association of Canada. Toronto: University of Toronto Press, 1968. 94 p. Charts. Tables. Bibliographic footnotes.

1920 to Present

18. Smith, R.M. CANADIAN ECONOMIC GROWTH AND DEVELOPMENT FROM 1939 to 1955. Royal Commission on Canada's Economic Prospects Study. Ottawa: Queen's Printer, 1956. 77 p. Tables.

19. Thompson, R.W. INTERNATIONAL TRADE AND DOMESTIC PROSPERITY, CANADA 1926-38. Canadian Studies in Economics, no. 22. Toronto: University of of Toronto Press, 1970. xi, 139 p. Tables. Bibliography, pp. 133-36.

V.A.i. General Works: The Maritimes

A good short introduction to the more recent economic history of the maritimes is provided in chapter 5 of II.A.i.1, especially pages 147-69; see also II.A.ii. 4, chapter 8. No really comprehensive twentieth-century economic history of the maritimes exists. For an analytic study of long-period change in the location of economic activities in the maritimes, see 21. A short statistical account of the Nova Scotian economy is provided by 24, and for Newfoundland, the new entrant into Confederation in 1949, 20, 22, and 23 provide some documentation of that province's more recent economic development. A collection of contemporary extracts dating from the 1930s, together with more recent commentary, are contained in 23.

V.A.i. General Works: The Maritimes

20. Copes, Parzival. ST. JOHN'S AND NEWFOUNDLAND, AN ECONOMIC SURVEY. St. John's: Newfoundland Board of Trade, 1961. xiii, 233 p. Illustrations. Maps. Charts. Tables. Bibliography.

21. Keirstead, B.S. "Temporal Shifts in Location: The Case of the Maritime Provinces." In his THE THEORY OF ECONOMIC CHANGE, pp. 267-313. Toronto: Macmillan of Canada, 1940.

22. McAllister, R.I., ed. NEWFOUNDLAND AND LABRADOR: THE FIRST FIFTEEN YEARS OF CONFEDERATION. St. John's, Newfoundland: Dicks and Co., 1964. 274 p. Illustrations. Diagrams. Maps.

23. Neary, Peter, ed. THE POLITICAL ECONOMY OF NEWFOUNDLAND 1929-1972. Issues in Canadian History. Toronto: Copp Clark, 1973. 264 p. Illustrations. Bibliography; pp. 262-64.

24. Nova Scotia. "The Provincial Economy." In REPORT OF THE ROYAL COMMISSION ON EDUCATION, PUBLIC SERVICES AND PROVINCIAL-MUNICIPAL RELATIONS. Vol. 2, chap. 2. Halifax, Nova Scotia: Queen's Printer, 1974.

1920 to Present

V.A.ii. General Works: Ontario and Quebec

For a brief introduction to the twentieth-century economic history of Ontario and Quebec, see chapter 5 of II.A.i.1, pages 169-94; see also II.A.ii.4, chapter 8. For Ontario, no general economic history has been written. A very brief introductory treatment is provided by 31. For a more complete and statistically documented account, see 29. For Quebec, the best analysis of economic development is supplied by the thorough and statistically well documented study, item 30, which includes the author's attempt to construct an input-output table for Quebec. For a short general view of Quebec's economic development within the context of Confederation, see 26. For another account, see 25. A systematic study of the impact of industrialization on French Canada is undertaken in 27, and a series of essays on political and economic aspects of contemporary Quebec are contained in 28. See also 32, 33, and 36 of II.A.ii for brief accounts of the contemporary Quebec economy.

V.A.ii. General Works: Ontario and Quebec

25. Daneau, Marcel. "Evolution économique du Québec 1950-1965." L'ACTUALITE ECONOMIQUE 41 (January-March 1966): 659-92.

26. Faucher, A[lbert], and Paquet, Gilles. L'experience economique du Québec et la Confederation. JOURNAL OF CANADIAN STUDIES 1 (November 1966): 16-30.

27. Hughes, Everett Cherrington. FRENCH CANADA IN TRANSITION. Chicago: University of Chicago Press, 1943. xi, 227 p. Frontispiece. Illustrations. Maps. Diagrams. Bibliography.

28. Migué, Jean-Luc, ed. LE QUEBEC D'AUJOURD-HUI. Montréal: Editions Hurtubise, 1971. 251 p.

29. Ontario. SUBMISSION OF ONTARIO TO THE ROYAL COMMISSION ON CANADA'S ECONOMIC PROSPECTS. Toronto: Queen's Printer, 1956. 202 p.

30. Raynauld, André. CROISSANCE ET STRUCTURE ECONOMIQUES DE LA PROVINCE DE QUEBEC. Québec: Ministere de l'Industrie et du Commerce, 1961. 657 p. Tables.

31. Richmond, D.R. THE ECONOMIC TRANSFORMATION OF ONTARIO: 1945-1973. The Evolution of Policy in Contemporary Ontario Series, Ontario Economic Council, no. 1. Toronto: 1974. 56 p. Tables.

V.A.iii. General Works: The West

For a short account of the twentieth-century economic development of the western provinces, see chapter 6 of II.A.i.1 and chapter 9 of II.A.ii.4. For the prairie provinces, see items 39, 41, 42, and 45 of II.A.ii and for a short analysis, see 32 below. For British Columbia, 38, 40, and 43 of II.A.ii provide good short treatments. In 33 below, British Columbia's economic structure is discerned from her pattern of external trade. Although mainly political, item 34 exposes well the nexus between government and business.

V.A.iii. General Works: The West

32. Britnell, George Edwin. "Perspective on Change in the Prairie Economy." CANADIAN JOURNAL OF ECONOMICS AND POLITICAL SCIENCE 19 (November 1953): 437-54.

33. Peters, J.E., and Shearer, R[onald] A. "The Structure of British Columbia's External Trade, 1939 and 1963." B. C. STUDIES 8 (1970-71): 34-46.

34. Robin, Martin. PILLARS OF PROFIT, THE COMPANY PROVINCE 1934-1972. Toronto: McClelland & Stewart, 1973. 351 p. Illustrations. Bibliographic footnotes.

V.B. STATISTICAL RECORD

Most of the major economic time series now published by Statistics Canada (formerly the Dominion Bureau of Statistics) originate in the early post-World War I years. The beginnings of a Canadian statistical organization are related in 4 and 12 below. Items 9 and 11 below discuss the National Accounts, the central focus of this statistical organization, which date from 1926. This new wealth of data is reflected in the main coverage provided by II.B.2 and continued in items 6 and 7 below. Annual totals of all the statistical series carried in the monthly issues of 6 are presented in 7 for the years 1926-71. For a full listing of the older statistical publications of the Dominion Bureau of Statistics, back to 1918, see 5. The data gathered by the Dominion Bureau of Statistics, and now by Statistics Canada, are presented monthly in 6, and annually in IV.B.3. From time to time, the availability of new series is highlighted and summarized in a professional journal such as the journals cited in 3, 8, 10, 13, 14, 15, 16, and 18. Much of this data, together with additional financial and banking statistics, is also presented monthly in 1 and 2. For interest rates alone during the years of the Great Depression, see 17.

1920 to Present

V.B. STATISTICAL RECORD

1. Bank of Canada. BANK OF CANADA REVIEW. Ottawa: 1972-- . Monthly.

2. _____. STATISTICAL SUMMARY. Ottawa: 1937-71. Monthly.

3. Blythe, C.D. "Statistics of Canada's Balance of Payments." CANADIAN JOURNAL OF ECONOMICS AND POLITICAL SCIENCE 19 (November 1953): 472-77.

4. Canada. Dominion Bureau of Statistics. DOMINION BUREAU OF STATISTICS, HISTORY FUNCTION AND ORGANIZATION. Ottawa: King's Printer, 1952. 341 p. Tables. Charts.

5. _____. HISTORICAL CATALOGUE OF DOMINION BUREAU OF STATISTICS PUBLICATIONS 1918-1960. D.B.S. cat. no. 11-504. Ottawa: 1966. xiv, 298 p.

6. Canada. Statistics Canada. CANADIAN STATISTICAL REVIEW. Ottawa: King's Printer, 1926-- . Monthly.

7. _____. "Historical Summary 1970." CANADIAN STATISTICAL REVIEW, August 1972, entire issue. Reprint as CANADIAN STATISTICAL REVIEW: HISTORICAL SUMMARY, 1970 EDITION. Ottawa: Queen's Printer, 1972. 148 p.

8. Editor. Canadian Journal of Economics. "Dominion Bureau of Statistics 1918-1968." CANADIAN JOURNAL OF ECONOMICS 1 (August 1968): 649-51.

9. Goldberg, Simon A. "The Development of National Accounts in Canada." CANADIAN JOURNAL OF ECONOMICS AND POLITICAL SCIENCE 15 (February 1949): 34-52.

10. _____. "Some Recent Developments in the Dominion Bureau of Statistics." CANADIAN JOURNAL OF ECONOMICS AND POLITICAL SCIENCE 21 (February 1955): 52-63.

11. Goldberg, S[imon] A., and Leacy, F.H. "The National Accounts: Whither Now?" CANADIAN JOURNAL OF ECONOMICS AND POLITICAL SCIENCE 22 (February 1956): 73-91.

12. Keyfitz, Nathan, and Greenway, H.F. "Robert Coats and the Organization of Statistics." CANADIAN JOURNAL OF ECONOMICS AND POLITICAL SCIENCE 27 (August 1961): 313-22. Bibliography of Coats's writings.

13. Lennox, Mary. "Recent Developments in the Work of the Dominion Bureau of Statistics." CANADIAN JOURNAL OF ECONOMICS AND POLITICAL SCIENCE 33 (February 1967): 88-98.

14. _____. "Recent Developments in the Work of the Dominion Bureau of Statistics." CANADIAN JOURNAL OF ECONOMICS 1 (February 1968): 114-21.

15. Marshall, Herbert. "The Role of the Dominion Bureau of Statistics in the Post-War World." CANADIAN JOURNAL OF ECONOMICS AND POLITICAL SCIENCE 19 (August 1953): 281-90.

16. Read, L.M. "The Development of National Transactions Accounts: Canada's Version of or Substitute for Money Flows Accounts." CANADIAN JOURNAL OF ECONOMICS AND POLITICAL SCIENCE 23 (February 1957): 42-56.

17. Stanley, Nixon. "The Course of Interest Rates in Canada 1929-1937." CANADIAN JOURNAL OF ECONOMICS AND POLITICAL SCIENCE 3 (August 1937): 421-34.

18. Tucker, Marjorie. "Recent Developments in the Work of the Dominion Bureau of Statistics." CANADIAN JOURNAL OF ECONOMICS AND POLITICAL SCIENCE 25 (November 1959): 497-501; 27 (February 1961): 85-91; 28 (February 1962): 147-54; 29 (February 1963): 90-98; 30 (February 1964): 110-15; 31 (February 1965): 118-24; 32 (February 1966): 66-76.

V.C. THESES OF ECONOMIC GROWTH

A number of major areas of interpretation and analysis of Canadian growth have emerged in the post-1920 period. The search for a new national policy in the face of continuing economic interdependence, particularly with the United States, has focused attention on the analysis of (1) the role of nationalism in general, (2) the role of the tariff in particular, and (3) the mechanisms of adjustments in the balance of payments. In all of these areas, and especially in (2) and (3), economists have expended substantial effort. The main topic of attention under (1) has been the impact of U.S. direct investment and increased trade with the United States. The size and structure of the manufacturing sector with and without tariffs has been examined under (2), while (3) has been investigated with the use of fairly sophisticated econometric models. Other areas to receive analytical attention are (4) regional growth patterns, (5) the role of money versus income and expenditure, and (6) differential economic growth in Quebec.

V.C.i. Theses of Economic Growth: The Role of Nationalism

The literature here is one-sided in the sense that attention given to nationalism per se is, with few exceptions, more polemic than analytic, and in general, fails to supply a satisfactory nationalist interpretation of twentieth-century Canadian economic development. In contrast, analytical studies, mostly by economists, have dwelt on the international as opposed to national elements of the growth story, and are mildly successful in revealing some positive, or at least nonnegative, roles played by international connections.

The trend of growing integration of the Canadian and American economies via trade and capital flows has been well documented. See, for example, II.G.iii. 1 and items 1, 2, 3, 7, 15, 16, and 17 below. Perhaps, the best overall view is provided by V.A.2. In addition, there is a whole series of short publications published jointly in the 1960s by the Private Planning Association of Canada and the National Planning Association of the United States under the auspices of the Canadian American Committee. Economic analyses of the trend toward integration are essentially of two kinds: (1) positive or explanatory, and (2) normative or welfare oriented. Contributing to the first kind are 9, 10, 13, 16, and 18. See especially the studies footnoted in 16. On the welfare issue, in addition to 16, see 1, 11, 14, 20, 21, and 22. Two exhaustive studies undertaken by the Canadian government are 5 and 6, referred to informally as the Gray Report and the Watkin's Report respectively.

For the treatment of nationalism per se, probably the best analysis is found in 4 and in II.E.iii.11; see also V.A.11. For a sweeping historical interpretation see II.E.iii.2, and for a different view, 8 below. Nationalist lament has made a voluminous penetration into the literature. For some of the many examples, see 11 and some of the later essays in 19. A good confrontation of viewpoints is also supplied by 19. For the evolution of the nationalist myth, see 12.

V.C.i. Theses of Economic Growth: The Role of Nationalism

1. Beigie, Carl E. CANADIAN-U.S. AUTOMOTIVE AGREEMENT, AN EVALUATION. Montreal: Canadian-American Committee, Private Planning Association of Canada, 1970. 167 p. Tables. Diagrams.

2. Bonin, B. L'INVESTISSEMENT ETRANGER A LONG TERM AU CANADA, SES CARACTERES ET SES EFFECTS SUR L'ECONOMIE CANADIENNE: AVEC ANNEXE SUR LES SYSTEME INTERNATION AUX DE POINTS DE BASE. Montréal: Les Presses de l'Ecole des Hautes Etudes Commerciales

1920 to Present

de Montréal, 1967. 462 p. Diagrams. Tables. Bibliography, pp. 423-45.

3. Brecher, I[rving]. CAPITAL FLOWS BETWEEN CANADA AND THE UNITED STATES. Montreal: Canadian-American Committee, Private Planning Association of Canada, 1965. xv, 141 p.

4. Breton, Albert. "The Economics of Nationalism." JOURNAL OF POLITICAL ECONOMY 72 (August 1964): 376-86.

5. Canada. Privy Council Office. FOREIGN DIRECT INVESTMENT IN CANADA. Ottawa: Queen's Printer, 1972. xi, 523 p. Tables.

6. Canada. Task Force on the Structure of Canadian Industry. FOREIGN OWNERSHIP AND THE STRUCTURE OF CANADIAN INDUSTRY. Ottawa: Queen's Printer, 1968. xi, 523 p. Tables.

7. Fayerweather, John. FOREIGN INVESTMENT IN CANADA, PROSPECTS FOR NATIONAL POLICY. Toronto: Oxford University Press, 1974. 200 p.

8. Fowke, V[ernon] C[lifford]. "The National Policy--Old and New." CANADIAN JOURNAL OF ECONOMICS AND POLITICAL SCIENCE 18 (August 1952): 271-86.

9. Kilduff, Vera Reynolds. "Economic Factors in the Development of Canadian-American Trade." SOUTHERN ECONOMIC JOURNAL 8 (October 1941): 201-17.

10. Knox, F[rank] A. "U.S. Capital Investments in Canada." AMERICAN ECONOMIC REVIEW 47 (May 1957): 596-609.

11. Levitt, Kari. SILENT SURRENDER; THE MULTINATIONAL CORPORATION IN CANADA. Preface by Melville Watkins. Toronto: Macmillan of Canada, 1970. 185 p. Illustrations. Bibliographic references.

12. Lower, Arthur R[eginald] M[arsden]. HISTORY AND MYTH, ARTHUR LOWER AND THE MAKING OF CANADIAN NATIONALISM. Edited by Welf H. Herick. Vancouver: University of British Columbia Press, 1975. 362 p.

13. Paquet, G[illes], ed. THE MULTINATIONAL FIRM AND THE NATION STATE. Don Mills, Ontario: Collier-Macmillan, 1972. x, 182 p. Selected bibliography, pp. 167-82.

1920 to Present

14. Penner, R[udolf] G. "The Benefits of Foreign Investment in Canada 1950-56." CANADIAN JOURNAL OF ECONOMICS AND POLITICAL SCIENCE 32 (May 1966): 172-83.

15. Radford, R.A. "Canada's Capital Inflow 1946-53." INTERNATIONAL MONETARY FUND STAFF PAPERS 4 (February 1955): 217-57.

16. Reuber, G[rant] L. "Foreign Investment in Canada: A Review." In ECONOMICS: CONTEMPORARY ISSUES IN CANADA, edited by D.A.L. Auld, pp. 161-80. Toronto: Holt, Rinehart and Winston, 1972.

17. _____. THE GROWTH AND CHANGING COMPOSITION OF TRADE BETWEEN CANADA AND THE UNITED STATES. Washington, D.C.: Canadian-American Committee, 1960. xii, 87 p. Diagrams.

18. Reuber, G[rant] L., and Roseman, F. THE TAKE-OVER OF CANADIAN FIRMS 1945-61. Economic Council of Canada Special Study, no. 10. Ottawa: Queen's Printer, 1969. 242 p. Tables. Statistical appendix, pp. 185-231.

19. Russell, P., ed. NATIONALISM IN CANADA, UNIVERSITY LEAGUE OF SOCIAL REFORM. Toronto: McGraw-Hill, 1966. xx, 377 p. Bibliographic references.

20. Safarian, A[lbert] E[dward]. FOREIGN OWNERSHIP OF CANADIAN INDUSTRY. Toronto: McGraw-Hill, 1966. 346 p. Tables. Bibliography, pp. 332-39.

21. _____. THE PERFORMANCE OF FOREIGN-OWNED FIRMS IN CANADA. Montreal: Canadian-American Committee, Private Planning Association of Canada, 1969. xvii, 123 p.

22. Shearer, R[onald] A. "Nationality, Size of Firm and Exploration of Petroleum in Western Canada, 1946-1964." CANADIAN JOURNAL OF ECONOMICS AND POLITICAL SCIENCE 30 (May 1964): 211-27.

V.C.ii. Theses of Economic Growth: The Role of the Tariff

Analysis of the Canadian tariff's impact begins with a path-breaking comparative study, item 3, most satisfactory for the period following 1920. A number of other attempts has been made to assess the tariff, either by the direct measurement of its costs, or by indirectly hypothesizing the resource reallocation effects of its removal. For a partial equilibrium welfare cost measurement, see 22. No general equilibrium assessment has yet been made, and for the hazards of applying the theory of effective protection, see 11. The latter includes the computation of effective rates on commodities for 1964.

The alternative approach for examining the effects of the tariff, namely studying the implications of its removal, is developed in detail in 21. For a different view, see 12. Taking trade liberalization as a point of departure for investigating the role of the tariff, the Private Planning Association of Canada sponsored a series of studies to explore the effects of tariff removal on various industries and regions, and on the ability of Canada to pursue her own economic policies: see 1, 6, 7, 8, 13, 14, 15, and 16. The results of these efforts are summed up in 18. Most of these studies, particularly those of individual industries and regions, provide a good short synopsis of their recent history. For some issues raised by the European Common Market, see 2 and 9.

Other hypotheses about the tariff relate to its effect on industrial organization. Pioneering studies in this direction include the essays reprinted in part 1 of 17, especially essays five and six. The detailed study of a number of manufacturing industries from the point of view of these essays is contained in 4. For a shorter similar treatment, see 5. For a case study in industrial reorganization following tariff modification, see chapter 11 in V.A.11; V.C.i.1; and 19 and 20 below. The tariff has also been linked to the spread of the multinational corporation in studies such as in II.D.ii.10. For another view, see 10 below.

V.C.ii. Theses of Economic Growth: The Role of the Tariff

1. Bond, David E., and Wonnacott, Ronald J. TRADE LIBERALIZATION AND THE CANADIAN FURNITURE INDUSTRY. Canada in the Atlantic Economy Series, no. 6. Published for the Private Planning Association of Canada. Toronto: University of Toronto Press, 1968. viii, 58 p. Bibliographic footnotes.

2. Caves, Richard E[arl]. "Europe's Unification and Canada's Trade." CANADIAN JOURNAL OF ECONOMICS AND POLITICAL SCIENCE 25 (August 1959): 249-58.

3. Dales, John H[arkness]. THE PROTECTIVE TARIFF IN CANADA'S DEVELOPMENT: EIGHT ESSAYS ON TARIFFS AND TRADE WHEN FACTORS MOVE WITH SPECIAL REFERENCE TO CANADIAN PROTECTIONISM 1870-1955. Toronto: Ryerson Press, 1966. vi, 168 p. Tables.

4. Eastman, H[arry] C., and Stykolt, S[tefan]. THE TARIFF AND COMPETITION IN CANADA. Toronto: Macmillan of Canada, 1967. ix, 400 p. Tables.

5. English, H[arry] E[dward]. INDUSTRIAL STRUCTURE IN CANADA'S INTERNATIONAL COMPETITIVE POSITION. Montreal: Canadian Trade Committee, 1964. xiv, 58 p.

6. Haviland, W.E., et al. TRADE LIBERALIZATION AND THE CANADIAN PULP AND PAPER INDUSTRY. Canada in the Atlantic Economy Series, no. 5. Published for the Private Planning Association of Canada. Toronto: University of Toronto Press, 1968. viii, 108 p. Bibliographic footnotes.

7. Johnson, Harry G[ordon], et al. HARMONIZATION OF NATIONAL ECONOMIC POLICIES UNDER FREE TRADE. Canada in the Atlantic Economy Series, no. 3. Published for the Private Planning Association of Canada. Toronto: University of Toronto Press, 1968. 84 p. Bibliographic footnotes.

8. MacFarlane, D.L., et al. TRADE LIBERALIZATION AND CANADIAN AGRICULTURE. Canada in the Atlantic Economy Series, no. 4. Published for the Private Planning Association of Canada. Toronto: University of Toronto Press, 1968. viii, 120 p. Bibliographic footnotes.

9. McIvor, R. Craig. "Canadian Foreign Trade and the European Common Market." INTERNATIONAL JOURNAL 13 (Winter 1957-58): 1-11.

10. McManus, John C. "The Theory of the International Firm." In THE MULTINATIONAL FIRM AND THE NATION STATE, edited by Gilles Paquet, pp. 66-93. Don Mills, Ontario: Collier-Macmillan, 1972. Selected bibliography, pp. 167-82.

11. Melvin, J[ames], and Wilkinson, Bruce [W.]. EFFECTIVE PROTECTION IN THE CANADIAN ECONOMY. Economic Council of Canada Special Study, no. 9. Ottawa: Queen's Printer, 1968. vii, 76 p. Bibliography, pp. 74-76.

12. Moore, Albert Milton. HOW MUCH COMPETITION? THE PREREQUISITES FOR AN EFFECTIVE CANADIAN COMPETITION POLICY. Montreal: McGill-Queen's University Press, 1970. xiv, 217 p. Bibliographic references.

13. Munro, John M. TRADE LIBERALIZATION AND TRANSPORTATION IN INTERNATIONAL TRADE. Canada in the Atlantic Economy Series, no. 8. Published for the Private Planning Association of Canada. Toronto: University of Toronto Press, 1969. viii, 204 p. Illustrations. Bibliographic footnotes.

14. Shearer, R.A., et al. TRADE LIBERALIZATION AND THE BRITISH COLUMBIA ECONOMY. Canada in the Atlantic Economy Series, no. 13. Published for the Private Planning Association of Canada. Toronto: University of Toronto Press, 1971. vi, 203 p.

15. Shibata, Hirofumi. FISCAL HARMONIZATION UNDER FREER TRADE: PRINCIPLES AND THEIR APPLICATIONS TO A CANADA-U.S. FREE TRADE AREA. Canada in the Atlantic Economy Series, no. 9. Published for the Private Planning Association of Canada. Toronto: University of Toronto Press, 1969. vi, 88 p. Bibliographic footnotes.

16. Singer, Jacques. TRADE LIBERALIZATION AND THE CANADIAN STEEL INDUSTRY. Canada in the Atlantic Economy Series, no. 7. Published for the Private Planning Association of Canada. Toronto: University of Toronto Press, 1969. viii, 142 p.

17. Stykolt, S[tefan]. EFFICIENCY IN THE OPEN ECONOMY. Edited, with an introduction by Anthony [Dalton] Scott and James D. Rae. Toronto: Oxford University Press, 1969. xi, 216 p.

18. Wilkinson, Bruce W.; Eastman, Harry C.; and English, H[arry] Edward. CANADA IN A WIDER ECONOMIC COMMUNITY. Canada in the Atlantic Economy Series, no. 13. Published for the Private Planning Association of Canada. Toronto: University of Toronto Press, 1973. viii, 151 p.

19. Wonnacott, Gordon Paul. "Canadian Automotive Protection: Content Provisions, the Bladen Plan, and Recent Tariff Changes." CANADIAN JOURNAL OF ECONOMICS AND POLITICAL SCIENCE 31 (February 1965): 98-116.

20. Wonnacott, G[ordon] P[aul], and Wonnacott, R[onald] J. "The Automotive Agreement of 1965." CANADIAN JOURNAL OF ECONOMICS AND POLITICAL SCIENCE 33 (May 1967): 269-84.

21. _____. FREE TRADE BETWEEN THE UNITED STATES AND CANADA, THE POTENTIAL ECONOMIC EFFECTS. Harvard Economic Studies, no. 129. Cambridge, Mass.: Harvard University Press, 1967. xx, 430 p. Illustrations. Map. Bibliographic footnotes.

22. Young, J.H. CANADIAN COMMERCIAL POLICY. Royal Commission on Canada's Economic Prospects Study. Ottawa: Queen's Printer, 1957. 233 p. Tables.

V.C.iii. Theses of Economic Growth: Trade, Cycles, and the Balance of Payments

Richard Caves, in chapter 3 of II.A.i.1, pointed out a fundamental consistency between models of short-run income determination for an open economy and models based on the staples approach to economic growth. The most striking example is the wheat boom for which the associated changes in the balance of payments are analyzed in IV.D.i.26 and IV.D.i.27. For further discussion of this example, see also 11 and 16 of IV.D.i. The background of these studies is a careful documentation of trade and capital flows for which the main sources were noted in V.C.i. For additional background see 1, 5, 7, 23, 27, and 32 below. A large number of the analytical studies attempt to estimate the relevant elasticities for predicting the effects of disturbances in the balance of payments. See, for example, 9, 13, 14, and 22. For overall views, see 28 and 29. Econometric models of Canadian income generation that incorporate explicit assumptions about the exchange rate are 19 and 24. Smaller scale models of trade and income include 8, 9, and 18. See 31 for a brief general essay on the typical trends and prices underlying the Canadian balance of payments.

Another strand of the literature examines the transmission of business cycles from abroad via balance of payments mechanisms, as in 4, 15, 16, 17, and 26 for the 1920s and 1930s, and in 3, 25, and 30 for more recent years. The role of capital flows and transfers are explored in 6, 7, 19, 20, 21, and 24. The associated market for foreign exchange, and the changing value of the Canadian dollar over time, are discussed in 10, 11, 12, 21, 33, and 34. For the balance of payments effects of the trade in petroleum, see 2.

V.C.iii. Theses of Economic Growth: Trade, Cycles, and the Balance of Payments

1. Anderson, R.V. THE FUTURE OF CANADA'S EXPORT TRADE. Royal Commission on Canada's Economic Prospects Study. Ottawa: Queen's Printer, 1957. 335 p. Tables. Bibliographic footnotes.

2. Bing, R.A. "Petroleum in Canada's Balance of International Payments." SOUTHERN ECONOMIC JOURNAL 19 (October 1952): 234-48.

3. Bonome, V., and Tanner, J.E. "Canadian Sensitivity to Economic Cycles in the United States." REVIEW OF ECONOMICS AND STATISTICS 54 (February 1972): 1-8.

4. Bryce, R.B. "The Effects on Canada of Industrial Fluctuations in the United States." CANADIAN JOURNAL OF ECONOMICS AND POLITICAL SCIENCE 5 (August 1939): 373-86.

1920 to Present

5. Canada. Dominion Bureau of Statistics. THE CANADIAN BALANCE OF INTERNATIONAL PAYMENTS 1926-1948. Ottawa: King's Printer, 1949. 192 p. Tables.

6. Caves, R[ichard] E[arl], and Reuber, G[rant] L. CANADIAN ECONOMIC POLICY AND THE IMPACT OF INTERNATIONAL CAPITAL FLOWS. Canada in the Atlantic Economy Series, no. 10. Published for the Private Planning Association of Canada. Toronto: University of Toronto Press, 1969. 82 p. Bibliographic footnotes.

7. _____. CAPITAL TRANSFERS AND ECONOMIC POLICY: CANADA 1951-1962. Harvard Economic Studies, vol. 135. Cambridge, Mass.: Harvard University Press, 1970. xviii, 432 p. Bibliography, pp. 413-23.

8. Chang, Tse-Chun. "A Note on Exports and National Income in Canada." CANADIAN JOURNAL OF ECONOMICS AND POLITICAL SCIENCE 13 (May 1947): 276-79.

9. de Vegh, Imre. "Imports and Income in the United States and Canada." REVIEW OF ECONOMICS AND STATISTICS 23 (August 1941): 130-46.

10. Eastman, Harry C. "Aspects of Speculation in the Canadian Market for Foreign Exchange." CANADIAN JOURNAL OF ECONOMICS AND POLITICAL SCIENCE 24 (August 1958): 355-72.

11. _____. "On Buying Cheap and Selling Dear: Professor Powrie's Paradox." CANADIAN JOURNAL OF ECONOMICS AND POLITICAL SCIENCE 30 (August 1964): 431-35.

12. Eastman, Harry C., and Stykolt, Stefan. "Exchange Stabilization in Canada 1950-4." CANADIAN JOURNAL OF ECONOMICS AND POLITICAL SCIENCE 22 (May 1956): 221-33.

13. Kemp, M.C. THE DEMAND FOR CANADIAN IMPORTS 1926-55. Canadian Studies in Economics, no. 15. Toronto: University of Toronto Press, 1962. 82 p. Bibliography, pp. 71-72. Bibliographic footnotes.

14. Malach, V[ernon] W[alter] "Elasticity of Demand for Canadian Exports." REVIEW OF ECONOMICS AND STATISTICS 39 (February 1957): 23-30.

15. _____. INTERNATIONAL CYCLES AND CANADA'S BALANCE OF PAYMENTS 1921-33. Toronto: University of Toronto Press, 1954. xii, 154 p. Diagrams. Tables. Bibliography.

16. _____. "The Mechanism of Adjustment in Canada's Balance of Payments 1921-9." CANADIAN JOURNAL OF ECONOMICS AND POLITICAL SCIENCE 18 (August 1952): 303-21.

17. Marcus, Edward. CANADA AND THE INTERNATIONAL BUSINESS CYCLE 1927-1939. New York: Bookman Associates, 1954. vi, 211 p. Bibliographic footnotes.

18. Munzer, E. "Exports and National Income in Canada." CANADIAN JOURNAL OF ECONOMICS AND POLITICAL SCIENCE 11 (February 1945): 35-47.

19. Officer, Lawrence H. AN ECONOMETRIC MODEL OF CANADA UNDER THE FLUCTUATING RATE. Harvard Economic Studies, no. 130. Cambridge, Mass.: Harvard University Press, 1968. 319 p.

20. Penner, Rudolph G. "The Inflow of Long-Term Capital and the Canadian Business Cycle, 1950-1960." CANADIAN JOURNAL OF ECONOMICS AND POLITICAL SCIENCE 28 (November 1962): 527-42.

21. Powrie, T.L. "Short-Term Capital Movements and the Flexible Canadian Exchange Rate 1953-1961." CANADIAN JOURNAL OF ECONOMICS AND POLITICAL SCIENCE 30 (February 1964): 76-94.

22. Reuber, Grant L. "Anglo-Canadian Trade: Prices and the Terms of Trade 1924-1954." REVIEW OF ECONOMICS AND STATISTICS 41, pt. 1, (May 1959): 196-99.

23. _____. BRITAIN'S EXPORT TRADE WITH CANADA. Canadian Studies in Economics, no. 12. Toronto: University of Toronto Press, 1960. 147 p. Bibliographic footnotes.

24. Rhomberg, R. "A Model of the Canadian Economy under Fixed and Fluctuation Exchange Rates." JOURNAL OF POLITICAL ECONOMY 72 (February 1964): 1-31.

25. Rosenbluth, G[ideon]. "Changes in Canadian Sensitivity to United States Business Cycles." CANADIAN JOURNAL OF ECONOMICS AND POLITICAL SCIENCE 23 (November 1957): 480-503.

26. Safarian, A[lbert] E[dward]. "Foreign Trade and the Level of Economic Activity in Canada in the 1930's." CANADIAN JOURNAL OF ECONOMICS AND POLITICAL SCIENCE 18 (August 1952): 336-44.

27. Slater, David W. CANADA'S IMPORTS. Royal Commission on Canada's Economic Prospects Study. Ottawa: Queen's Printer, 1957. 219 p. Tables. Bibliographic footnotes. Bibliography, pp. 217-19.

28. _____. PERSPECTIVES ON CANADA'S INTERNATIONAL PAYMENTS, A BACKGROUND SKETCH AND SURVEY. Economic Council of Canada Special Study, no. 3. Ottawa: Queen's Printer, 1965. 91 p. Tables.

29. Walter, Edward A. "The Vulnerability of the Canadian Economy." CANADIAN JOURNAL OF ECONOMICS AND POLITICAL SCIENCE 20 (February 1954): 10-18.

30. Watts, G.S. "The Canadian Balance of International Payments 1950-2, and the Mechanism of Adjustments." CANADIAN JOURNAL OF ECONOMICS AND POLITICAL SCIENCE 20 (February 1954): 19-26.

31. _____. "Some Longer-Term Factors in the Canadian Balance of International Payments." CANADIAN JOURNAL OF ECONOMICS AND POLITICAL SCIENCE 16 (February 1950): 12-21.

32. Wilkinson, Bruce W. CANADA'S INTERNATIONAL TRADE: AN ANALYSIS OF RECENT TRENDS AND PATTERNS. Montreal: Private Planning Association of Canada, 1968. 200 p. Illustrations.

33. Wonnacott, Gordon Paul. THE CANADIAN DOLLAR 1948-1958. Canadian Studies in Economics, no. 13. Toronto: University of Toronto Press, 1960. xii, 162 p. Tables. Diagrams. Bibliography included in notes, pp. 143-59.

34. _____. THE CANADIAN DOLLAR, 1948-1962. Toronto: University of of Toronto Press, 1965. 339 p. Illustrations. Incorporates as part 1 Wonnacott's THE CANADIAN DOLLAR 1948-1958, cited above.

V.C.iv. Theses of Economic Growth: Quantity Theory vs. Income Expenditure

In a series of articles, 4, 5, 6, and 7, George Macesich develops a test of the quantity theory of money for Canada. See also the critical note, 1. In 8, Macesich develops a supply and demand analysis of the Canadian money supply from 1868 to 1958, including a data series of the money supply over this interval. For an older attempt over a shorter period, see 2. For an analysis of the supply side of the Canadian money supply 1925-34, see 3.

V.C.iv. Theses of Economic Growth: Quantity Theory vs. Income Expenditure

1. Barber, C[larence] L. "The Quantity Theory and the Income Expenditure Theory in an Open Economy, 1926-1958: A Comment." CANADIAN JOURNAL OF ECONOMICS AND POLITICAL SCIENCE 32 (August 1966): 375-77.

2. Buck, Hart. "Means of Payments and Prices in Canada, 1900-46." CANADIAN JOURNAL OF ECONOMICS AND POLITICAL SCIENCE 13 (May 1947): 197-207.

3. Courchene, T.J. "An Analysis of the Canadian Money Supply: 1925-1934." JOURNAL OF POLITICAL ECONOMY 77 (May/June 1969): 363-91.

4. Macesich, George. "Determinants of Monetary Velocity in Canada 1926-1958." CANADIAN JOURNAL OF ECONOMICS AND POLITICAL SCIENCE 28 (May 1962): 245-54.

5. _____. "Empirical Testing and the Income Expenditure Theory." CANADIAN JOURNAL OF ECONOMICS AND POLITICAL SCIENCE 32 (August 1966): 377-79.

6. _____. "The Quantity Theory and the Income Expenditure Theory in an Open Economy: Canada, 1926-1958." CANADIAN JOURNAL OF ECONOMICS AND POLITICAL SCIENCE 30 (August 1964): 368-90.

7. _____. "The Rate of Change in Money Stock as a Leading Canadian Indicator." CANADIAN JOURNAL OF ECONOMICS AND POLITICAL SCIENCE 28 (August 1962): 424-30.

8. _____. "Supply and Demand for Money in Canada." In VARIETIES OF MONETARY EXPERIENCE, edited by D. Meiselman, pp. 251-95. Chicago: University of Chicago Press, 1970.

V.C.v. Theses of Economic Growth: Regional Growth Patterns

A difference in the pattern of regional growth between Canada and the United States was first noted in 7, a comprehensive comparative study of many countries using alternative measures of regional income inequality. This finding is largely substantiated in 5 and 3, and in the corresponding fuller accounts, 6 and 2. For a tentative hypothesis about Canadian regional growth, see 2 and 3. See also IV.A.8. For a criticism of 6, see 4. An interesting thesis about the perpetuation of regional disparities is proposed in 1.

V.C.v. Theses of Economic Growth: Regional Growth Patterns

1. Breton, Albert. DISCRIMINATORY GOVERNMENT POLICIES IN FEDERAL COUNTRIES. Montreal: Private Planning Association of Canada, 1967. xiii, 77 p. Bibliographic footnotes.

2. Green, Alan G. REGIONAL ASPECTS OF CANADA'S ECONOMIC GROWTH. Canadian Studies in Economics, no. 21. Toronto: University of Toronto Press, 1971. xi, 116 p. Bibliographic references.

3. _____. "Regional Inequality, Structural Change and Economic Growth in Canada 1890-1956." ECONOMIC DEVELOPMENT AND CULTURAL CHANGE 17 (July 1969): 567-83.

4. Lemelin, Charles. "Comment on Professor McInnis' Paper." CANADIAN JOURNAL OF ECONOMICS 1 (May 1968): 471-73.

5. McInnis, R. M[arvin]. "Regional Income Differentials in Canada 1911-1961." JOURNAL OF ECONOMIC HISTORY 26 (December 1966): 586-88.

6. _____. "The Trend of Regional Income Differentials in Canada." CANADIAN JOURNAL OF ECONOMICS 1 (May 1968): 440-73.

7. Williamson, Jeffrey G. "Regional Inequality and the Process of National Development." ECONOMIC DEVELOPMENT AND CULTURAL CHANGE 13 (July 1965): pt. 2.

V.C.vi. Theses of Economic Growth: Quebec

The effect of modern industrialism on Quebec and the possible effect of French Canadian culture on Quebec's industrialization have been controversial. For an introductory summary view, see V.A.16, chapter 3. For statistical background on the structure of post-World War II manufacturing in the two provinces, see 1, 2, and 3. For early views that Quebec's culture was unique and stood in the way of industrialization, see 4 and 5. The same view is refined for the mid-1950s in 2. On the other side of the issue, see IV.D.ii.6 and IV.A.ii.16.

V.C.vi. Theses of Economic Growth: Quebec

1. Chateau, J.P. "Croissance et structure des industries manufacturieres au Québec et en Ontario, 1949-63. L'ACTUALITE ECONOMIQUE 44 (July-September 1968): 273-89; (October-December 1968): 492-527.

2. Dales, J[ohn] H[arkness]. "A Comparison of Manufacturing in Quebec and Ontario, 1952." In CANADIAN DUALISM, edited by Mason Wade, pp. 203-21. Toronto: University of Toronto Press, 1960.

3. Hughes, Everett C[herrington], and McDonald, M.L. "French and English in the Economic Structure of Montreal." CANADIAN JOURNAL OF ECONOMICS AND POLITICAL SCIENCE 7 (November 1941): 493-505.

4. Melancon, Jacques. "Retard de croissance de l'entreprise canadienne-française." L'ACTUALITE ECONOMIQUE 31 (January-March 1956): 503-22.

5. Taylor, Norman W. "French Canadians as Industrial Entrepreneurs." JOURNAL OF POLITICAL ECONOMY 68 (February 1960): 37-52.

V.D. SECTORS AND INDUSTRIES

Although the secondary sector continues after the 1920s to dominate primary production in relative importance, many secondary industries depend heavily on natural resources, and diversification remains incomplete in comparison with some other advanced industrial economies. The service sector maintains the position of importance it acquired in the late nineteenth century.

V.D.i. Sectors and Industries: Primary Industry

Wheat continues to be an important export commodity after 1920, but other resources, particularly oil, gas, and other minerals, begin to assume growing importance. The grain trade after 1930 is recorded in 24 and 37, and the agricultural sector as a whole is brought up to the present in 1, 12, 14, 18, 20, and 31. Regional competition is discussed in 7. The surpassing of agriculture by secondary industry as the leading sector is discussed in 8 and 13. The change is also foretold in the composition of exports: see 36, and for British Columbia, 32. For several short essays on agricultural development, see I.B.2 for 1945, pages 188-91; for 1957-58, pages 392-96; and for 1960, pages 434-39.

Fishing and forestry operations are still important in some regions. For fisheries overall since 1926, see 4, and in Newfoundland, 6 and 27; see also I.B.2 for 1943-44, pages 277-79; and for 1960, pages 625-30. For an overview of the development of forest industries since 1926, see item 11 below and I.B.2 for 1951, pages 425-37.

Perhaps the most spectacular development in the mineral area is the discovery and production of petroleum and natural gas. The best overall treatment is 17; see also 25 and 5. A useful statistical account, and an analysis that includes coal, hydroelectricity, and atomic power as well as oil and gas, is 9. The processing industries are also covered in 9. For the development of the uranium industry, see 19, and for its significance, 22. For a complete account of the growth of all minerals production, see 10 supplemented with 21. The annual issues of 3 are also excellent and detailed. The discovery, mining, and refining of nickel is discussed in 23, 26, and 38. For iron and steel, see 30 and 39. For one account of nonferrous metals in Noranda, Quebec, see 34, and for the prairie provinces, see 35. For short treatments, see also I.B.2 for 1939, pages 309-10, giving a short historical sketch of the development of the Canadian mineral industry; for 1940, pages 298-309, on mineral resources and the war effort; for 1942, pages 279-82 on wartime controls over nonferrous metals and fuels; for 1946, pages 302-14 dealing with the postwar outlook, and pages 337-47 on coal; for 1950, pages 505-13 on the Quebec-Labrador iron ore resources; for 1952-53, pages 476-95 on the postwar mineral expansion, and pages 524-27 on petroleum; and for 1954, pages 540-44 on petroleum.

A characteristic of many of these mineral developments has been the presence of American capital and the prospect of an American market. This aspect of mineral growth is discussed in 2, 15, 16, and 29. For particular reference to petroleum, gas, and electricity, see 28 and 33. For a recent study which deals with North American policy with reference to energy minerals, see V.E.iii.20.

V.D.i. Sectors and Industries: Primary Industry

1. Britnell, G[eorge] E[dwin], and Fowke, V[ernon] C[lifford]. CANADIAN AGRICULTURE IN WAR AND PEACE, 1935-50. Palo Alto, Calif.: Stanford University Press, 1962. xiv, 502 p. Tables. Map. Bibliographic footnotes. Bibliography, pp. 469-77.

2. Burton, Ian, and Kates, Robert W. "Canadian Resources and American Requirements." CANADIAN JOURNAL OF ECONOMICS AND POLITICAL SCIENCE 30 (May 1964): 265-69.

3. Canada. Department of Energy, Mines and Resources. CANADIAN MINERALS YEARBOOK. Ottawa: Queen's Printer, 1954-- . Annual.

4. Canada. Department of Fisheries. THE COMMERCIAL FISHERIES OF CANADA. Royal Commission on Canada's Economic Prospects Study.

Ottawa: Queen's Printer, 1956. 191 p. Tables. Bibliographic footnotes.

5.   Cochrane, H.G. "The Natural Gas Story. CANADIAN BUSINESS 29 (March 1956): 12-22.

6.   Copes, Parzival. "The Development of the Newfoundland Fishing Economy." PROCEEDINGS AND TRANSACTIONS OF THE ROYAL SOCIETY OF CANADA, 4th ser. 10 (1972): 309-17.

7.   Craddock, W.J. INTERREGIONAL COMPETITION IN CANADIAN CEREAL PRODUCTION. Economic Council of Canada Special Study, no. 12. Ottawa: Queen's Printer, 1970. vii, 257 p. Illustrations. Maps (some in color). Bibliography, pp. 245-47.

8.   Daly, D.J. "Aspects of the Decline in Employment in Canadian Agriculture." CANADIAN JOURNAL OF AGRICULTURAL ECONOMICS 3, no. 2 (1955): 19-31.

9.   Davis, John [S.]. CANADIAN ENERGY PROSPECTS. Royal Commission on Canada's Economic Prospects Study. Ottawa: Queen's Printer, 1957. 390 p. Tables. Diagrams. Bibliography, pp. 384-89.

10.   _____. MINING AND MINERAL PROCESSING IN CANADA. Royal Commission on Canada's Economic Prospects Study. Ottawa: Queen's Printer, 1957. ix, 397 p. Tables. Maps. Diagrams. Chapter bibliographies.

11.   Davis, J[ohn S.]., et al. THE OUTLOOK FOR THE CANADIAN FOREST INDUSTRIES. Royal Commission on Canada's Economic Prospects Study. Ottawa: Queen's Printer, 1957. 259 p. Tables. Diagrams. Maps. Bibliographic footnotes.

12.   Dawson, John. CHANGES IN AGRICULTURE TO 1970. Economic Council of Canada Staff Study, no. 11. Ottawa: Queen's Printer, 1964. 26 p.

13.   Drummond, W[illiam] M[alcolm]. "The Impact of the Post-War Industrial Expansion on Ontario's Agriculture." CANADIAN JOURNAL OF ECONOMICS AND POLITICAL SCIENCE 24 (February 1958): 84-92.

14.   _____. PROGRESS AND PROSPECTS OF CANADIAN AGRICULTURE. Royal Commission on Canada's Economic Prospects Study. Ottawa: Queen's Printer, 1957. 421 p. Tables. Bibliographic footnotes.

1920 to Present

15. Eldon, D. AMERICAN INFLUENCE IN THE CANADIAN IRON AND STEEL INDUSTRY. University of Rochester Canadian Studies, no. 5. Rochester, N.Y.: University of Rochester Press, 1954. ix, 574 p. Microprint copy of typescript, 14 cards. Maps. Diagrams. Tables. Bibliography, pp. 565-74.

16. Goodman, Bernard. INDUSTRIAL MATERIALS IN CANADIAN AMERICAN RELATIONS. Wayne State University Center for Economic Studies, Monograph no. 2. Detroit: Wayne State University Press, 1961. xvii, 217 p. Maps. Diagrams. Tables. Bibliography, pp. 204-15.

17. Hanson, E.J. DYNAMIC DECADE. Toronto: McClelland & Stewart, 1958. 314 p. Illustrations.

18. Hudson, S.C. FUTURE MARKET OUTLETS FOR CANADIAN WHEAT AND OTHER GRAINS. Economic Council of Canada Special Study, no. 11. Ottawa: Queen's Printer, 1970. xxiv, 326 p.

19. Hunter, W.D.G. "The Development of the Canadian Uranium Industry: An Experiment in Public Enterprise." CANADIAN JOURNAL OF ECONOMICS AND POLITICAL SCIENCE 28 (August 1962): 329-52.

20. Kerr, Donald [G.G.]. "The Physical Basis of Agriculture in British Columbia." ECONOMIC GEOGRAPHY 28 (July 1952): 229-39.

21. Langford, George Burwash. OUT OF THE EARTH: THE MINERAL INDUSTRY OF CANADA. Toronto: University of Toronto Press, 1954. xiv, 125 p. Illustrations. Maps (1 folding). Diagrams. Tables. Bibliography.

22. Le Bourdais, D[onat] M[arc]. CANADA AND THE ATOMIC REVOLUTION. Toronto: McClelland & Stewart, 1959. xix, 199 p. Plates. Portraits. Maps. Maps on lining papers. Bibliography, pp. 185-88.

23. _____. THE SUDBURY BASIN: THE STORY OF NICKEL. Toronto: Ryerson Press, 1953. 210 p. Illustrations

24. MacGibbon, D[uncan] A[lexander]. THE CANADIAN GRAIN TRADE 1931-1951. Toronto: University of Toronto Press, 1952. ix, 227 p. Bibliographic footnotes.

25. McGillivray, A.A., and Lipsett, L.R. ALBERTA'S OIL INDUSTRY. Report of the Alberta Royal Commission. Edmonton, Alberta: King's Printer, 1940. 287 p. Tables.

26. Main, Orrin William. THE CANADIAN NICKEL INDUSTRY; A STUDY IN MARKET CONTROL AND PUBLIC POLICY. Canadian Studies in Economics, no. 4. Toronto: University of Toronto Press, 1955. 168 p.

27. Mayo, H.B. The Economic Problem of the Newfoundland Fisheries." CANADIAN JOURNAL OF ECONOMICS AND POLITICAL SCIENCE 17 (November 1951): 482-93.

28. Miller, John T., Jr. FOREIGN TRADE IN GAS AND ELECTRICITY IN NORTH AMERICA, A LEGAL AND HISTORICAL STUDY. New York: Praeger, 1970. xix, 316 p.

29. Moore, Elwood S. AMERICAN INFLUENCE IN CANADIAN MINING. Political Economy Series, no. 9. Toronto: University of Toronto Press, 1941. xx, 144 p. Illustrations. Maps. Bibliographic footnotes.

30. Morgan, L. THE CANADIAN PRIMARY IRON AND STEEL INDUSTRY. Royal Commission on Canada's Economic Prospects Study. Ottawa: Queen's Printer, 1956. 101 p. Tables. Diagrams. Bibliographic references.

31. Morrissette, Hughes. LES CONDITIONS DU DEVELOPPEMENT AGRICOLE AU QUEBEC. Québec: Les Presses de l'Université Laval, 1972. xviii, 173 p.

32. Peters, J.E., and Shearer, R[onald] A. "The Structure of British Columbia's Trade 1939-1963." B.C. STUDIES 8 (Winter 1970-71): 34-64.

33. Plotnick, Alan R. PETROLEUM, CANADIAN MARKETS AND UNITED STATES FOREIGN POLICY. Seattle: University of Washington Press, 1964. 172 p. Maps. Bibliography, pp. 153-65.

34. Roberts, Leslie. NORANDA. Toronto: Clarke Irwin, 1956. xiii, 223 p. Illustrations. Plates. Frontispiece portrait. Maps. Maps on end papers. Chart.

35. Siebert, Fred V. "50th Anniversary Review of Mineral Development in the Prairie Provinces." CANADIAN MINING JOURNAL 76 (August 1955): 49-53.

36. Slater, David W. "Changes in the Structure of Canada's International Trade." CANADIAN JOURNAL OF ECONOMICS AND POLITICAL SCIENCE 31 (February 1955): 1-19.

1920 to Present

37. Swanson, William Walker, and Armstrong, P.C. WHEAT. Toronto: Macmillan of Canada, 1930. xiii, 320 p. Maps. Diagrams.

38. Thompson, John Fairfield, and Beasley, Norman. FOR THE YEARS TO COME, A STORY OF INTERNATIONAL NICKEL OF CANADA. New York: Putnam, 1960. 374 p.

39. Warsbrough, V.C. "Implications of Canadian Iron Ore Production." CANADIAN JOURNAL OF ECONOMICS AND POLITICAL SCIENCE 16 (August 1950): 334-39.

V.D.ii. Sectors and Industries: Secondary Industry

The preeminence of manufacturing activities after 1920 has been extensively documented by detailed quantitative descriptions of a large number of individual industries. For a brief overview, see I.B.2 for 1943-44, pages 354-62, and for 1945, pages 364-81. The majority of recent surveys are studies undertaken as a part of the Royal Commission on Canada's Economic Prospects reporting in 1956, summarized and reviewed in 17. For the separate industries covered by these studies, see 1, 3, 9, 10, 18, 20, 22, 23, and 25. All of these studies include industry statistics back to at least 1926, together with some analysis of the markets for their products. In addition, the farm machinery industry has received comprehensive treatment in 2. For the pulp and paper industry, in addition to V.D.i.11, see items 5, 12, 13, and 24 below. A brief account of the pulp and paper industry is given in I.B.2 for 1952-53, pages 467-75. Though old, 13 still provides the most complete analysis of the growth of the newsprint industry. For other brief accounts of the auto, steel, and chemical industries, see I.B.2 for 1947, pages 521-25; for 1959, pages 618-25; and for 1948-49, pages 532-50 respectively. The interrelations among these industries were first studied in 1947, producing the first input-output table for Canada, discussed in 4. The composition of the manufacturing sector is related to the presence of hydroelectric power, as analyzed in 6. The location of industry relative to urban centers is studied in 14 and 21. For Quebec's urbanization, see 19. The differential pattern of manufacturing growth in central Canada and the maritimes is examined in detail in 11.

Most recently, technical studies have attempted to specify and estimate the production relations of Canadian manufacturing: see 15 and 16. For an early attempt, see 8. For a more descriptive and less technical approach, see 17.

V.D.ii. Sectors and Industries: Secondary Industry

1. Barber, Clarence L. THE CANADIAN ELECTRICAL MANUFACTURING INDUSTRY. Royal Commission on Canada's Economic Prospects Study. Ottawa: Queen's Printer, 1956. 85 p. Tables Bibliographic footnotes.

1920 to Present

2. Canada. Privy Council Office. ROYAL COMMISSION OF FARM MACHINERY. 13 vols. Ottawa: Queen's Printer, 1969.

3. Canadian Business Service Ltd. THE ELECTRONICS INDUSTRY IN CANADA. Royal Commission on Canada's Economic Prospects Study. Ottawa: Queen's Printer, 1956. 81 p. Tables.

4. Caves, Richard E[arl]. "The Inter-Industry Structure of the Canadian Economy." CANADIAN JOURNAL OF ECONOMICS AND POLITICAL SCIENCE 23 (August 1957): 313-30.

5. Dagenais, M.G. "The Short Run Determinants of Output and Shipments in the North American Newsprint Industry." YALE ECONOMIC ESSAYS 4 (Fall 1964): 280-328.

6. Dales, J[ohn] H[arkness]. "Fuel, Power and Industrial Development in Central Canada." AMERICAN ECONOMIC REVIEW 43 (May 1953): 181-98.

7. Daly, D.J., et al. SCALE AND SPECIALIZATION IN CANADIAN MANUFACTURING. Economic Council of Canada Staff Study, no. 21. Ottawa: Queen's Printer, 1968. 97 p. Tables. Bibliographic footnotes.

8. Daly, Patricia, and Douglas, Paul H. "The Production Function for Canadian Manufacturers." JOURNAL OF THE AMERICAN STATISTICAL ASSOCIATION 38 (June 1943): 178-86.

9. Davis, John [S.]. THE CANADIAN CHEMICAL INDUSTRY. Royal Commission on Canada's Economic Prospects Study. Ottawa: Queen's Printer, 1957. 178 p. Tables. Bibliography, pp. 181-82.

10. Fullerton, D.H., and Hampson, H.A. CANADIAN SECONDARY MANUFACTURING INDUSTRY. Royal Commission on Canada's Economic Prospects Study. Ottawa: Queen's Printer, 1957. 272 p. Tables. Statistical appendix, pp. 208-72.

11. George, Roy E. A LEADER AND A LAGGARD, MANUFACTURING INDUSTRY IN NOVA SCOTIA, QUEBEC AND ONTARIO. Toronto: University of Toronto Press, 1970. viii, 220 p. Statistical appendix.

12. Guthrie, John A. AN ECONOMIC ANALYSIS OF THE PULP AND PAPER INDUSTRY. Pullman: Washington State University Press, 1972. 235 p.

1920 to Present

13. _____. THE NEWSPRINT PAPER INDUSTRY, AN ECONOMIC ANALYSIS. Harvard Economic Studies, vol. 68. Cambridge, Mass.: Harvard University Press, 1941. xxiii, 274 p. Illustrations. Maps. Tables. Diagrams. Bibliography, pp. 253-65.

14. Hay, K[eith] A. J. "Trends in the Location of Industry in Ontario 1945-59." CANADIAN JOURNAL OF ECONOMICS AND POLITICAL SCIENCE 31 (August 1965): 368-81.

15. Kotowitz, Y. "Capital Labour Substitution in Canadian Manufacturing 1926-39 and 1946-61." CANADIAN JOURNAL OF ECONOMICS 1 (August 1968): 619-32.

16. Lithwick, N.H., et al. "Post War Production Relationships in Canada." In THE THEORY AND EMPIRICAL ANALYSIS OF PRODUCTION, edited by M. Brown, pp. 139-273. National Bureau of Economic Research Studies in Income and Wealth, vol. 31. New York: Columbia University Press, 1967.

17. Markham, Jesse W. "Canada's Economic Prospects: A Survey of Ten Industries." CANADIAN JOURNAL OF ECONOMICS AND POLITICAL SCIENCE 27 (May 1961): 261-67.

18. National Industrial Conference Board. THE CANADIAN PRIMARY TEXTILES INDUSTRY. Royal Commission on Canada's Economic Prospects Study. Ottawa: Queen's Printer, 1956. 103 p. Tables.

19. Polèse, Mario, and Toupin, Pierre. "L'Evolution de la hiérarchie tertiaire des villes: Le Case de la région du sud-est de Montréal, 1931-1966." L'ACTUALITE ECONOMIQUE 48 (October-December 1972): 398-413.

20. Royal Bank of Canada. THE CANADIAN CONSTRUCTION INDUSTRY. Royal Commission on Canada's Economic Prospects Study. Ottawa: Queen's Printer, 1956. 230 p. Tables. Bibliographic footnotes. Statistical bibliography, pp. 221-22. Nonstatistical bibliography, pp. 223-24.

21. Slater, David W. "Decentralization of Urban Peoples and Manufacturing Activity in Canada." CANADIAN JOURNAL OF ECONOMICS AND POLITICAL SCIENCE 27 (February 1961): 72-84.

22. Sun Life Assurance Company of Canada. THE CANADIAN AUTOMOTIVE INDUSTRY. Royal Commission on Canada's Economic Prospects Study. Ottawa: Queen's Printer, 1956. 117 p. Tables.

1920 to Present

23. Urwick, Currie, Ltd. THE CANADIAN INDUSTRIAL MACHINERY INDUSTRY. Royal Commission on Canada's Economic Prospects Study. Ottawa: Queen's Printer, 1956. 29 p. Tables. Charts.

24. Wiegman, C. TREES TO NEWS. Toronto: McClelland & Stewart, 1953. 364 p. Illustrations. Maps on lining papers.

25. Woods, J.D., and Gordon Company. THE CANADIAN AGRICULTURE MACHINERY INDUSTRY. Royal Commission on Canada's Economic Prospects Study. Ottawa: Queen's Printer, 1956. 45 p. Tables. Map. Charts.

V.D.iii. Sectors and Industries: Tertiary Industry

Transportation and banking developments continue to dominate the literature. In the transportation area, the most comprehensive description and economic analysis of the recent development and operation of all modes of transport is 3. A somewhat shorter, but still comprehensive treatment is 13. Of special interest for the post-1920 period are the further development of the St. Lawrence waterway analyzed in 18 and 20, the extension of a railway to Hudson's Bay described in 6, an era of electric interurban railways described in 4, and the emergence of air travel described in 1 and 5. See items 2 and 16 of II.D.iii, and IV.D.iii.13 for further discussion of transportation.

In the field of banking and financial intermediation, the best single treatments are probably 13, 14, and 15 of II.D.iii. For a brief overview, see 14 below. A detailed study with much institutional and statistical documentation is provided by 9. For the working of the Canadian banking system in particular, see 7 and 11. A specialized study of the interrelation of capital markets in Canada and the United States is provided by 8. For a view of the postwar housing market, see 16, and for life insurance, see 10 and 17. For retail and wholesale trade, see 15. Items 2, 12, and 19 treat the post-World War II growth of the service industries, defined comprehensively as including retail and wholesale trade; banking; commercial and personal services; and medical, legal, and educational services. These provide some analysis of the growth in relative importance of services.

V.D.iii. Sectors and Industries: Tertiary Industry

1. Ashley, Charles A[llan]. THE FIRST TWENTY-FIVE YEARS: A STUDY OF TRANS CANADA AIR LINES. Toronto: Macmillan of Canada, 1963. 72 p.

2. Bank of Montreal. THE SERVICE INDUSTRIES. Royal Commission on Canada's Economic Prospects Study. Ottawa: Queen's Printer, 1956.

1920 to Present

      161 p. Tables. Charts. Bibliography, pp. 157-61.

3. Currie, Archibald William. CANADIAN TRANSPORTATION ECONOMICS. Toronto: University of Toronto Press, 1967. 719 p. Bibliographic references included in notes, pp. 643-707.

4. Due, John Fitzgerald. THE INTERCITY ELECTRIC RAILWAY INDUSTRY IN CANADA. Toronto: University of Toronto Press, 1966. 118 p. Illustrations.

5. Ellis, Frank H. CANADA'S FLYING HERITAGE. Rev. ed. Toronto: University of Toronto Press, 1961. xiv, 388 p. Portraits. Illustrations.

6. Fleming, Howard A. CANADA'S ARCTIC OUTLET: A HISTORY OF THE HUDSON BAY RAILWAY. Berkeley and Los Angeles: University of California Press, 1957. 129 p. Map. Bibliography, pp. 115-21.

7. Galbraith, John Alexander. THE ECONOMICS OF BANKING OPERATIONS, A CANADIAN STUDY. Montreal: McGill University Press, 1963. xvii, 510 p. Bibliography, pp. 477-93.

8. Helleiner, G.K. "Connection between United States and Canadian Capital Markets 1952-60." YALE ECONOMICS ESSAYS 2 (Fall 1962): 351-400.

9. Hood, William C. FINANCING OF ECONOMIC ACTIVITY IN CANADA. Royal Commission on Canada's Economic Prospects Study. Ottawa: Queen's Printer, 1959. xv, 700 p. Diagrams. Tables. Bibliography, pp. 493-94.

10. Hood, W[illiam] C., and Main, O[rrin] W[illiam]. "The Role of Canadian Life Insurance Companies in the Post-War Capital Market." CANADIAN JOURNAL OF ECONOMICS AND POLITICAL SCIENCE 22 (November 1956): 467-80.

11. Jamieson, Archibald Black. CHARTERED BANKING IN CANADA. Toronto: Ryerson Press, 1953. x, 394 p.

12. Lang, Vernon. THE SERVICE STATE EMERGES IN ONTARIO 1945-1973. The Evolution of Policy in Contemporary Ontario Series, Ontario Economic Council, no. 3. Toronto: 1974. 83 p. Tables.

13. Lessard, J.C. TRANSPORTATION IN CANADA. Royal Commission on Canada's Economic Prospects Study. Ottawa: Queen's Printer, 1956. 158 p. Tables.

14. McIvor, R. Craig. "Postwar Trends in the Financing of Canadian Economic Activity." PROCEEDINGS AND TRANSACTIONS OF THE ROYAL SOCIETY OF CANADA, 4th ser. 11 (1973): 199-227.

15. Moyer, M.S., and Snyder, G. TRENDS IN CANADIAN MARKETING. 1961 Census Monograph. Ottawa: Dominion Bureau of Statistics, 1967. xxi, 321 p. Tables.

16. Oksanen, Ernest H. "Housing Demand in Canada 1947 to 1962: Some Preliminary Experimentation." CANADIAN JOURNAL OF ECONOMICS AND POLITICAL SCIENCE 32 (August 1966): 302-18.

17. Poapst, James V. "Life Insurance Savings in Canada." CANADIAN JOURNAL OF ECONOMICS AND POLITICAL SCIENCE 19 (May 1953): 202-9.

18. Sydor, Leon P. "The St. Lawrence Seaway: National Shares in Seaway Wheat Benefits." CANADIAN JOURNAL OF ECONOMICS 4 (November 1971): 543-55.

19. Worton, D.A. "The Service Industries in Canada, 1946-66." In PRODUCTION AND PRODUCTIVITY IN THE SERVICE INDUSTRIES, edited by V.R. Fuchs, pp. 237-86. National Bureau of Economic Research Studies in Income and Wealth, vol. 34. New York: Columbia University Press, 1969.

20. Wright, C.P. THE ST. LAWRENCE DEEP WATER-WAY: A CANADIAN APPRAISAL. Toronto: Macmillan of Canada, 1935. xxi, 450 p.

V.E. ECONOMIC ORGANIZATION

Most of the literature in this period deals with some aspect of government intervention in the economy, reflecting a growth in the public sector in both absolute and relative terms: see IV.E.iii.14.

V.E.i. Economic Organization: Industrial Organization

The main literature here considers the connection between industrial organization and the tariff: see 4, 5, 12, and 17 of V.C.ii. For placing the evolution of industrial organization in historical perspective, see II.E.i.1. For a definitive study of concentration in manufacturing in the 1950s, see 1 below. For a more recent analysis, see 4. A comparison of concentration in Canadian and American industry is made in 2, and the connection between foreign control and concentration is explored in 3.

V.E.i. Economic Organization: Industrial Organization

1. Rosenbluth, G[ideon]. CONCENTRATION IN CANADIAN MANUFACTURING INDUSTRIES. National Bureau of Economic Research General Series, no. 61. Princeton, N.J.: Princeton University Press, 1957. xv, 152 p. Tables. Bibliographic footnotes.

2. _____. "Industrial Concentration in Canada and the United States." CANADIAN JOURNAL OF ECONOMICS AND POLITICAL SCIENCE 20 (August 1954): 332-46.

3. _____. "The Relation between Foreign Control and Concentration in Canadian Industry." CANADIAN JOURNAL OF ECONOMICS 3 (February 1970): 14-38.

4. Stewart, Max D. "Concentration in Canadian Manufacturing and Mining Industries." Economic Council of Canada Background Paper. Ottawa: Queen's Printer, 1970. 147 p. Mimeographed. Tables.

V.E.ii. Economic Organization: Labor Organization

In the absence of a definitive history of the twentieth-century Canadian labor movement, the literature is small and specialized. One theme has been the difficulty of achieving unity in the labor movement, discussed in 5. Another has been the controversial role played by international unions; see 4, or the shortened version 3, and the analysis provided in 8. For a statistical summary of union growth and industrial disputes, see 1 and 2 below, and II.E.ii.4, chapter 5. Efforts of the labor movement to establish itself as a political force are discussed in 6. For a useful collection of essays on various topics in labor history, see 7.

V.E.ii. Economic Organization: Labor Organization

1. Canada. Department of Labour. STRIKES AND LOCKOUTS IN CANADA. Ottawa: Queen's Printer, 1969. 70 p.

2. _____. UNION GROWTH IN CANADA 1921-1967. Ottawa: Queen's Printer, 1970. 106 p. Tables. Graphs.

1920 to Present

3. Crispo, J. [H.G.] INTERNATIONAL UNIONISM, A STUDY IN CANADIAN-AMERICAN RELATIONS. Toronto: McGraw-Hill, 1967. viii, 327 p. Bibliography, pp. 325-27.

4. _____. THE ROLE OF INTERNATIONAL UNIONISM IN CANADA. Washington, D.C.: Canadian-American Committee, 1967. 59 p. Colored frontispiece.

5. Forsey, Eugene. "The Movement towards Labour Unity in Canada: History and Implications." CANADIAN JOURNAL OF ECONOMICS AND POLITICAL SCIENCE 24 (February 1958): 70-83.

6. Horowitz, Gad. CANADIAN LABOUR IN POLITICS. Studies in the Structure of Power: Decision-making in Canada, no. 4. Toronto: University of Toronto Press, 1968. 273 p. Bibliographic footnotes.

7. Miller, Richard Ulric, and Isbester, A. Fraser, eds. CANADIAN LABOUR IN TRANSITION. Toronto: Prentice-Hall of Canada, 1971. xviii, 266 p. Bibliographic footnotes.

8. Montagne, J.T. "International Unions and the Canadian Labour Movement." CANADIAN JOURNAL OF ECONOMICS AND POLITICAL SCIENCE 33 (February 1957): 69-82.

V.E.iii. Economic Organization: The Role of Government

By the mid-twentieth century, government intervention in some form had proliferated into almost every area of economic activity. For an overview, see 6, 28, and 55. The depression of the 1930s provided an immediate impetus for expanded government activity. The most extensive and complete discussion of new attitudes toward economic policy is found in 5 and 39. For the creation and management of the Bank of Canada, the best source is 52; see also the older study, 64. On exchange control, see 27. See also the brief articles in I.B.2 for 1937, pages 881-85 for the role of the Bank of Canada; for 1941, pages 833-35 for foreign exchange control; for 1942, pages 803-6 for the central bank in wartime, 830-33 for exchange control; and for 1954, pages 1061-64 for immediate postwar federal public finance. For an overview of the "New Deal" legislation of Prime Minister Bennett, see 70, and for summary of views, 71. The constitutional problems encountered by this legislation are treated in 60. For an economic evaluation, see 14. The most direct effects of depression were experienced on the prairies. The main policy response to these effects is discussed in 3, 4, 17, 18, 44, 46, and 48; see also II.E.iii.8. For brief accounts, see I.B.2 for 1938, pages 223-30; for 1945, pages 188-91; for 1954, pages 366-70; for 1956, pages 917-22; for 1960, pages 957-60; and for 1961, pages 399-402. For the effects of war, see 26.

1920 to Present

For a discussion of early and proposed social welfare measures, see 9. The long delayed entry of government into the housing market has been widely discussed. See, for example, 29 and 53. For recent prices and incomes policies, see 33. Welfare legislation in general is mostly discussed in the context of Dominion-Provincial fiscal relations. A good starting point is IV.A.4, followed by 61 and 67 below. See also 8 and 46 below, and volume 2 of II.E.iii.18 regarding welfare legislation. An excellent older study illustrating the special constitutional problems in this area is 12; see also 59. For the Social Credit experiment, see 31, 36, and 37. A different political approach is described in 50. For the basis of Newfoundland's entry into Confederation, see 47.

The literature in well-established areas of government concern such as trade, transportation, immigration, labor, and competition is fairly extensive. For an early discussion of tariff policy, see 3. More recent issues surrounding nontariff barriers are discussed in 63. See also the items listed in V.C.ii on the role of the tariff. The commercial policies of Canada's principal trading partners have also received attention. See, for example, 7, 16, 19, 40, and 58. The policy impact of capital flows is discussed in 10. The best work on transportation policy is probably 54; see also V.D.iii.3. An authoritative analysis of immigration policy is provided by 11. See also I.B.2 for 1931, pages 189-92, on immigration. On the development of labor policy, II.E.iii.26 is the best single source; see also 43 below. In the area of competition policy, in addition to II.E.iii.22, see 2 and 65 below.

Governments have increasingly engaged directly in the productive process. These activities fall under the title of crown corporations and are comprehensively treated in 61; see also 21, 24, 29, 35, 38, 51, 52, 55, 69, and 73. The development of this form of activity was especially notable under the sponsorship of C.D. Howe: see 56. See also I.B.2 for 1955, pages 840-51, on the formation of the Canadian National Railways. For the contribution of government to capital formation, see 23 and 66. For the St. Lawrence Seaway, see also I.B.2 for 1955, pages 885-88; for 1956, pages 821-29; and for 1960, pages 851-60.

A relatively new area of government concern has been science and technology. See 73 for an overview. For a political analysis, see 15 and 32, and for an economic view, see 42. For an economic analysis of patent policy, see 22.

Explicitly regional policies also multiply in this period. For a description and analysis of these see II.E.iii.6 and V.C.v.1. In addition, see 45 for the tariff, and 13 and 44 for freight rate regulation. For regional policies and Nova Scotia, see 30.

For resource development policies, the literature is diverse and fragmentary. The best single source for Ontario is II.E.iii.16. For Canada as a whole, a good narrative of the evolution of public property rights is IV.E.iii.23. For forests see 49, and for oil and energy resources see 1 and 20. For government involvement in the development of the Columbia River, see 41.

V.E.iii. Economic Organization: The Role of Government

1. Aitken, Hugh G.J. The Midwestern Case." CANADIAN JOURNAL OF ECONOMICS AND POLITICAL SCIENCE 25 (May 1959): 129-43.

2. Ball, J.A. CANADIAN ANTI-TRUST LEGISLATION. Baltimore, Md.: Williams and Wilkins, 1934. vii, 105 p.

3. Bladen, V[incent] W[heeler]. "Tariff Policy and Employment in Depression." CANADIAN JOURNAL OF ECONOMICS AND POLITICAL SCIENCE 6 (February 1940): 72-78.

4. Booth, J.F. "The Canadian Agricultural Price Support Programme." CANADIAN JOURNAL OF ECONOMICS AND POLITICAL SCIENCE 17 (August 1951): 334-43.

5. Brecher, I[rving]. MONETARY AND FISCAL THOUGHT AND POLICY IN CANADA 1919-1939. Canadian Studies in Economics, no. 8. Toronto: University of Toronto Press, 1957. xii, 337 p. Tables. Diagrams. Bibliographic references in notes, pp. 243-331.

6. Brewis, T[homas] N., et al. CANADIAN ECONOMIC POLICY. Rev. ed. Toronto: Macmillan of Canada, 1965. xv, 463 p. Statistical appendix by J.E. Gander. Bibliography, pp. 430-43.

7. Britnell, G[eorge] E[dwin]. "The Implications of U.S. Policy for the Canadian Wheat Economy." CANADIAN JOURNAL OF ECONOMICS AND POLITICAL SCIENCE 22 (February 1956): 1-16.

8. Buck, Arthur Eugene. FINANCING CANADIAN GOVERNMENT. Chicago: Public Administration Service, 1949. xi, 367 p. Selected bibliography, pp. 349-57.

9. Cassidy, Harry M. SOCIAL SECURITY AND RECONSTRUCTION IN CANADA. Toronto: Ryerson Press, 1943. x, 197 p. Bibliographic footnotes.

10. Caves, Richard E[arl] and Reuber, Grant L. CANADIAN ECONOMIC POLICY AND THE IMPACT OF INTERNATIONAL CAPITAL FLOWS. Canada in the Atlantic Economy Series, no. 10. Published for the Private Planning Association of Canada. Toronto: University of Toronto Press, 1969. vii, 82 p. Bibliographic footnotes.

11. Corbett, D.C. CANADIAN IMMIGRATION POLICY: A CRITIQUE. Published for the Canadian Institute of International Affairs. Toronto: University of Toronto Press, 1957. xii, 215 p. Tables. Bibliography, pp. 201-8.

12. Corry, James Alexander. DIFFICULTIES OF DIVIDED JURISDICTION. Royal Commission on Dominion-Provincial Relations, Appendix 7. Ottawa: King's Printer, 1939. 44 p.

13. Currie, A[rchibald] W[illiam]. "Freight Rates and Regionalism." CANADIAN JOURNAL OF ECONOMICS AND POLITICAL SCIENCE 14 (November 1948): 427-40.

14. Curtis, C[lifford] A. "Dominion Legislation of 1935: An Economist's Review." CANADIAN JOURNAL OF ECONOMICS AND POLITICAL SCIENCE 1 (November 1935): 599-608.

15. Doern, G. Bruce. SCIENCE AND POLITICS IN CANADA. Montreal and London: McGill-Queen's University Press, 1972. xiv, 231 p.

16. Drummond, Ian M[acdonald]. IMPERIAL ECONOMIC POLICY, 1917-1939: STUDIES IN EXPANSION AND PROTECTION. London: Allen and Unwin, 1974. 496 p. Bibliographic references.

17. Drummond, W[illiam] M[alcolm]. "Objectives of an Agricultural Price Support Policy." CANADIAN JOURNAL OF ECONOMICS AND POLITICAL SCIENCE 17 (August 1951): 344-51.

18. Easterbrook, W[illiam] T[homas]. "Agricultural Debt Adjustment." CANADIAN JOURNAL OF ECONOMICS AND POLITICAL SCIENCE 2 (August 1936): 390-403.

19. Egerer, Gerald. "Protection and Imperial Preference in Britain: The Case of Wheat 1925-1960." CANADIAN JOURNAL OF ECONOMICS AND POLITICAL SCIENCE 31 (August 1965): 382-89.

20. Erickson, Edward W., and Waverman, Leonard, eds. THE ENERGY QUESTION: AN INTERNATIONAL FAILURE OF POLICY: VOLUME 2, NORTH AMERICA. Toronto: University of Toronto Press, 1974. xxiii, 390 p.

21. Ferguson, D.A. "The Industrial Development Bank of Canada." JOURNAL OF BUSINESS 21 (October 1948): 214-29.

1920 to Present

22. Firestone, O[tto] J[ack]. ECONOMIC IMPLICATIONS OF PATENTS. Ottawa: University of Ottawa Press, 1971. xi, 398 p. Tables. Bibliographic footnotes.

23. Firestone, O[tto] J[ack] and Urquhart, M.C. PUBLIC INVESTMENT AND CAPITAL FORMATION, A STUDY OF PUBLIC AND PRIVATE INVESTMENT OUTLAY, CANADA 1926-1941. Dominion-Provincial Conference on Reconstruction. Ottawa: King's Printer, 1945. 128 p. Tables.

24. Fouriner, Leslie Thomas. RAILWAY NATIONALIZATION IN CANADA; THE PROBLEM OF THE CANADIAN NATIONAL RAILWAYS. Publications of the International Finance Section of the Department of Economics and Social Institutions in Princeton University, vol. 5. Toronto: Macmillan of Canada, 1935. ix, 358 p. Bibliography, pp. 351-53.

25. Fowke, V[ernon] C[lifford]. "Dominion Aids to Wheat Marketing, 1929-39." CANADIAN JOURNAL OF ECONOMICS AND POLITICAL SCIENCE 6 (August 1940): 390-402.

26. _____. "Economic Effects of the War on the Prairie Economy." CANADIAN JOURNAL OF ECONOMICS AND POLITICAL SCIENCE 11 (August 1945): 373-87.

27. Gibbons, Alan O. "Foreign Exchange Control in Canada, 1939-51." CANADIAN JOURNAL OF ECONOMICS AND POLITICAL SCIENCE 19 (February 1953): 35-54.

28. Gibson, J[ames] D[ouglas] "Post-war Economic Development and Policy in Canada." CANADIAN JOURNAL OF ECONOMICS AND POLITICAL SCIENCE 20 (November 1954): 439-55.

29. Gilles, J. "Some Financial Aspects of the Canadian Government Housing Program: History and Prospective Developments." JOURNAL OF FINANCE 8 (March 1953): 22-33.

30. Graham, John F. FISCAL ADJUSTMENT AND ECONOMIC DEVELOPMENT, A CASE STUDY OF NOVA SCOTIA. Toronto: University of Toronto Press, 1963. xviii, 278 p. Diagrams. Tables. Bibliography, pp. 261-70.

31. Hanson, E.J. "Public Finance in Alberta since 1935." CANADIAN JOURNAL OF ECONOMICS AND POLITICAL SCIENCE 18 (August 1952): 322-35.

32. Hayes, F. Ronald. THE CHARMING OF PROMETHEUS: EVOLUTION OF A POWER STRUCTURE FOR CANADIAN SCIENCE. Toronto: University of Toronto Press, 1973. xix, 209 p. Bibliographic notes.

33. Haythorne, George V. "Prices and Incomes Policy: The Canadian Experience, 1969-1972." INTERNATIONAL LABOUR REVIEW 108 (December 1973): 485-503.

34. Higgins, Benjamin, and Higgins, Jean. CANADA'S TRADE POLICY IN THE SECOND DEVELOPMENT DECADE. Montreal: Private Planning Association of Canada, 1970. xv, 70 p.

35. Hodgetts, J.E. "The Public Corporation in Canada." In GOVERNMENT ENTERPRISE: A COMPARATIVE STUDY, edited by W. Friedmann and J[ohn] F. Garner, pp. 201-26. London: Stevens and Sons, 1970.

36. Irving, John A. "The Evolution of the Social Credit Movement." CANADIAN JOURNAL OF ECONOMICS AND POLITICAL SCIENCE 14 (August 1948): 321-41.

37. _____. THE SOCIAL CREDIT MOVEMENT IN ALBERTA. Toronto: University of Toronto Press, 1959. xi, 369 p. Bibliographic footnotes.

38. Kilbourn, W[illiam]. PIPELINE; TRANSCANADA AND THE GREAT DEBATE, A HISTORY OF BUSINESS AND POLITICS. Toronto: Clarke Irwin, 1970. xiii, 222 p. Illustrations (some in color). Group portraits. Bibliographic references.

39. Knox, F[rank] A. "Dominion Monetary Policy, 1929-34." Royal Commission on Dominion-Provincial Relations. Ottawa: King's Printer, 1939. 92 p. Tables. Mimeographed.

40. Kottman, Richard N. RECIPROCITY AND THE NORTH ATLANTIC TRIANGLE 1932-1938. Ithaca, N.Y.: Cornell University Press, 1968. ix, 294 p. Bibliography, pp. 283-89.

41. Krutilla, John A. THE COLUMBIA RIVER TREATY: THE ECONOMICS OF AN INTERNATIONAL RIVER BASIN DEVELOPMENT. Baltimore, Md.: Johns Hopkins Press, 1967. xv, 211 p. Tables.

42. Lithwick, N.H. CANADA'S SCIENCE POLICY AND THE ECONOMY. Toronto: Methuen, 1969. ix, 176 p. Illustrations. Bibliography, pp. 159-69.

43. Logan, Harold Amos. STATE INTERVENTION AND ASSISTANCE IN COLLECTIVE BARGAINING: THE CANADIAN EXPERIENCE 1843-1954. Canadian Studies in Economics, no. 6. Toronto: University of Toronto Press, 1956. 176 p. Tables.

44. McDougall, J[ohn] L[orne]. "The Relative Level of Crows' Nest Grain Rates in 1899-1968." CANADIAN JOURNAL OF ECONOMICS AND POLITICAL SCIENCE 32 (February 1966): 46-54.

45. MacGregor, D.C. "The Provincial Incidence of the Canadian Tariff." CANADIAN JOURNAL OF ECONOMICS AND POLITICAL SCIENCE 1 (August 1935): 384-95.

46. Maxwell, J[ames] A[ckley]. "Canadian Dominion-Provincial Relations." QUARTERLY JOURNAL OF ECONOMICS 55 (August 1941): 584-610.

47. Mayo, H.B. "Newfoundland's Entry into the Dominion." CANADIAN JOURNAL OF ECONOMICS AND POLITICAL SCIENCE 15 (November 1949): 505-22.

48. Menzies, M.W. "Wheat Prices and Marketing Policies since 1930." CANADIAN JOURNAL OF AGRICULTURAL ECONOMICS 3, no. 1 (1955): 32-50.

49. Moore, A[lbert] M[ilton]. FORESTRY TENURES AND TAXES IN CANADA. Toronto: Canadian Tax Foundation, 1957. 315 p. Tables.

50. Morton, William Lewis. THE PROGRESSIVE PARTY IN CANADA. Social Credit in Alberta, Its Background and Development, no. 1. 1950. Reprint, with corrections. Toronto: University of Toronto Press, 1967. xiii, 331 p. Bibliographic essay, pp. 307-18.

51. Musolf, L.D. "Canadian Public Enterprise: A Character Study." AMERICAN POLITICAL SCIENCE REVIEW 50 (June 1956): 405-21.

52. Neufeld, E[dward] P[eter]. BANK OF CANADA OPERATIONS, 1935-54. Rev. ed. Canadian Studies in Economics, no. 5. Toronto: University of Toronto Press, 1958. 253 p. Illustrations.

53. Poapst, J[ames] V. "The National Housing Act, 1954." CANADIAN JOURNAL OF ECONOMICS AND POLITICAL SCIENCE 22 (May 1956): 234-43.

54. Purdy, Harry Leslie. TRANSPORT, COMPETITION AND PUBLIC POLICY IN CANADA. Vancouver: University of British Columbia Press, 1972. xv, 327 p. Bibliographic footnotes.

55. Rea, Kenneth J., and McLeod, J.T. BUSINESS AND GOVERNMENT IN CANADA: SELECTED READINGS. Toronto: Methuen, 1969. xiv, 412 p. Bibliographies.

56. Roberts, Leslie. THE LIFE AND TIMES OF CLARENCE DECATUR HOWE. Toronto: Clarke Irwin, 1957. 246 p. Illustrations.

57. Rosenbluth, G[ideon], and Thorburn, H.G. "Canadian Anti-Combines Administration, 1952-1960." CANADIAN JOURNAL OF ECONOMICS AND POLITICAL SCIENCE 27 (November 1961): 498-508.

58. Scheinberg, Stephen. "Invitation to Empire: Tariffs and American Economic Expansion." In ENTERPRISE AND NATIONAL DEVELOPMENT; ESSAYS IN CANADIAN BUSINESS AND ECONOMIC HISTORY, edited by Glenn Porter and Robert D. Cuff, pp. 218-38. Toronto: Hakkert, 1973. Bibliographic references. Reprinted from BUSINESS HISTORY REVIEW 47 (Summer 1973).

59. Scott, F[rank] R. "The Constitutional Background of Taxation Agreements." MCGILL LAW JOURNAL 2 (Autumn 1955): 1-10.

60. _____. "The Privy Council and Mr. Bennett's 'New Deal' Legislation." CANADIAN JOURNAL OF ECONOMICS AND POLITICAL SCIENCE 3 (May 1937): 234-41.

61. Smiley, D[onald] V. CONSTITUTIONAL ADAPTATION AND CANADIAN FEDERALISM SINCE 1945. Royal Commission on Bilingualism and Biculturalism, document no. 4. Ottawa: Queen's Printer, 1970. viii, 155 p. Bibliographic footnotes.

62. Stager, David. "Federal Government Grants to Canadian Universities 1951-66." CANADIAN HISTORICAL REVIEW 54 (September 1973): 287-97.

63. Stegemann, Klaus. CANADIAN NON-TARIFF BARRIERS TO TRADE. Published for the Canadian Economic Policy Committee. Montreal: Private Planning Association of Canada, 1973. xi, 158 p. Tables.

64. Stokes, Milton L. THE BANK OF CANADA: THE DEVELOPMENT AND PRESENT POSITION OF CENTRAL BANKING IN CANADA. Toronto: Macmillan of Canada, 1939. xii, 382 p. Frontispiece plate. Bibliography, pp. 371-75.

65. Thorburn, H.G. "Pressure Groups in Canadian Politics: Recent Revisions of the Anti-Combines Legislation." CANADIAN JOURNAL OF ECONOMICS AND POLITICAL SCIENCE 30 (May 1964): 157-274.

66. Urquhart, M.C. "Public Investment in Canada." CANADIAN JOURNAL OF ECONOMICS AND POLITICAL SCIENCE 11 (November 1945): 535-53.

67. Waines, W.J. "Dominion-Provincial Financial Arrangements: An Examination of Objectives." CANADIAN JOURNAL OF ECONOMICS AND POLITICAL SCIENCE 19 (August 1953): 304-15.

68. Wallace, W.J. "Recent Power Legislation in Ontario." CANADIAN JOURNAL OF ECONOMICS AND POLITICAL SCIENCE 2 (May 1936): 212-15.

69. Weir, E. Austin. THE STRUGGLE FOR NATIONAL BROADCASTING IN CANADA. Toronto: McClelland & Stewart, 1965. xiv, 477 p.

70. Wilbur, [J.] R. [H.]. THE BENNETT ADMINISTRATION, 1930-35. Canadian Historical Association Booklet, no. 24. Ottawa: Canadian Archives, 1969. 21 p.

71. _____, ed. THE BENNETT NEW DEAL: FRAUD OF PORTENT? Issues in Canadian History. Toronto: Copp Clark, 1968. 250 p.

72. Willoughby, William. THE ST. LAWRENCE SEAWAY: A STUDY IN POLITICS AND DIPLOMACY. Madison: University of Wisconsin Press, 1961. 381 p. Illustrations. Bibliography.

73. Wilson, Andrew H. SCIENCE, TECHNOLOGY AND INNOVATION. Economic Council of Canada Special Study, no. 8. Ottawa: Queen's Printer, 1968. vi, 134 p. Bibliographic references. Bibliography, pp. 119-28.

V.F. TECHNOLOGY, PRODUCTIVITY CHANGE, AND WELFARE

The technical literature measuring changes in productivity, both at the aggregate and at the industry level, is much more extensive in this time period than earlier. For the economy as a whole, the main studies of changes in income per capita, and/or in total factor productivity are 4, 17, 26, 30, 35, and 39. A shortened version of 26 appears as 27. See 21 and 16 for a controversy over 17. Along similar lines, the very recent past has been examined in 40 and 41. Comparisons with the United States and other countries have also been made: see V.C.ii.3, and items 9, 10, and 31 below. For a comparative study restricted to manufacturing productivity, see 15.

A number of studies have assessed changes in agricultural productivity. See, for example, 1, 12, 28, 29, and 42. Productivity change in manufacturing is studied from 1935 to 1948 in 32, and from 1947 to 1956 in 36. See also 22 for an assessment of technical change. On innovations, see 11. Decreasing returns to scale are found to characterize Canadian manufacturing from 1926 to 1972 in 24.

With respect to the distribution of the gains from productivity growth, see 13 and 14. For the share going to agriculture, see 18, 23, 25, and 29. A comparison with the United States is part of 25. The experience of the wage share is documented in 20.

On the stability versus instability of economic growth, a good starting point is 38, a standard treatment of the 1930s depression period. An impressionistic study of the same period is 19. A careful documentation of business cycles since 1919, using a National Bureau of Economic Research framework, is 6. A general analysis of cyclical behavior in the first half of the twentieth century is given in 37. Several studies examine aspects of the business cycle: see 33 for savings, 5 for technical change in agriculture, and 2 for inventories. Long cycles are detected and analyzed in 8.

Regional aspects of changing welfare have also generated a literature. See, in particular, the listings in V.C.v. In addition, regional differences are studied in 7, and the case of British Columbia is examined in 3.

An almost completely unstudied area, except for 34, is the influence of falling transaction costs on economic growth.

V.F. TECHNOLOGY, PRODUCTIVITY CHANGE, AND WELFARE

1. Anderson, W.J. "Productivity of Labour in Canadian Agriculture."

CANADIAN JOURNAL OF ECONOMICS AND POLITICAL SCIENCE
21 (May 1955): 228-36.

2. Barber, Clarence L. INVENTORIES AND THE BUSINESS CYCLE, WITH SPECIAL REFERENCE TO CANADA. Canadian Studies in Economics, no. 10. Toronto: University of Toronto Press, 1958. xii, 132 p. Charts. Tables. Bibliographic references in notes, pp. 125-30.

3. Blain, L.; Paterson, D.G.; and Rae, J[ames] D. "The Regional Impact of Economic Fluctuations during the Inter-war Period: The Case of British Columbia." CANADIAN JOURNAL OF ECONOMICS 7 (August 1974): 381-401.

4. Brown, T.M. CANADIAN ECONOMIC GROWTH. Ottawa: Queen's Printer, 1965. ix, 316 p. Tables.

5. Butlin, J.A. "The Effect of Canadian Business Cycles on the Adoption of Technological Innovations in Canadian Agriculture 1926-1967." THE CANADIAN JOURNAL OF AGRICULTURAL ECONOMICS 19 (October 1971): 61-71.

6. Chambers, E.J. "Canadian Business Cycles since 1919: A Progress Report." CANADIAN JOURNAL OF ECONOMICS AND POLITICAL SCIENCE 24 (May 1958): 166-89.

7. Chernick, S.E. INTERREGIONAL DISPARITIES IN INCOME. Economic Council of Canada Staff Studies, no. 14. Ottawa: Queen's Printer, 1966. v, 91 p. Tables. Map. Bibliographic footnotes.

8. Daly, D.J. "Long Cycles and Recent Canadian Experience." In APPENDIX VOLUME, appendix K, pp. 279-301. Report of Royal Commission on Banking and Finance. Ottawa: Queen's Printer, 1964.

9. Domar, Evsey D., et al. "Economic Growth and Productivity in the United States, Canada, United Kingdom, Germany, and Japan in the Post-war Period." REVIEW OF ECONOMICS AND STATISTICS 46 (February 1964): 33-40.

10. Due, Jean Mann. "Consumption Levels in Canada and the United States." CANADIAN JOURNAL OF ECONOMICS AND POLITICAL SCIENCE 21, (May 1955): 174-82.

11. Firestone, O[tto] J[ack]. "Innovations and Economic Development--The Canadian Case." THE REVIEW OF INCOME AND WEALTH, 18th ser. 8 (December 1972): 399-419.

12. Furniss, I.F. "Productivity Change of Canadian Agriculture, 1935-1960, A Quarter Century of Change." CANADIAN JOURNAL OF AGRICULTURAL ECONOMICS 12, no. 2 (1964): 41-53.

13. Goldberg, Simon A. "Long Run Changes in the Distribution of Income by Factor Shares in Canada." In THE BEHAVIOR OF INCOME SHARES, SELECTED THEORETICAL AND EMPIRICAL ISSUES, pp. 189-285. National Bureau of Economic Research Studies in Income and Wealth, vol. 27. Princeton, N.J.: Princeton University Press, 1964. Bibliographic footnotes.

14. Goldberg, S[imon] A., and Poduluk, J.R. "Income Size Distribution Statistics in Canada." In INCOME AND WEALTH SERIES, no. 6, edited by Milton Gilbert and Richard Stone, pp. 155-201. London: Bowes and Bowes, 1957.

15. Heath, J.B. "British-Canadian Manufacturing Productivity." ECONOMIC JOURNAL 67 (December 1957): 665-91.

16. Hood, W[illiam] C. "Rejoinder." CANADIAN JOURNAL OF ECONOMICS AND POLITICAL SCIENCE 27 (February 1961): 106-8.

17. Hood, William C., and Scott, Anthony [Dalton]. OUTPUT, LABOUR AND CAPITAL IN THE CANADIAN ECONOMY. Royal Commission on Canada's Economic Prospects Study. Ottawa: Queen's Printer, 1957. 510 p. Tables. Charts. Bibliographic footnotes.

18. Hope, E.C. "Agriculture's Share of the National Income." CANADIAN JOURNAL OF ECONOMICS AND POLITICAL SCIENCE 9 (August 1943): 384-93.

19. Horn, Michael Steven Daniel, ed. THE DIRTY THIRTIES: CANADIANS IN THE GREAT DEPRESSION. Toronto: Copp Clark, 1972. xxx, 728 p. Illustrations. Bibliographic references.

20. Hotson, J.H. "The Constancy of the Wage Share: The Canadian Experience." REVIEW OF ECONOMICS AND STATISTICS 45 (February 1963): 84-91.

21. Johnson, Harry G[ordon]. "Factor Mobility and Rates of Technical Progress: A Critical Note on 'Output, Labour and Capital in the Canadian Economy'." CANADIAN JOURNAL OF ECONOMICS AND POLITICAL SCIENCE 27 (February 1961): 101-5.

# 1920 to Present

22. Kotowitz, Y. "Technical Progress, Factor Substitution and Income Distribution in Canadian Manufacturing 1926-39 and 1946-61." CANADIAN JOURNAL OF ECONOMICS 2 (February 1969): 106-14.

23. Kulshrestha, S.T.J. "Measuring the Relative Income of Farm Labour, 1941-1961." CANADIAN JOURNAL OF AGRICULTURAL ECONOMICS 15, no. 1 (1967): 28-43.

24. LaTourette, John E. "Economies of Scale and Capital Utilization in Canadian Manufacturing 1926-72." CANADIAN JOURNAL OF ECONOMICS 8 (August 1975): 448-55.

25. Lerohl, M.L., and MacEachern, G.A. "Factor Shares in Agriculture: The Canada-United States Experience." CANADIAN JOURNAL OF AGRICULTURAL ECONOMICS 15, no. 1 (1967): 1-20.

26. Lithwick, N.H. ECONOMIC GROWTH IN CANADA. 2d ed. Canadian Studies in Economics, no. 19. Toronto: University of Toronto Press, 1970. xiv, 145 p. Bibliography, pp. 135-36.

27. _____. "Labour, Capital and Growth: The Canadian Experience." In GROWTH AND THE CANADIAN ECONOMY, edited by T.N. Brewis, pp. 65-75. Carleton Library, no. 39. Toronto: McClelland & Stewart, 1968.

28. Lok, Siepko H. "An Enquiry into the Relationship between Changes in Overall Productivity and Real Net Return per Farm, and between Changes in Total Output and Real Gross Returns, Canadian Agriculture 1926-1957." Ottawa: Department of Agriculture, 1961. x, 175 p. Mimeographed. Charts. Tables. Bibliographic footnotes. Bibliography, pp. 118-27.

29. Mackenzie, W. "The Terms of Trade, Productivity and Income of Canadian Agriculture." CANADIAN JOURNAL OF AGRICULTURAL ECONOMICS 9, no. 2 (1961): 1-13.

30. Maddison, A. "Productivity in an Expanding Economy." ECONOMIC JOURNAL 62 (September 1952): 584-94.

31. _____. "Productivity in Canada, the United Kingdom and the United States." OXFORD ECONOMIC PAPERS 4 (October 1952): 235-42.

32. _____. "Productivity in Canadian Manufacturing, 1935-1948." CANADIAN JOURNAL OF ECONOMICS AND POLITICAL SCIENCE 19 (May 1953): 222-25.

1920 to Present

33. Maywald, Karel. "National Savings and Changing Employment in Canada 1926-54." CANADIAN JOURNAL OF ECONOMICS AND POLITICAL SCIENCE 22 (May 1956): 174-82.

34. Pennie, T.E. "The Influence of Distribution Costs and Direct Investments on British Exports to Canada." OXFORD ECONOMIC PAPERS 8 (October 1956): 229-45.

35. Pentland, H[arry] C[lare]. "Physical Productivity in Canada 1935-52." ECONOMIC JOURNAL 64 (June 1954): 399-404.

36. Postner, Harry H. AN ECONOMIC ANALYSIS OF CANADIAN MANUFACTURING PRODUCTIVITY, SOME PRELIMINARY RESULTS. Economic Council of Canada Staff Study, no. 37. Ottawa: Queen's Printer, 1971. v, 119 p. Tables.

37. Rosenbluth, G[ideon]. "Changing Structural Factors in Canada's Cyclical Sensitivity 1903-54." CANADIAN JOURNAL OF ECONOMICS AND POLITICAL SCIENCE 24 (February 1958): 21-43.

38. Safarian, Albert Edward. THE CANADIAN ECONOMY IN GREAT DEPRESSION. Canadian Studies in Economics, no. 11. Toronto: University of Toronto Press, 1959. xii, 185 p. Tables. Bibliography. New ed. Carleton Library, no. 54. Toronto: McClelland & Stewart, 1970. 261 p. Illustrations.

39. Sutton, G.D. "Productivity in Canada." CANADIAN JOURNAL OF ECONOMICS AND POLITICAL SCIENCE 19 (May 1953): 185-201.

40. Walters, D. CANADIAN GROWTH REVISITED 1950-1967. Economic Council of Canada Staff Study, no. 28. Ottawa: Queen's Printer, 1970. v, 68 p. Bibliographic footnotes.

41. _____. CANADIAN INCOME LEVELS AND GROWTH: AN INTERNATIONAL PERSPECTIVE. Economic Council of Canada Staff Study, no. 23. Ottawa: Queen's Printer, 1968. 272 p. Tables. Bibliographic footnotes. Appendix by E.C. West. "Real Output Comparison, Canada and the United States, 1966 and Selected Years Back to 1950."

42. Wampack, J. "Les Tendences dans le productivité totale dans l'agriculture: Canada, Ontario, Québec, 1926-1964." CANADIAN JOURNAL OF AGRICULTURAL ECONOMICS 15, no. 1 (1967): 119-30.

V.G. RESOURCES

Population growth and capital formation have proceeded at a relatively rapid rate, particularly since World War II, and have been the focus of considerable research. Natural resource discovery, however, has been less dramatic; increasing relative resource scarcity has been common often accompanied by detailed stock-taking efforts, and concern for future supplies.

V.G.i. Resources: Land and Its Endowments

Chapter 5 of II.G.i.8 provides a useful summary of changing natural resource availability in the postwar period. A more exhaustive and detailed examination is provided in 1 below. The conference for which the studies included in 1 were prepared addresses both stocktaking and questions of policy. Other useful sources, in addition to the general references listed under II.G.i, include V.D.i.10 for minerals, V.D.i.9 for energy, and V.D.i.11 for forest resources. See also V.D.i.4 for fisheries. For an interpretive and theoretical discussion, see II.D.i.4.

V.G.i. Resources: Land and Its Endowments

1. Canada. Department of Northern Affairs and National Resources. RESOURCES FOR TOMORROW; CONFERENCE BACKGROUND PAPERS AND PROCEEDINGS. Montreal Conference, October 23-28, 1961. 3 vols. Ottawa: Queen's Printer, 1961. Vols. 1 and 2, 1,061 p.; vol. 3, 519 p.

V.G.ii. Resources: Population

For a brief overview of changes in the population and labor force, see chapters 2 and 6 respectively of II.G.i.8. The best comprehensive treatment is II.G.ii.13. See also 13 below. For detailed sources on recent population changes, see the 1961 census monographs II.G.ii.7 and II.G.ii.19.

For the war and immediate post war period, 9 below provides a good overview. For birth rate changes, see 7. Internal migration has been separately analyzed in 1 and 8. A topic of special concern has been the international flow of skilled manpower: see 12. On the mix and assimilation of immigrants, see 14. For pioneering settlement, 15 and 16 of II.G.ii and 4 below discuss the topic until the late 1930s. On the Indian question, see 2. Occupational shifts in the labor force are documented and discussed in 10. For the labor supply in agriculture, see 5, and for the labor supply in general, see 11. Aspects of demographic change in Quebec have been extensively researched. See, for example, 3, 6, and 15.

V.G.ii. Resources: Population

1. Anderson, I.B. "Internal Migration in Canada, 1931-1961." Economic Council of Canada Staff Study, no. 13. Ottawa: Queen's Printer, 1966. ix, 87 p. Tables. Bibliographic footnotes.

2. Deprez, Paul. "The Economic Development of the Canadian North: With or Without the Indians?" ANNALS OF REGIONAL SCIENCE 5 (December 1971): 8-16.

3. Dumareau, Pierre. "L'Aspect et l'avenir demographiques du Canada français." L'ACTUALITE ECONOMIQUE 28 (April-June 1952): 5-26.

4. England, Robert. "Land Settlement in Northern Areas of Western Canada, 1925-35." CANADIAN JOURNAL OF ECONOMICS AND POLITICAL SCIENCE 1 (November 1935): 578-87.

5. Haythorne, George V. LABOR IN CANADIAN AGRICULTURE. Harvard Studies in Labor in Agriculture. Cambridge, Mass.: Harvard University Press, 1960. 122 p. Bibliographic footnotes.

6. Henripin, Jacques. "Observations sur la situations de démographique des Canadiens français." L ACTUALITE ECONOMIQUE 31 (January-March 1957): 559-80.

7. Hurd, W. Burton. "The Decline in the Canadian Birth Rate." CANADIAN JOURNAL OF ECONOMICS AND POLITICAL SCIENCE 3 (February 1937): 40-57.

8. Hurd, W. Burton, and Cameron, J.C. "Population Movements in Canada, 1921-31: Some Further Considerations." CANADIAN JOURNAL OF ECONOMICS AND POLITICAL SCIENCE 1 (May 1935): 222-45.

9. Le Neveu, A.H., and Kasahara, Y. "Demographic Trends in Canada, 1941-56, and Some of Their Implications." CANADIAN JOURNAL OF ECONOMICS AND POLITICAL SCIENCE 24 (February 1958): 9-20.

10. Meltz, Noah M. CHANGES IN THE OCCUPATIONAL COMPOSITION OF THE CANADIAN LABOR FORCE, 1931-1961. Canada, Department of Labour, Economic and Research Branch Occasional Paper, no. 2. Ottawa: Queen's Printer, 1965. 136 p. Illustrations. Bibliography, pp. 133-36.

11. _____. MANPOWER IN CANADA, 1931 TO 1961; HISTORICAL STATISTICS OF THE CANADIAN LABOUR FORCE. Issued by Canadian Department of Manpower and Immigration, Program Development, Research Branch. Ottawa: Queen's Printer, 1969. v, 288 p. Bibliographic references.

12. Parai, L. IMMIGRATION AND EMIGRATION OF PROFESSIONAL AND SKILLED MANPOWER DURING THE POST WAR PERIOD. Economic Council of Canada Special Study no. 1. Ottawa: Queen's Printer, 1965. v, 248 p. Tables. Charts. Bibliographic footnotes.

13. Veyret, Paul. LA POPULATION DU CANADA. Publications de la Faculté des Lettres de l'Université de Grénoble, VII. Paris: Presses Universitaires de France, 1953. 158 p. Map. Diagrams. Bibliography, pp. 157-58.

14. Younge, Eva R. "Population Movements and the Assimilation of Alien Groups in Canada." CANADIAN JOURNAL OF ECONOMICS AND POLITICAL SCIENCE 10 (August 1944): 372-80.

15. Zay, N. "Analyse, statistique du travail de la femme mariée dans la province de Québec." L'ACTUALITE ECONOMIQUE 32 (October-December 1956): 488-501.

V.G.iii. Resources: Capital Formation

The documentation and interpretation of capital formation since 1920 is incomplete. For a brief introduction, see II.G.i.8, chapter 7. The best and most comprehensive statistical study for the manufacturing sector is item 6 below. Other estimates are provided in V.F.17 and IV.B.6. See 7 below for measurement problems. In a different way, and across a wider spectrum of activities, capitalization is documented and compared with the United States in 4 and 5. The contribution of public investment is discussed in V.E.iii.66 below. More specialized studies examine personal savings, dwelling starts, and education: see 2, 8, and 3 respectively. In 1, an assessment of educational contribution to recent economic growth is made; see also V.F.26.

V.G.iii. Resources: Capital Formation

1. Bertram, G[ordon] W. THE CONTRIBUTION OF EDUCATION TO ECONOMIC GROWTH. Economic Council of Canada Staff Study, no. 12. Ottawa: Queen's Printer, 1966. vii, 146 p. Tables. Charts. Bibliographic footnotes. Statistical appendix, pp. 65-92.

1920 to Present

2. Humphreys, D.J.R. "Personal Saving in Canada: Direct Estimates, 1939-1953." In PROCEEDINGS OF THE BUSINESS AND ECONOMIC STATISTICS SECTION, AMERICAN STATISTICAL ASSOCIATION, pp. 207-14. Montreal, 10-13 September 1954. Washington, D.C.: American Statistical Association, 1954.

3. Illing, Wolfgang M., and Zsigmond, Zoltan E. ENROLLMENT IN SCHOOL AND UNIVERSITIES 1951-52 TO 1975-76. Economic Council of Canada Staff Study, no. 20. Ottawa: Queen's Printer, 1967. xvii, 161 p. Tables. Charts.

4. LaTourette, J[ohn] E. "Aggregate Factors in the Trends in Capital Output Ratios." CANADIAN JOURNAL OF ECONOMICS 3 (May 1970): 255-75.

5. _____. "Trends in the Capital-Output Ratio: United States and Canada 1926-65." CANADIAN JOURNAL OF ECONOMICS 2 (February 1969): 35-51.

6. Rymes, T.K. FIXED CAPITAL FLOWS AND STOCKS MANUFACTURING CANADA 1926-1960, METHODOLOGY. Dominion Bureau of Statistics. Ottawa: Queen's Printer, 1967. 257 p. Bibliography, p. 257.

7. Scott, Anthony [Dalton]. "Canada's Reproducible Wealth." In THE MEASUREMENT OF NATIONAL WEALTH, edited by R. Goldsmith and G. Saunders, pp. 193-216. Income and Wealth Series 8. London: Bowes and Bowes, 1959.

8. Steele, M.L. "Estimates of Dwelling Starts in Canada 1921-1940." In PROCEEDINGS OF THE FIRST CANADIAN CONFERENCE IN APPLIED STATISTICS, edited by C.S. Carter et al., pp. 379-92. Montreal: 1972.

AUTHOR INDEX

This index lists authors, editors, compilers, and other contributors to works cited in the text. Alphabetization is letter by letter and numbers refer to pages.

A

Abella, Irving Martin 3, 24
Acheson, Thomas William 81
Aitken, Hugh G.J. 6, 26, 34, 49, 53, 56, 59, 94, 127
Albion, Robert Greenhalgh 45
Allin, Celphas Daniel 53
Anderson, I.B. 140
Anderson, R.V. 107
Anderson, W.J. 134
Angers, Francois Albert 20
Ankli, Robert 53
Annett, Douglas Rudyard 26, 81
Armstrong, C. 81
Armstrong, Frederick H. 1, 20, 53, 65
Armstrong, P.C. 118
Ashley, Charles Allan 81, 121
Ashton, E.J. 58
Asimakopulos, A. 73
Atwood, Wallace Walter 31
Auld, D.A.L. 103

B

Babcock, Robert H. 79
Balawyder, A. 79
Ball, J.A. 127
Ball, N.R. 30
Balls, H.R. 53
Bancroft, Hubert Howe 42
Bank of Canada 99
Bank of Montreal 121
Barber, Clarence L. 111, 118, 135
Bates, Stewart 81
Beach, E.F. 87
Beasley, Norman 118
Beauroy, J. 58
Beigie, Carl E. 101
Bennett, M.D. 70
Bercuson, David J. 79
Berton, Pierre 75
Bertram, Gordon W. 68, 70, 73, 141
Bhagwati, Jagdish N. 68
Bicha, Karel Denis 87
Biggar, Henry Percival 51
Bing, R.A. 107
Bird, Richard M. 81
Biss, Irene M. 81
Bladen, Vincent Wheeler 7, 81, 127
Blain, Jean 44
Blain, L. 135
Blake, Gordon 26
Bliss, John William Michael 3, 81, 85
Blythe, C.D. 99
Bond, David E. 22, 104
Bonin, B. 101
Bonome, V. 107
Booth, J.F. 127
Bracken, John 70
Brady, Alexander 27, 73
Brebner, John Bartlet 7, 38
Brecher, Irving 94, 102, 127

Author Index

Breckenridge, Roeliff Morton 49, 75
Breen, David H. 87
Breton, Albert 102, 112
Brewis, Thomas N. 2, 27, 127, 137
British Columbia. Economic Council 65
Britnell, George Edwin 62, 98, 114, 127
Brown, George William 7, 53
Brown, John James 29
Brown, M. 120
Brown, Robert Craig 62, 81-82
Brown, T.M. 135
Bryce, R.B. 107
Buck, Arthur Eugene 127
Buck, Hart 111
Buckley, Kenneth A.H. 13, 14, 32, 66, 87, 90
Buller, Arthur Henry Reginald 70
Burley, Kevin H. 62
Burt, Alfred LeRoy 40
Burton, F.W. 18, 45
Burton, Ian 114
Burton, Thomas L. 27
Butlin, J.A. 135
Butlin, Noel G. 75

C

Cairncross, Alexander Kirkland 90
Calvin, Delano Dester 45
Cameron, J.C. 140
Camu, P. 31
Canada. Department of Agriculture 43, 67
Canada. Department of Energy, Mines and Resources 31, 114
Canada. Department of Fisheries 114
Canada. Department of Labour 124
Canada. Department of Northern Affairs and National Resources 139
Canada. Department of Trade and Commerce 3, 67
Canada. Dominion Bureau of Statistics 18, 32, 63, 65, 99, 108
Canada. Privy Council Office 102, 119
Canada. Royal Commission on Dominion-Provincial Relations 62

Canada. Statistics Canada 99
Canada. Task Force on the Structure of Canadian Industry 102
Canadian Business Service Ltd. 119
Canadian Economic Association 3
Careless, James Maurice Stockford 1, 7, 40, 62
Carrothers, W.A. 17, 18, 19, 66
Carter, C.S. 142
Cassidy, Harry M. 127
Caves, Richard Earl 5, 68, 104, 107, 108, 119, 127
Chadwick, St. John 63
Chambers, E.J. 70, 73, 85, 135
Chang, Tse-Chun 108
Charbonneau, Hubert 58
Chateau, J.P. 113
Chernick, S.E. 135
Clark, Andrew H. 58
Clark, Jane 4
Clark, Samuel Delbert 77, 82
Coats, Robert Hamilton 32, 43, 62, 67, 88
Cochrane, H.G. 115
Colquette, R.D. 78
Comeau, Robert 11
Cook, Ramsey 62
Cooper, J.I. 54
Copes, Parzival 96, 115
Copp, John Terry 85
Corbett, D.C. 32, 128
Corry, James Alexander 82, 128
Courchene, T.J. 111
Cowan, Helen I. 58-59
Crabbé, Philippe 18
Craddock, W.J. 115
Craig, Gerald Marquis 40
Craig, Roland D. 86
Crean, J.F. 48
Creighton, Donald Grant, 4, 7, 37, 38, 40, 41, 42, 47, 54, 62, 63
Crispo, J.[H.G.] 125
Croil, James 75
Cross, Michael Sean 14, 52
Cuff, Robert D. 81, 132
Currie, Archibald William 6, 22, 31, 76, 82, 122, 128
Curtis, Clifford Austin 22, 67, 128
Cuthbertson, George A. 22

Author Index

D

Dagenais, M.G. 119
Dales, J[ohn] H[arkness] 63, 68, 70, 73, 104, 113, 119
Daly, D.J. 115, 119, 135
Daly, Patricia 119
Daneau, Marcel 97
Davidson, Gordon Charles 51
Davis, John S. 72, 115, 119
Dawson, Carl Addington 88
Dawson, John 115
Defebaugh, James Elliot 70
Delage, D. 40
Demsetz, Harold 54
Denison, Merrill 20, 22, 82
Denton, Frank T. 32
Deprez, Paul 140
Deutsch, J.J. 82
de Vegh, Imre 108
Doern, G. Bruce 128
Domar, Evsey D. 135
Dominion Bank 77
Donald, William John Alexander 20
Dougall, Herbert Edward 82
Doughty, Arthur G. 8, 11
Douglas, Paul H. 119
Drummond, Ian Macdonald 3, 6, 76, 128
Drummond, William Malcolm 49, 115, 128
Due, Jean Mann 135
Due, John Fitzgerald 122
Dumareau, Pierre 140
Durocher, René 4, 11

E

Earl, David W.L. 54
Easterbrook, William Thomas 2, 4, 6, 14-15, 20, 76, 128
Easterlin, Richard A. 88
Eastman, Harry C. 72, 104, 106, 108
Eccles, William John 40
Economic Council of Canada 94
Editor. Canadian Journal of Economics 99
Egerer, Gerald 128
Eldon, D. 116
Elliott, G.R. 51

Ellis, Frank H. 122
Ellis, Lewis Ethan 82
England, Robert 88, 140
English, Harry Edward 94, 105, 106
Erickson, Edward W. 128
Espessat, Hélène 79

F

Fairweather, S.W. 23
Falardeau, J.C. 73
Farnie, D.A. 46
Faucher, Albert 7, 10, 49, 54, 64, 73, 97
Fauteux, Joseph Noel 48
Fay, Charles Ryle 9, 15, 63
Fayerweather, John 102
Ferguson, D.A. 128
Firestone, Otto Jack 19, 20, 48, 66, 67, 70, 129, 135
Fleming, Howard A. 122
Flenley, Ralph 31
Forsey, Eugene 24, 73, 125
Fouriner, Leslie Thomas 129
Fowke, Vernon Clifford 27, 40, 68, 80, 82, 102, 114, 129
Fox, Harold George 27
Frégault, Guy 40
French, Goldwin S. 65
Friedmann, W. 130
Fuchs, V.R. 123
Fulford, Robert 4
Fullerton, D.H. 119
Furniss, I.F. 136

G

Galarmeau, Claude 46
Galbraith, John Alexander 88, 122
Gallaway, L.E. 34
Garner, John F. 54, 130
Gates, Lillian Frances 54
George, M.V. 33
George, Peter J. 1, 2, 76
George, Roy E. 119
Gibbon, John Murray 76
Gibbons, Alan O. 129
Gibson, James Douglas 95, 129
Gidney, Robert D. 34

Author Index

Gilbert, Milton 136
Gilles, J. 129
Gilmour, James M. 73
Glazebrook, George Parkin de Twenebroker 22, 73
Gold, N.L. 88
Goldberg, Simon A. 99, 136
Goldsmith, R. 142
Goodman, Bernard 116
Goodwin, Craufurd D.W. 68
Gordon, Donald F. 23
Gordon, Donald F. 70
Gordon Company 121
Gourlay, Robert Fleming 43
Graham, Gerald Sandford 38, 54
Graham, John F. 129
Grant, George Parkin 29
Grant, Ruth Fulton 63
Gray, John Morgan 59
Green, Alan G. 33, 62, 112
Greenway, H.F. 100
Guillet, Edwin Clarence 49
Guthrie, John A. 119-20

H

Hamelin, Jean 41, 46, 64
Hammond, Bray 49
Hampson, H.A. 119
Hansen, Marcus Lee 33
Hanson, E.J. 116, 129
Hardy, Jean-Pierre 79
Harkness, J.P. 15
Harris, C.A. 63
Harris, Curtis C. 71
Harris, Richard Colebrook 41, 54, 58
Hartland, P.E. 15, 70
Hartz, Louis 16
Harvey, Fernand 11
Harvey, Pierre 10
Haviland, W.E. 105
Hay, Keith A.J. 85-86, 120
Hayes, F. Ronald 130
Haythorne, George V. 88, 130, 140
Heath, J.B. 136
Heaton, Herbert 88
Hedges, James Blaine 83, 88
Helleiner, G.K. 122
Henderson, George Fletcher 67
Henripin, Jacques 32, 33, 73, 140

Herick, Welf H. 102
Higgins, Benjamin 130
Higgins, Jean 130
Hind, Henry Youle 43
Hodgetts, J.E. 54, 130
Hoffman, Arnold David 18
Hoffman, Irwin D. 18
Holton, Richard H. 5
Hood, William C. 122, 136
Hope, E.C. 86, 136
Horn, Michael Steven Daniel 136
Horowitz, Gad 125
Hotson, J.H. 136
Howay, Frederic William 12
Howland, R.D. 7
Hudson, S.C. 116
Hughes, Everett Cherrington 97, 113
Humphreys, D.J.R. 142
Hunter, W.D.G. 116
Hurd, W. Burton 140

I

Illing, Wolfgang M. 142
Ingram, J.C. 71
Innis, Harold Adams 1, 10, 11, 15, 18, 22-23, 25, 27, 33, 44, 55, 63, 71, 76, 93
Innis, Mary Q. 8, 48
Irving, John A. 130
Irwin, Leonard Bertrain 49
Isbester, A. Fraser 125

J

Jackson, James A. 12
Jacobsen, M.W. 71
James, Robert Warren 95
Jamieson, Archibald Black 122
Jamieson, Stuart Marshall 25, 79
Jecchinis, Chris 86
Jenks, Leland Hamilton 60
Joerg, W.L.G. 33, 83, 88
Johnson, Harry Gordon 27, 95, 105, 136
Jones, George M. 53
Jones, Lawrence F. 18
Jones, Robert Leslie 46, 55
Judah, Charles Burnett, Jr. 55

Author Index

K

Kalbach, Warren E. 33
Kasahara, Y. 140
Kates, Robert W. 114
Keefer, Thomas Coltrin 50
Keirstead, B.S. 96
Kemp, M.C. 108
Kennedy, Douglas Ross 79
Kerr, Donald G.G. 13, 116
Kerr, Wilfred Brenton 38
Kesterton, Wilfred N. 23
Keyfitz, Nathan 33, 100
Kilbourn, William 20, 30, 130
Kilduff, Vera Reynolds 102
Kingsford, William 50
Knorr, Klaus Eugen 55
Knowles, C.M. 8
Knowles, Lilian Charlotte Anne 8
Knox, Frank A. 20, 83, 102, 130
Kotowitz, Y. 120, 137
Kottman, Richard N. 130
Krutilla, John A. 130
Kulshrestha, S.T.J. 137
Kuznets, Simon 67

L

La Forest, Gerard V. 83
Lambert, Richard Stanton 27
Lamontagne, Maurice 10, 73
Landon, Fred 65
Lang, Vernon 122
Langford, George Burwash 116
Langlois, Georges 89
LaTourette, John E. 137, 142
Lavoie, Elzear 46
Lavoie, Yolande 58
Lawr, Douglas A. 34, 71
Lawson, Murray E. 55
Leach, Richard H. 95
Leacy, F.H. 99
LeBlaut, Robert 46
Le Bourdais, Donat Marc 19, 116
Légaré, Jacques 59
Legget, Robert Ferguson 50
Lemelin, Charles 112
Le Neveu, A.H. 140
Lennox, Mary 100
Lerohl, M.L. 137

Lessard, J.C. 122
Letarte, Jacques 64
Letourneau, Firmin 19
Levitt, Kari 102
Linteau, Paul-André 4, 11
Lipsett, L.R. 116
Lithwick, N.H. 120, 130, 137
Logan, Harold Amos 25, 131
Lok, Siepko H. 137
Lonn, George 18
Lounsbury, Ralph Greenbe 46
Lower, Arthur Reginald Marsden 1, 8, 17, 19, 31, 33, 44, 45, 46, 59, 102
Lyons, Cicely 12

M

McAllister, R.I. 96
Macaulay, R.H.H. 19
McCalla, D. 51
McDiarmid, Orville John 27
Macdonald, L.R. 55
McDonald, M.L. 113
MacDonald, Norman 59, 89
McDougall, Duncan M. 74, 89
McDougall, John Lorne 15, 76, 131
MacEachern, G.A. 137
Macesich, George 111
MacFarlane, D.L. 105
MacGibbon, Duncan Alexander 71, 116
McGillivray, A.A. 116
MacGregor, D.C. 131
MacGregor, James G. 12
MacInnes, T.R.L. 27
McInnis, Edgar 8
McInnis, R. Marvin 20, 89, 112
McIvor, R. Craig 23, 105, 123
MacKay, Douglas 19
MacKay, Robert Alexander 9
Mackenzie, W. 137
Mackintosh, William Archibald 1, 15, 33, 63, 78, 83, 88
MacKirdy, Kenneth A. 16, 66
MacLean, Guy 42
MacLean, M.C. 32, 33
McLean, Simon James 83
McLeod, J.T. 132
McLuhan, Marshall 15, 16
McManus, John C. 55, 105

Author Index

Macmillan, David S. 1, 8
MacNutt, William Stewart 38
McRae, K.D. 16
McVey, Wayne W. 33
Maddison, A. 137
Main, Orrin William 117, 122
Malach, V[ernon] W[alter] 108-9
Malenbaum, Wilfred 71
Mandron, Robert 2
Marcus, Edward 109
Markham, Jesse W. 120
Marsh, Leonard C. 88
Marshall, Herbert 20, 100
Martin, Chester Bailey 59, 83, 95
Masters, Donald Campbell 7, 55, 74, 79
Mavor, James 83
Maxwell, James Ackley 83, 131
Mayo, H.B. 117, 131
Maywald, Karel 138
Mealing, S.R. 43
Meier, Gerald M. 71
Meiselman, D. 111
Melancon, Jacques 113
Meltz, Noah M. 140-41
Melvin, James 105
Menzies, M.W. 131
Mercer, Lloyd J. 76
Migue, Jean-Luc 97
Miller, John T., Jr. 117
Miller, Richard Ulric 125
Minville, Esdras 19, 74
Mitchell, H. 67, 71
Montagne, J.T. 125
Moore, Albert Milton 105, 131
Moore, Elwood S. 117
Morgan, L. 117
Morrissette, Hughes 117
Morton, Arthur S. 42, 83
Morton, William Lewis 4, 8, 12, 38, 40, 41, 42, 43, 47, 62, 63, 131
Moyer, M.S. 123
Munro, John M. 105
Munro, William Bennett 52, 55-56
Munzer, E. 109
Murchie, Robert Welch 71
Musolf, L.D. 131
Myers, Gustavas 35

N

Nader, George A. 74
National Industrial Conference Board 120
Neary, Peter 96
Neatby, Hilda 40
Neill, Robin F. 2, 28
Nelles, H.V. 28, 50, 81, 83
Nelson, J.G. 82
Neufeld, Edward Peter 21, 23, 131
Nicholson, Norman L. 8
Nish, Cameron 4, 11, 41
Norrie, K.H. 83, 89
North, Douglas C. 57, 86
Nova Scotia 96

O

Officer, Lawrence H. 56, 109
Oksanen, Ernest H. 1, 2, 123
Oliver, Peter N. 65
Olson, Marcus 71
Ontario 97
Ormsby, Margaret A. 12
Ostry, Bernard 83-84
Ostry, Sylvia 29, 32, 73, 86
Ouellet, F. 41, 46

P

Paltiel, Khayyan Zev 28
Paquet, Gilles 1, 2, 41, 44, 46-47, 56, 89, 97, 102, 105
Parai, L. 141
Parenteau, Roland 20
Parker, John P. 50
Parker, Keith Alfred 47
Paterson, D.G. 135
Patton, Harold S. 78
Penner, Rudolph G. 103, 109
Pennie, T.E. 138
Pentland, Harry Clare 60, 79, 138
Perlman, M. 88
Perren, Richard 71
Perry, John Harvey 28
Peters, J.E. 98, 117
Petersen, J.O. 30
Phillips, Paul Chrisler 47, 56

Author Index

Phillips, William Gregory 21
Pickett, J. 89, 90
Plotnick, Alan R. 117
Plumptre, Arthur Fitzwalter Wynne 84, 95
Poapst, James V. 123, 131
Poduluk, J.R. 136
Polèse, Mario 120
Porritt, Edward 84
Porter, Glenn 81, 132
Postner, Harry H. 138
Powrie, T.L. 109
Preston, Richard Arthur 8
Pritchett, John Perry 43
Pross, Paul 27
Purdy, Harry Leslie 132

Q

Quinn, Magella 91

R

Radford, R.A. 103
Radosh, Ronald 78
Rae, James D. 106, 135
Rawlyk, G.A. 10
Ray, Arthur I. 47
Raynauld, Andre 95, 97
Rea, Kenneth J. 95, 132
Read, L.M. 100
Regehr, T.D. 76
Reid, Allana G. 47
Reid, D.J. 74
Reisman, S.S. 94
Reuber, Grant L. 103, 108, 109, 127
Reynolds, Lloyd G. 84
Rhomberg, R. 109
Rich, Edwin Ernest 47, 56
Richardson, Harry Ward 89
Richmond, D.R. 97
Ritchie, Thomas 21
Roberts, Leslie 117, 132
Robin, Martin 66, 79, 98
Robinson, John Lewis 31
Roby, Y[ves] 64
Rose, J. Holland 8
Roseman, F. 103
Rosenbluth, Gideon 109, 124, 132, 138

Rosenfeld, Barry D. 84
Ross, C.M. 95
Ross, Victor Harold 71, 77
Rostow, Walt W. 68
Rothney, Gordon Oliver 10
Rotstein, Abraham 3, 29
Royal Bank of Canada 120
Ruddell, Thierry 79
Russell, P. 103
Rutherford, John Gunion 72
Rutter, William Pickering 72
Ryan, William F. 64
Ryder, N.B. 34
Ryerson, Stanley Brehaut 41
Rymes, T.K. 27, 73, 142

S

Safarian, Albert Edward 103, 109, 138
Sage, Walter Noble 16
Saint-Germain, Maurice 11
Saul, Samuel Berrick 72
Saunders, G. 142
Saunders, Stanley Alexander 10, 17, 19, 56, 64
Savage, Rosemary Lorna 77
Scace, R.C. 82
Scheinberg, Stephen 132
Schlote, Werner 72
Scott, Anthony Dalton 24, 28, 29, 106, 136, 142
Scott, Frank R. 28, 132
Sequin, Maurice 10, 47
Sharp, Paul Fredrick 66, 78
Shearer, Ronald A. 22, 98, 103, 106, 117
Shepherd, James F. 48, 57
Shibata, Hirofumi 106
Shortt, Adam 8, 11
Shotwell, James Thompson 25
Shoyama, T.K. 28
Siebert, Fred V. 117
Silver, A.I. 89
Simon, M. 91
Sinclair, B. 30
Singer, Jacques 106
Skelton, Oscar Douglas 42, 50, 77
Skeoch, L.A. 28
Slater, David W. 95, 110, 117, 120

Author Index

Smails, Reginald George Hampden 81
Smiley, Donald V. 62
Smith, L. 56
Smith, R.M. 96
Smith, William 50
Snyder, G. 123
Southworth, Constant 84
Spelt, Jacob 74
Splane, Richard B. 56
Spry, Irene M. 18
Stabler, Jack C. 89
Stager, David 132
Stamp, Robert M. 91
Stanley, George Francis Gilman 16, 28, 43
Stanley, Nixon 100
Staples, Melville H. 78
Steele, M.L. 142
Stegemann, Klaus 132
Stetler, Gilbert 74
Stevens, George Roy 21, 23, 77
Stevens, Wayne Edson 48
Stevenson, Hugh A. 65
Stewart, Max D. 124
Stokes, Milton L. 133
Stone, Leroy O. 34, 74
Stone, Richard 136
Stovel, John A. 72
Strong, Margaret Kirkpatrick 28
Studness, C.M. 89
Stykolt, Stefan 104, 106, 108
Sun Life Assurance Company of Canada 120
Sutton, G.D. 138
Swainson, Donald 12, 83
Swanson, William Walker 118
Sydor, Leon P. 123

T

Talman, J.J. 51
Tanner, J.E. 107
Taylor, Kenneth Wiffin 67
Taylor, Norman W. 10, 113
Thomas, Brinley 34, 90
Thomas, Dorothy Swaine 88
Thompson, John Fairfield 118
Thompson, R.W. 96
Thorburn, H.G. 132, 133

Timlin, Mabel Frances 34, 84, 90
Tory, H.M. 30
Trotter, Reginald George 9
Trudel, Marcel 42, 56
Truesdell, Leon Edgar 34
Tucker, G.N. 56
Tucker, Marjorie 100

U

Underhill, Frank Hawkins 9
Upton, L.F.S. 28
Urquhart, M.C. 13, 129, 133
Urwick, Currie, Ltd. 121

V

Vedder, R.K. 34
Veyret, Paul 141
Vicero, Ralph D. 90
Vickery, Edward 16
Viner, Jacob 72

W

Wade, Mason 9
Waines, W.J. 90, 133
Waite, Peter B. 38, 63
Wallace, Frederick William 50
Wallace, W.J. 133
Wallace, W. Stewart 22
Wallot, Jean-Pierre 41, 44, 46-47, 56, 84
Walter, Edward A. 110
Walters, D. 138
Walton, Gary M. 57
Wampack, J. 138
Ware, Norman J. 25
Warkentin, John 31, 58
Warsbrough, V.C. 118
Watkins, Melville H. 2, 3, 16, 30, 84, 101, 102
Watt, F.W. 84
Watts, G.S. 110
Waverman, Leonard 128
Weir, E. Austin 133
Weldon, J.C. 87
Westcott, F.J. 84
White, Aubrey 56
Whitelaw, William Menzies 38

Author Index

Whitford, H.N. 86
Wiegman, C. 121
Wilbur, J.R.H. 133
Wilgus, William John 23
Wilkes, George C. 85
Wilkins, Mira 24
Wilkinson, Bruce W. 105, 106, 110
Willcox, Walter F. 88
Williamson, Jeffrey G. 112
Willoughby, William 133
Wilson, Alan 10, 57
Wilson, Andrew H. 133
Wilson, George W. 31
Wilson, John Donald 35
Wilson, Roland 90
Winks, R.W. 2
Wolfe, R.I. 9
Wonnacott, Gordon Paul 106, 110
Wonnacott, Ronald J. 104, 106
Wood, L.A. 78

Wood, William 4, 23
Woods, H.D. 29, 86
Worton, D.A. 123
Wright, C.P. 72, 123
Wright, J.F.C. 12
Wrong, George MacKinnon 42

Y

Young, J.H. 16, 106
Young, W.R. 85
Younge, Eva R. 141

Z

Zaidi, Mahmood A. 29, 86
Zaslow, Morris 16, 63, 65
Zay, N. 141
Zsigmond, Zoltan E. 142

TITLE INDEX

This index includes books cited in the text. In some cases titles have been shortened. Alphabetization is letter by letter and numbers refer to pages.

A

Agrarian Revolt in Western Canada, a Survey Showing American Parallels, The 78
Agricultural Co-Operation in Western Canada 78
Agricultural Implement Industry in Canada, The 21
Agricultural Progress on the Prairie Frontier 71
Alberta's Oil Industry 116
All Afloat 23
American Born in Canada, The 32
American Capital and Canadian Resources 34
American Economic Impact on Canada, The 94
American Farmer and the Canadian West, 1896-1914, The 87
American Influence in Canadian Mining 117
American Influence in the Canadian Iron and Steel Industry 116
Analysis of Stages in the Growth of Population in Canada 33
Anatomy of Poverty 85
Annexation, Preferential Trade and Reciprocity 53
Approaches to Canadian Economic History 2
Approaches to Canadian History 2

Aspects of Nineteenth Century Ontario 65
Atlantic Provinces, the Emergence of Colonial Society 1712-1857, The 38
Atlas d'Histoire Economique et Sociale du Québec 1951-1901 64
Atlas Historique du Canada Français des Origines a 1867 42

B

Bank of Canada, The 133
Bank of Canada Operations, 1935-54 131
Bank of Canada Review 99
Barley and Steam 20
Beginnings of New France, 1524-1663, The 42
Bennett Administration, 1930-35, The 133
Bennett New Deal, The 133
Bias of Communications, The 15
Birth of Western Canada, A History of the Riel Rebellions, The 43
Boundaries of Canada, its Provinces and Territories, The 8
Britain's Export Trade with Canada 109
British Colonial Theories, 1570-1850 55
British Columbia 12

Title Index

British Columbia and the United States 12
British Columbia Fisheries, The 18
British Emigration to British North America, 1783-1837 58
British Fishery at Newfoundland, 1634-1763, The 46
British Immigration before Confederation 59
British Immigration to British North America 59
British North America at Confederation 37
British Overseas Trade from 1700 to the 1930's 72
British Policy and Canada 1774-1791, a Study in 18th Century Trade Policy 54
British Preference in Canadian Commercial Policy 81
British Preferences in Canadian Commercial Policy 26
Building the Canadian West 88
Business and Government in Canada 132

C

Canada 7
Canada, a Modern History 7
Canada: An Appraisal of its Needs and Resources 31
Canada, a Political and Social History 8
Canada: A Story of Challenge 7
Canada: Immigration and Colonization 1841-1903 89
Canada and Its Provinces, a History of the Canadian People and their Institutions 8
Canada and Newfoundland 8
Canada and the Atomic Revolution 116
Canada and the International Business Cycle 1927-1939 109
Canada and the New International Economy 94
Canada before Confederation, a Study in Historical Geography 58
Canada Builds 1867-1967 21
Canada 1874-1896, Arduous Destiny 63
Canada 1896-1921 62
Canada in a Changing World Economy 95
Canada in a Wider Economic Community 106
Canada in Peace and War 95
Canada in the World Economy 72
Canada Permanent Story, 1855-1955, The 77
Canada, 1763-1841 59
Canada's Arctic Outlet 122
Canada's Balance of International Indebtedness, 1900-1913 72
Canada's Economic Development, 1867-1953 with Special Reference to Changes in the Country's National Product and National Wealth 67
Canada's Economy in a Changing World 95
Canada's First Bank 22
Canada's First Century 1867-1967 62
Canada's Flying Heritage 122
Canada's Imports 110
Canada's International Trade 110
Canada's National Policy, 1883-1900 81
Canada's Science Policy and the Economy 130
Canada's Trade Policy in the Second Development Decade 130
Canada under Louis XIV, 1663-1701 40
Canada-United States Economic Relations 94
Canada Year Book 3
Canada Year Book, The 67
Canadian Agricultural Policy, the Historical Pattern 27
Canadian Agriculture in War and Peace, 1935-50 114
Canadian Agriculture Machinery Industry, The 121
Canadian-American Industry 20
Canadian Anti-Trust Legislation 127
Canadian Atlantic Fishery, The 63
Canadian Automotive Industry, The 120

Title Index

Canadian Balance of International Payments 1926-1948, The 108
Canadian Banking System 1817-1890 49
Canadian Born in the United States, The 34
Canadian Business History Selected Studies 1497-1971 8
Canadian Canals, The 50
Canadian Chemical Industry, The 119
Canadian Commercial Policy 106
Canadian Commercial Revolution 1845-1851 56
Canadian Construction Industry, The 120
Canadian Crown Corporations 81
Canadian Dollar 1948-1958, The 110
Canadian Dollar 1948-1962, The 110
Canadian Economic Development 6
Canadian Economic Growth and Development from 1939 to 1955 96
Canadian Economic Growth 135
Canadian Economic History 6
Canadian Economic Policy 127
Canadian Economic Policy and the Impact of International Capital Flows 108, 127
Canadian Economic System, The 95
Canadian Economic Thought 68
Canadian Economy, The 5
Canadian Economy in Great Depression, The 138
Canadian Economy, Organization and Development, The 6
Canadian Education 35
Canadian Electrical Manufacturing Industry, The 118
Canadian Energy Prospects 115
Canadian Federation, Its Origins and Achievement 9
Canadian Graduate Theses 1919-1967 4
Canadian Grain Trade, The 71
Canadian Grain Trade 1931-1951, The 116
Canadian Growth Revisited 1950-1967 138
Canadian Immigration Policy 128
Canadian Income Levels and Growth 138

Canadian Industrial Machinery Industry, The 121
Canadian Iron and Steel Industry, The 20
Canadian Labour in Politics 125
Canadian Labour in Transition 125
Canadian Manufacturers' Association, The 77
Canadian Minerals Yearbook 114
Canadian Monetary, Banking and Fiscal Development 23
Canadian National Railways 23
Canadian Nickel Industry 117
Canadian Non-Tariff Barriers to Trade 132
Canadian Pacific, a Brief History 76
Canadian Primary Iron and Steel Industry, The 117
Canadian Primary Textile Industry, The 120
Canadian Quandary, The 95
Canadians 1867-1967, The 62
Canadian Secondary Manufacturing Industry 119
Canadian Society in the French Regime 40
Canadian Statistical Review 99
Canadian Transportation Economics 122
Canadian-U.S. Automotive Agreement 101
Canadian Wheat Pools, The 78
Canals of Canada, their Prospects and Influence, The 50
Capital Flows between Canada and the United States 102
Capital Formation in Canada 1896-1930 90
Capital Transfers and Economic Policy 108
Cattle Trade of Western Canada, The 72
Census of Canada 1870-71 43
Centennial History of Manitoba, The 12
Challenge of Agriculture, the Story of the United Farmers of Ontario, The 78
Changes in Agriculture to 1970 115

Title Index

Changes in the Occupational Composition of the Canadian Labor Force, 1931-1961 140
Changing Perspectives in Canadian History 16
Channel Islands and Newfoundland 9
Charming of Prometheus, The 130
Chartered Banking in Canada 122
Chronological Record of Canadian Mining Events from 1604 to 1947 and Historical Tables of Mineral Production in Canada 18
Clergy and Economic Growth in Quebec 1896-1914, The 64
Clergy Reserves of Upper Canada, The 57
Cod Fisheries 18
Colonization of Western Canada, The 88
Colony to Nation 8
Columbia River Treaty, The 130
Commercial Empire of the St. Lawrence, 1760-1850, The 40
Commercial Fisheries of Canada, The 114
Commercial Policy in the Canadian Economy 27
Concentration in Canadian Manufacturing Industries 124
Constitutional Adaptation and Canadian Federalism since 1945 132
Contemporary Canada 95
Contribution of Education to Economic Growth, The 141
Contributions to Canadian Economics 4
Control of Competition in Canada, The 84
Critical Years, The 41
Croissance et Structure Economiques de la Province de Quebec 97
Crop Production in Western Canada 70

D

Dairy Industry in Canada, The 18
Demand for Canadian Imports 1926-55, The 108
Demographic Basis of Canadian Society, The 33

Development of Canada's Staples 1867-1939, The 62
Development of the Fraser River Salmon Canning Industry 1885-1913, The 74
Difficulties of Divided Jurisdiction 128
Dirty Thirties, The 136
Discriminatory Government Policies in Federal Countries 112
Documents Relating to the Seigneurial Tenure System in Canada 1598-1854 56
Does Canada Need More People? 34
Dominion Bureau of Statistics 99
Dominion of the North 7
Dynamic Decade 116

E

Early Trading Companies of New France, The 51
Econometric Model of Canada under the Fluctuating Rate, An 109
Economic Analysis of Canadian Manufacturing Productivity, An 138
Economic Analysis of the Pulp and Paper Industry, An 119
Economic Background of Dominion Provincial Relations, The 63
Economic Development of the British Overseas Empire, The 8
Economic Geography of Canada (Camu) 31
Economic Geography of Canada (Currie) 31
Economic Growth in Canada 137
Economic History of Canada, An 8
Economic Implications of Patents 129
Economic Nationalism in Old and New States 27
Economics of Banking Operations, The 122
Economics of Immigration 33
Economics of Take-Off into Sustained Growth, The 68
Economics of the Canadian Financial System, The 22

Title Index

Economic Transformation of Ontario, The 97
Economic Welfare of the Maritime Provinces, The 64
Economie et Societe en Nouvelle-France 41
Economie Quebecoise 11
Educating Canadians 34
Effective Protection in the Canadian Economy 105
Efficiency in the Open Economy 106
Eighty Years' Progress in British North America 43-44
Electronics Industry in Canada, The 119
Elements Combined, a History of the Steel Company of Canada, The 20
Emergence of Multinational Enterprise, The 24
Empire and Communications 15
Empire of the North Atlantic 38
Energy Question, The 128
English Colonial Policy and the North American Fishery Industry 1498-1713 55
Enrollment in School and Universities 1951-52 to 1975-76 142
Essai sur l'Industrie au Canada sous le Régime Français 48
Essays in Canadian Economic History 15
Essays in Political Economy 15
Essays in Transportation in Honour of W.T. Jackman 23
Essays on Wheat, including the Discovery and Introduction of Marquis Wheat, the Early History of Wheat Growing in Manitoba, Wheat in Western Canada, etc. 70
Explorers of North America, 1492-1806, The 38

F

Family Compact, The 54
Farm Credit in Canada 76
Federal Railway Land Subsidy Policy of Canada, The 83
Federal Royal Commissions in Canada 1867-1966 67

Federal Subsidies to the Provincial Governments in Canada 83
Fifth Annual Review 94
Fifty Years of Banking Service, 1871-1921 77
Financial History of Canadian Governments 81
Financial System of Canada, Its Growth and Development, The 23
Financing Canadian Government 127
Financing of Economic Activity in Canada 122
Finding List of Canadian Railway Companies before 1915 75
First Fifty Years, a History of the United Grain Growers Limited, The 78
First Twenty-Five Years, The 121
Fiscal Adjustment and Economic Development, a Case Study of Nova Scotia 129
Fiscal Harmonization under Freer Trade 106
Fixed Capital Flows and Stocks Manufacturing Canada 1926-1960, Methodology 142
Foreign Direct Investment in Canada 102
Foreign Investment in Canada, Prospects for National Policy 102
Foreign Ownership and the Structure of Canadian Industry 102
Foreign Ownership of Canadian Industry 103
Foreign Trade in Gas and Electricity in North America 117
Forestry Tenures and Taxes in Canada 131
Forests and Sea Power 45
Forests of British Columbia 86
For the Years to Come, a Story of International Nickel of Canada 118
Franchise and Politics in British North America 1755-1867, The 54
Free Gold 18
Free Trade between the United States and Canada, the Potential Economic Effects 106

Title Index

French Canada in Transition 97
Freshwater 22
Frontier Thesis and the Canadas, The 14
Fur: A Study in English Mercantilism 55
Fur Trade, The 47
Fur Trade and the Northwest to 1857, The 47
Fur Trade in Canada, The 18
Future Market Outlets for Canadian Wheat and Other Grains 116
Future of Canada's Export Trade, The 107

G

Global Corporation, a History of the International Development of Massey-Ferguson Ltd., A 21
Government Intervention, Railways and Canadian Economic Development 76
Grain Growers' Co-Operation in Western Canada 78
Grand Trunk Railway of Canada, The 22
Great Britain's Woodyear, British America and the Timber Trade 1763-1867 46
Growth and Changing Composition of Trade between Canada and the United States, The 103
Growth of Government of Spending in Canada, The 81
Growth of Manpower in Canada, The 32

H

Harmonization of National Economic Policies under Free Trade 105
Harvest Triumphant 20
Histoire de l'Agriculture (Canada Français) 19
Histoire de la Population Canadienne-Francaise 89
Histoire du Québec, Bibliographie Selective (1867-1970) 4
Histoire Economique du Québec 1851-1896 64

Histoire Economique et Sociale du Québec 1760-1850 41
Histoire Economique et Unité Canadienne 7
Historical Atlas of Canada, A 13
Historical Catalogue of Dominion Bureau of Statistics Publications 1918-1960 99
Historical Essays on the Atlantic Provinces 10
Historical Essays on the Prairie Provinces 12
Historical Estimates of the Canadian Labour Force 32
Historical Highlights of Canadian Mining 18
Historical Statistics of Canada 13
History and Myth, Arthur Lower and the Making of Canadian Nationalism 102
History of Agriculture in Ontario 1613-1880 46
History of Alberta, A 12
History of Banking in Canada, The 75
History of British Columbia 1792-1887 42
History of Canada, A 4
History of Canadian Wealth 35
History of Farmers' Movements in Canada 78
History of Journalism in Canada, A 23
History of Prairie Settlement and "Dominion Lands" Policy 83
History of Science in Canada 30
History of the Canadian Bank of Commerce, with an Account of the Other Banks That Now Form Part of Its Organization, A 77
History of the Canadian Pacific Railway 76
History of the Canadian West to 1870-71, A 42
History of the Hudson's Bay Company 1670-1870, The 47
History of the Lumber Industry in America 70
History of the Post Office in British North America 1639-1870 50

Title Index

History of Trade Union Organization in Canada, The 25
History of Transportation in Canada, A 22
Honourable Company, The 19
How Much Competition? 105
Hydroelectricity and Industrial Development 73

I

Ideas in Exile 29
Image of Confederation, The 9
Immigration and Emigration of Professional and Skilled Manpower during the Post War Period 141
Impact of Immigration on Canada's Population, The 33
Imperial Economic Policy, 1917-1939 128
Indians in the Fur Trade 47
Industrial Materials in Canadian American Relations 116
Industrial Relations in Canada 25
Industrial Structure in Canada's International Competitive Position 105
Industry and Education 20
Influence of the United States on Canadian Development, The 8
Intercity Electric Railway Industry in Canada, The 122
Internal Migration in Canada, a Demographic Analysis 33
International Cycles and Canada's Balance of Payments 1921-33 108
International Trade and Domestic Prosperity, Canada 1926-38 96
International Unionism, a Study in Canadian-American Relations 125
Interregional Competition in Canadian Cereal Production 115
Interregional Disparities in Income 135
Introduction to New France 42
Introduction to Political Economy, An 7
Inventories and the Business Cycle 135
Inventors, The 29

K

Kingdom of Canada 8
Knights of Labour in Canada, The 79

L

Labor in Canadian Agriculture 140
Labour Economics in Canada 86
Labour in Canadian-American Relations 25
Labour Policy in Canada 29
La Forêt 19
La "National Canadienne" et l'Agriculture 1760-1850 47
Land and Labour, a Social Survey of Agriculture and Farm Labour Market in Central Canada 88
Land Policies of Upper Canada 54
La Population du Canada 141
Last Spike; The Great Railway, 1881-1885, The 75
Leader and a Laggard, Manufacturing Industry in Nova Scotia, Quebec and Ontario A 119
Le XVIIIe Siècle Canadien 40
Le Québec d'Aujourd'Hui 97
Le "Retard" du Québec et l'Inferiorité Economique des Canadiens-Français 11
Les Bourgeois--Gentilshommes de la Nouvelle-France 1729-1748 41
Les Conditions du Developpement Agricole au Québec 117
Let Us Be Honest and Modest, Technology and Society in Canada 30
Life and Labour in Newfoundland 9
Life and Times of Clarence Decatur Howe, The 132
Life and Times of Sir Alexander Tillock Galt, The 42
L'Investissement Etranger à Long Term au Canada, ses Caractères et ses Effects sur l'Economie Canadienne 101
Living Profit, A 85
Lord Selkirk of Red River 59
Lord Selkirk's Work in Canada 59

Title Index

M

Making of the Maritime Provinces 1713-1784, The 38
Manitoba 12
Manpower in Canada, 1931 to 1961 141
Maritime Provinces in their Relation to the National Economy of Canada 63
Maritime Provinces of British North America and the American Revolution, The 38
Maritimes and Canada before Confederation, The 38
Metals and Men 19
Migration and Economic Growth 34
Migration in Canada, Some Regional Aspects 34
Migration of British Capital to 1875, The 60
Mingling of the Canadian and American Peoples, The 33
Mining and Mineral Processing in Canada 115
Mobilizing Canada's Resources for War 95
Monetary and Fiscal Thought and Policy in Canada 1919-1939 127
Money and Banking in Canada 23
Monopolies and Patents 27
Montréal Economique 74
Multinational Firm and the Nation State, The 102

N

National Atlas of Canada, The 31
National Dream, The 75
Nationalism, Communism and Canadian Labour 24
Nationalism in Canada, University League of Social Reform 103
National Policy and the Wheat Economy, The 82
Natural Resource Development in Canada 18
Natural Resource Policy in Canada 27
Natural Resources 28
Natural Resources and Public Property under the Canadian Constitution 83
New Brunswick 38
New England's Outpost 38
Newfoundland 9
Newfoundland and Labrador 96
Newfoundland from International Fishery to Canadian Province 10
Newfoundland, Island into Province 63
Newsprint Paper Industry, an Economic Analysis, The 120
New Theory of Value, the Canadian Economics of H.A. Innis 2
Niagara in Politics 83
Noranda 117
North American Assault on the Canadian Forest, The 19
North Atlantic Triangle 7
North West Company, The 51
Northwest Fur Trade 1763-1800, The 48

O

Ogilvie in Canada--Pioneer Millers, 1801-1951 21
Old Province of Quebec, The 40
Ontario since 1867, a Bibliography 65
Opening of the Canadian North 1870-1914, The 63
Origins of the International Labor Organization, The 25
Outlook for the Canadian Forest Industries, The 115
Out of the Earth 116
Output, Labour and Capital in the Canadian Economy 136

P

Pacific Railways and Nationalism in the Canadian-American Northwest, 1845-1873 49
Patronage et Pouvoir dans le Bas Canada 1794-1812 56
People's Power, the History of Ontario Hydro, The 82

Title Index

Performance of Foreign-Owned Firms in Canada, The 103
Perspectives on Canada's International Payments, a Background Sketch and Survey 110
Petroleum, Canadian Markets and United States Foreign Policy 117
Petroleum in Canada 71
Philosophy of Railroads and Other Essays 50
Physiographic Provinces of North America, The 31
Pillars of Profit, the Company Province 1934-1972 98
Pioneering in the Prairie Provinces 88
Pioneer Public Service 54
Pipeline 130
Political Economy in the Modern State 27
Political Economy of Newfoundland 1929-1972, The 96
Political Economy of the Canadian North, The 95
Political Party Financing in Canada 28
Politics of Development, Forest, Mines, and Hydro-Electric Power in Ontario 1849-1941, The 28
Prairie Provinces in their Relation to the National Economy of Canada, The 65
Prairie Settlement 33
Precarious Homestead, The 29
Problems of Staple Production in Canada 18
Profiles of a Province, Studies in the History of Ontario 65
Progress and Prospects of Canadian Agriculture 115
Progressive Party in Canada, The 131
Protective Tariff in Canada's Development, The 104
Public Investment and Capital Formation 1926-1941 129
Public Welfare Administration in Canada 28

Q

Québec en Amerique au XIXe Siècle 64

R

Radical Politics and Canadian Labour 1880-1930 79
Railway Builders, a Chronicle of Overland Highways, The 50
Railway Interrelations of the United States and Canada, The 23
Railway Nationalization in Canada 129
Rapport sur les Activites du Centre de Recherche en Histoire Economique du Canada Française, 1965-1969 11
Read Canadian, a Book about Canadian Books 4
Recent Trends and New Literature in Canadian History 2
Reciprocity and the North Atlantic Triangle 1932-1938 130
Reciprocity 1846-1911 55
Reciprocity 1911 82
Reciprocity Treaty of 1854, The 55
Red River Valley, 1811-1849, The 43
Reference Aids in Canadian History 4
'Regional Aspects of Canada's Economic Growth 112
Regional Economic Policies in Canada 27
Regionalism in the Canadian Community 1867-1967 9
Renewing Nature's Wealth 27
Report of the Royal Commission on Dominion-Provincial Relations (Book I-III) 62
Resources for Tomorrow 139
Resources of the Canadian Shield 31
Restrictive Trade Practices in Canada 28
Revue d'Histoire de l'Amerique Francaise 4
Rideau Waterway 50
Rise and Fall of New France, The 42
Rise of Toronto 1850-1890, The 74
Role of International Unionism in Canada, The 125
Romantic History of the Canadian Pacific, The 76

Title Index

Royal Commission on Farm Machinery 119
Rush for Spoils, the Company Province 1871-1933, The 66

S

Saga of the St. Lawrence, A 45
Sails of the Maritimes 50
St. John's and Newfoundland, an Economic Survey 96
St. Lawrence Deep Water-Way, The 123
St. Lawrence Seaway, The 133
Salmon, Our Heritage, the Story of a Province and an Industry 12
Saskatchewan, the History of a Province 12
Scale and Specialization in Canadian Manufacturing 119
Science and Politics in Canada 128
Science, Technology and Innovation 133
Sea Power and British North America 1783-1820 54
Seigneurial Regime, The 56
Seigneurial System in Canada, The 55
Seigneurial System in Early Canada, The 54
Select Documents in Canadian Economic History, 1497-1783 44
Select Documents in Canadian Economic History, 1783-1885 44
Service Industries, The 121
Service State Emerges in Ontario 1945-1973, The 122
Settlement and the Forest Frontier of Eastern Canada 33
Settlement of the Peace River Country, The 88
Seventh Annual Review 94
Shipping, Maritime Trade, and Economic Development of Colonial North America 57
Short History of the Canadian Constitution, A 28
Silent Surrender 102
Sixty Years of Protection in Canada, 1846-1907 84
Social Credit Movement in Alberta, The 130
Social Security and Reconstruction in Canada 127
Social Welfare in Ontario, 1791-1893 56
Some Regional Aspects of Canada's Economic Development 7
Spatial Evolution of Manufacturing, Southern Ontario 1851-1891 73
Spatial Interaction in the Economic History of Canada, 1800-1867 9
Stages of Economic Growth, a Non-Communist Manifesto, The 68
Staple Industries and Economic Development, Canada 1841-1867, The 47
State and Economic Growth, The 26
State Intervention and Assistance in Collective Bargaining 131
Statistical Abstract and Record 67
Statistical Account of Upper Canada, Compiled with a View to a Grand System of Emigration 43
Statistical Summary 99
Statistical Yearbook of the Province of Quebec 67
Statistics of Banking 67
Statistics of Industry in British Columbia 1871-1934 65
Statistics of Trade 67
Statistiques Manufacturieres du Québec, 1665-1948 20
Steam Navigation, and Its Relation to the Commerce of Canada and the United States 75-76
Story of Canadian Roads, The 49
Story of Toronto, The 73
Strikes and Lockouts in Canada 124
Struggle for National Broadcasting in Canada, The 133
Studies in the Economy of the Maritime Provinces 10
Submission of Ontario to the Royal Commission on Canada's Economic Prospects 97
Sudbury Basin, The 116
Summary. Seventh Census of Canada, 1931 32

Title Index

T

Take-Over of Canadian Firms 1945-61, The 103
Tariff and Competition in Canada, The 104
Tariff History of Canada, The 83
Taxes, Tariffs, and Subsidies 28
Technology and Empire 29
Theoretical, Historical and Planning Perspectives 74
Times of Trouble: Labour Unrest and Industrial Conflict in Canada 1900-1966 79
Towards the Discovery of Canada 7
Trade Liberalization and Canadian Agriculture 105
Trade Liberalization and the British Columbia Economy 106
Trade Liberalization and the Canadian Furniture Industry 104
Trade Liberalization and the Canadian Pulp and Paper Industry 105
Trade Liberalization and the Canadian Steel Industry 106
Trade Liberalization and Transportation in International Trade 105
Trade Unions in Canada 25
Transatlantic Economic Community 94
Transportation in Canada 122
Transport, Competition and Public Policy in Canada 131
Trees to News 121
Trends and Factors of Fertility in Canada 33
Trends in Canadian Marketing 123

U

Une Economie a Liberer, le Quebec Analyse dans ses Structures Economiques 11

Unequal Union 41
Union Growth in Canada 1921-1967 124
Union of the Canadas, The 40
Upper Canada, the Formative Years 1784-1841 40
Urban Development in Canada 74
Urban Development in South Central Ontario 74

W

Wartime Economic Co-Operation 95
Welland Canal Company, The 49
West and Confederation 1857-71, The 43
Western Ontario and the American Frontier 65
Wheat 118
Wheat Economy, The 62
Wheat-Growing in Canada, the United States and Argentina 72
Wholesale Prices in Canada 1890-1909 67
Whoop-Up Country 66
Winnipeg General Strike, The (Balawyder) 79
Winnipeg General Strike, The (Masters) 79
Wooden Ships and Iron Men 50
Workingman in the Nineteenth Century, The 52
World Trade and Economic Growth 95
World Wheat Economy 1885-1939, The 71

Y

Yearbook and Almanac of Canada, The 44

SUBJECT INDEX

This index follows letter by letter alphabetization. Underlined numbers refer to pages of main emphasis within the subject area.

A

Acadia 38
Agricultural cooperatives 78
Agricultural credit
   confederation to 1920 76
   1920 to the present 128
Agricultural implement industry 21, 119, 121
   tariff in 83
Agricultural labor 88, 140
   income of 137
   productivity of 134
Agriculture 19
   colonial period to 1867 46, 47, 51, 55
   confederation to 1920 70, 71, 78, 85, 86, 88
   national income and 86, 136
   1920 to the present 105, 114, 115, 116, 127, 128, 135, 136, 137, 140
   policies for 27
   productivity of 136, 137, 138
   societies 51, 78
   tariff in 55, 105
   technology in 135
   See also Cattle industry and trade; Dairy industry; Farm products
Air line industry 121, 122
Alberta
   economic history of 12
   petroleum industry in 116
   public finance in 129
Americans in Canada 32, 33
   confederation to 1920 87, 88
Antitrust legislation. See Trusts, industrial
Assimilation 141
Automobile industry 120
   international agreements in 101, 106

B

Balance of payments 20
   confederation to 1920 70, 71, 72, 83
   1920 to the present 99, <u>107-10</u>
Balance of trade, confederation to 1920 70
Bank of Canada 131, 133
Bank of Montreal 22
Banks and banking 22, 23
   colonial period to 1867 49
   confederation to 1920 67, 75, 77
   1920 to the present 99, 122, 128, 131
   See also Currency; Finance; Interest rates; Monetary policy
Barter and exchange 66
Bennett 132, 133

Subject Index

Birth rate, decline of 140
Bladen Plan 106
Branch Factory System 78
British Columbia
  agriculture in 116
  economic history of 12, 42
  fishing industry in 18
  forests of 86
  industry in 65
  lumber industry in 19
  trade of 66, 98, 106, 117
British in Canada
  colonial period to 1867 58-59
  confederation to 1920 89
Broadcasting industry 133
Business. See Industry
Business cycles 85, 86, <u>107-10</u>, 135, 138
Businessmen, economic conditions of 85

C

Canada. See Acadia; Maritime Provinces; New France; United Province of Canada; Western provinces; specific names of individual provinces
Canada Permanent Mortgage Corp. 77
Canadian Annexation Movement (1849-50) 53
Canadian Bank of Commerce 77
Canadian Congress of Labour 24
Canadian Manufacturers' Association 77, 82
Canadian Northern Railway 76
Canadian Pacific Railway 76, 88
Canadians in the U.S. 34
Canals 50. See also Welland Canal Co.
Canning industry 74
Capital 136, 137
  flow of 102, 103, 108, 109, 122, 127, 142
  utilization of in manufacturing 137
Capital formation 34-35
  colonial period to 1867 59-60
  confederation to 1920 90-91

  1920 to the present 129, <u>141-42</u>
Capitalism 131
Catholic Church. See Church
Cattle industry and trade 71, 72
Channel Islands, economic history of 9
Chemical industry 119
Church
  economic role of in Quebec 64
  land policies and the 57
Clergy reserves. See Church, land policies and the
Climate, economics of 29
Coats, Robert 100
Cod fisheries. See Fishing industry
Collective bargaining 79
  government intervention in 131
  political pressure and 77
Colonization. See Economic history, colonial period to 1867; France, relations with New France; Great Britain in Canadian economic history; Seigneurial system
Columbia River Treaty 130
Commerce, colonial period to 1867 46, 47, 48, 51, 54, 56
  confederation to 1920 70, 71, 75-76, 81
  1920 to the present 95, 96, 98, 102, 103, 104, 105, 106, <u>107-10</u>, 117, 130, 132
  policies in 26, 27, 51, 54, 81, 106, 130
  politics and 54
  with the U.S. 71
  See also Customs administration; Free trade and protection; Reciprocity; Subsidies; Tariff
Common Market. See European Economic Community, Canadian commerce and
Communications, in economic growth 14, 15, 16
Communism, labor and 24
Company towns 74
Comparative economics. See Economics, comparative
Competition 105, 115
  control of 84

Subject Index

tariff and 104
in transportation 131
Congress of Industrial Organizations 24
Conservation, economics of 28. See also Natural resources
Construction industry 120
Consumption, levels of 135
Corporations 130. See also Crown corporations, administration and control of; Industry; Monopoly; Multinational corporations; Trusts, industrial
Credit. See Social Credit movement
Crown corporations, administration and control of 81, 130, 132
Currency 22
Customs administration 26
colonial period to 1867 53

D

Dairy industry 18
Demography. See Birth rate, decline of; Fertility, human; Population resources
Depression (1929) 127, 132, 133, 136, 138
Distribution of goods, costs of 138
Dominion Bureau of Statistics 99, 100
Dominion-provincial relations 131
financial 133

E

Economic geography. See Geography, economic
Economic growth and development 2, 7, 14-16, 86
colonial period to 1867 44, 57, 60
confederation to 1920 66, 67-68, 70, 71, 76, 84
immigration and 32
migration and 34
1920 to the present 96, 100-113, 129, 135, 137, 138, 140, 141
Economic history
general 1-2, 6-12, 17-23

bibliography 1, 2-4
statistics 13, 20
textbooks 5-6
colonial period to 1867 37-43
statistics 43-44
confederation to 1920 61-66
bibliography 65
statistics 63, 66-67
1920 to the present 93-98
statistics 98-100
See also Capital formation; Government, role in economic organization; Industry; Labor economics; Nationalism, economic; Population resources; Regionalism in economics; Science and technology
Economic interdependence
colonial period to 1867 55
Economic organization
government in 25-29
colonial period to 1867 52-57
confederation to 1920 79-85
1920 to the present 125-33
industrial 23-24
colonial period to 1867 51
confederation to 1920 77-78
1920 to the present 123-24
labor 24-25
colonial period to 1867 52
confederation to 1920 78-79
1920 to the present 124-25
Economic policy
confederation to 1920 68, 81, 84, 91
1920 to the present 102, 105, 108, 127, 128, 129
Economics, comparative 27
Education 20
confederation to 1920 91
history of 34, 35
1920 to the present 96, 141, 142
See also Universities and colleges, federal grants to
Electrical manufacturing industry 118
Electric power industry 117. See also Hydro-electric power
Electric railroads 122
Electronics industry 119

Subject Index

Employment
 changes in 138
 in the depression of 1929 127
 of women 141
Energy resources 115, 119, 128
Entrepreneurship 14
European Economic Community,
  Canadian commerce and 104, 105
Explorers and exploration 38
Extractive industries 24. See also Mining and mineral industries

F

Farming. See Agriculture
Farm products
 prices of 46, 71
 price supports for 127, 128
 See also Grain trade; Wheat trade
Fertility, human 33
Finance 22, 23, 122, 123, 127, 129
 history of public 81
First Dominion Companies Act 82
Fiscal policy 28, 127, 129. See also Monetary policy
Fishing industry 12, 18
 colonial period to 1867 46, 55
 confederation to 1920 63, 74
 1920 to the present 114, 115, 117
Foreign exchange 108, 109, 110, 129
Foreign investment. See Investment, foreign
Forests
 in British Columbia 86
 management 27, 28, 85
 tenures and taxes 131
 See also Lumber industry; Pulp and paper industry
France
 in Canadian economic development 91
 relations with New France 47, 55
Franchise. See Suffrage, colonial period to 1867
Fraser River 74
Free trade and protection
 colonial period to 1867 54
 confederation to 1920 84
 1920 to the present 104, 105, 106, 128

Freight rates 13
 oceanic 86
French Canadians
 demographic characteristics of 140
 as industrial entrepreneurs 113
 labor movement and the 79
 population statistics and movements of 89, 90
 See also New France; Quebec
Frontier thesis in Canadian economic history 14, 15, 16
Fuel. See Energy resources
Furniture industry, trade liberalization in 104
Fur trade 18
 colonial period to 1867 46, 47, 48, 55

G

Galt, Alexander Tillock 42
Gas industry 117
Geography, economic <u>30-31</u>, 58
Gompers, Samuel 79
Government
 business and 132
 grants to education 132
 role in economic organization 25-29
  colonial period to 1867 52-57
  confederation to 1920 79-85
  1920 to the present 125-33
 spending policies of 81, 84
 See also Dominion-provincial relations
Government, provincial, federal subsidies to 83. See also Provincial-municipal relations
Grain trade
 confederation to 1920 71, 78
 1920 to the present 115, 116, 131
 See also Wheat trade
Grand Trunk Railway 22
Great Britain in Canadian economic history 7, 11, 26, 29
 colonial period to 1867 45, 46, 54, 55, 60
 confederation to 1920 71, 72,

Subject Index

81, 89, 90, 91, 109
1920 to the present 128, 138
See also British in Canada
Great Lakes 22, 23
Gross national product 67

H

Harbors. See Ports of entry
Hat manufacture 48
Highways. See Roads, colonial period to 1867
Housing
  demand for 123
  financial aspects of 129
  laws and legislation 131
  statistics 142
Howe, Clarence Decatur 132
Hudson Bay Co. 19, 47, 88
Hudson Bay Railway 122
Hydro-electric power 28, 82. See also Ontario Hydro-electric Power Commission

I

Immigration and emigration 32, 33, 34, 43
  colonial period to 1867 58, 59
  confederation to 1920 84, 88, 89, 90
  1920 to the present 128, 141
  See also Americans in Canada; British in Canada; Canadians in the U.S.
Income
  confederation to 1920 67, 86
  1920 to the present 108, 109, 112, 130, 135, 136, 137, 138
Income expenditure theory 110-11
Indians
  economic development and 140
  in the fur trade 47, 55
  government policies toward 27, 28
Industrial Development Bank of Canada 128
Industry
  economic history of 17-23
    colonial period to 1867 45-50
    confederation to 1920 68, 69-77
    1920 to the present 105, 113-23, 136, 137
  location of 120
  organization of 23-24
    colonial period to 1867 51
    confederation to 1920 77-78
    1920 to the present 124
  production function of 119, 120
  productivity of 73, 74, 136, 137, 138
  specialization of 119
  See also Corporations; Crown Corporations; Monopoly; Multinational corporations; Trusts, industrial; names of industries and companies
Inland water transportation 22, 23. See also Rideau Waterway
Innis, Harold Adams 14, 15
Insurance industry
  confederation to 1920 76
  1920 to the present 122, 123
Interest rates 100
International economic relations 94. See also Great Britain in Canadian economic history; United States in Canadian economic history
International Labor Organization 25
International Nickel Company of Canada Ltd. 118
Inventories 135
Inventors and inventions 29
Investment 20, 129, 133, 138
  foreign 90, 91, 101, 102, 103, 124
Iron and steel industry 20, 117
  American influence on 116
  productivity of 118
  trade liberalization and 106

J

Journalism 23

K

Knights of Labour 79

169

Subject Index

L

Labor economics <u>24-25</u>, 29
   colonial period to 1867 52
   confederation to 1929 <u>79</u>, 83, 84
      86
   1920 to the present <u>124-25</u>,
      136, 137
   manpower studies 32, 88, 141
   politics and 79, 83-84, 125
   See also Agricultural labor; Collective bargaining; Occupations, changes in; Strikes and lockouts; Wages
Labor-management relations 25
Labrador, in the confederation 96
Land policies and settlement
   colonial period to 1867 49, 54, 56, 57, 58, 59
   confederation to 1920 61, 83, 87, 88
   1920 to the present 140
   railroads and 83, 88
   See also Geography, economic; Public lands, management of
Lower, Arthur 102
Lower Canada (1791-1840) 41, 44
   agriculture in 46, 47
   economic history of 56
   land tenure in 56
   politics in 56
   shipbuilding in 49
   See also Quebec
Lumber industry 19
   colonial period to 1867 45, 46, 56
   confederation to 1920 70, 115
   the Royal Navy and 45
   settlement and 33
   See also Forests; Pulp and paper industry

M

Machinery industry 121
McInnis, R. Marvin 112
Manitoba, economic history of 12
Manpower. See Labor economics
Manufacturing. See Industry
Maritime Provinces
   economic history of 9-10
      colonial period to 1867 38
      confederation to 1920 63-64
      1920 to the present 96
   industrialization of 81
   lumber industry in 19
   shipping in 50
   See also Acadia; New Brunswick; Newfoundland; Nova Scotia, economic development of
Marketing 123
Massey-Ferguson Ltd. 21
Massey-Harris Co. 20
Meat industry and trade. See Cattle industry and trade
Mercantilism. See France, relations with New France; Great Britain in Canadian economic history; Seigneurial system
Merchant Marine. See Shipping industry
Migration, internal 33, 34
   confederation to 1920 87, 88, 89, 90
   1920 to the present 140, 141
Milling trade 21
Mining and mineral industries 18, 19
   development policies for 28
   land settlement and 33
   1920 to the present 114, 115, 116, 117
   See also names of mining industries
Molson Breweries 20
Monetary policy 127, 130. See also Currency; Fiscal policy; Foreign exchange; Quantity theory of money
Monopoly 27. See also Trusts, industrial
Montreal 74
   economic structure of 113
   urbanization of 120
   working class in 85
Multinational corporations 24, 102, 105

N

National Housing Act (1954) 131

Subject Index

Nationalism, economic 27, 29
  colonial period to 1867 49
  labor and 24
  1920 to the present 101-3
National parks, policies for 82
Natural gas. See Gas industry
Natural resources
  availability of 139
  conservation of 28
  development of 18
  policies for 27, 82
  See also Energy resources; Population resources; Wildlife, management of
New Brunswick 38
Newfoundland
  economic history of 8, 96
  entry into the Dominion 131
  fisheries of 46, 115, 117
New France
  economic history of 39, 40, 41, 42, 44
  industry in 48
  lumbering in 46
  relations with France 47, 55
  settlement of 58
  wheat supply in 45
  See also Ontario; Quebec
Newsprint paper industry. See Pulp and paper industry
Nickel industry 116, 117, 118
Northwest Co. 51
Nova Scotia, economic development of 129

O

Occupations, changes in 140
Oil industry. See Petroleum industry
Ontario
  agriculture in 46, 71, 78, 85, 115
  economic history of 11
    confederation to 1920 <u>64-65</u>, 83
    1920 to the present 97
  federal system and 81
  forest policy in 85
  hydro-electric power in 73, 82
  industry in 73, 113, 120
  natural resource management in 27
  urban development in 74
  See also United Province of Canada; Upper Canada; names of cities in Ontario
Ontario Hydro-electric Power Commission 73, 81

P

Paper industry. See Pulp and paper industry
Parks. See National parks, policies for
Patents and patent law 27, 129
Peace River region 88
Petroleum industry
  confederation to 1920 71
  1920 to the present 103, 107, 116, 117, 130
Political parties
  financing of 28
  See also Progressive Party
Politics
  collective bargaining and 77
  commerce and 54
  labor and 79, 83-84, 125
  in Lower Canada 56
  pressure groups in 133
  in science and technology 128
  See also Suffrage, colonial period to 1867
Poor 85
Population resources 29, 31-34
  colonial period to 1867 58-59
  confederation to 1920 86-90
  1920 to the present 139-41
  in rural areas 85
  See also Birth rate, decline of
Ports of entry 53
Post office
  colonial period to 1867 50
  confederation to 1920 76
Prairie provinces. See Western provinces
Pressure groups, in politics 133
Prices
  colonial period to 1867 46
  confederation to 1920 67, 71
  1920 to the present 127, 128, 130, 131
Private enterprise. See Capitalism; Entrepreneurship

Subject Index

Productivity
   agricultural 136, 137, 138
   industrial 73, 74, 118, 136, 137, 138
Progressive Party 131
Property, right of 54, 81
Provincial-municipal relations 96.
      See also Dominion-provincial relations; Government, provincial, federal subsidies to
Public lands, management of 27.
      See also Forests; National parks, policies for
Public services and service 28
   colonial period to 1867 54
   1920 to the present 96
Public welfare. See Social welfare
Pulp and paper industry
   confederation to 1920 73, 84
   1920 to the present 105, 119, 120, 121

Q

Quantity theory of money 110-11
Quebec
   agriculture in 19, 117
   demography of 33
   economic growth of 113
   economic history of 4, 10-11
      confederation to 1920 64
      1920 to the present 97
   employment statistics of 141
   foreign investment in 91
   hydro-electric power in 73
   industry in 20
   shipbuilding in 49
   See also French Canadians; Lower Canada; Montreal; New France; United Province of Canada
Quebec, Old Province of (1759-1791) 40, 41
   agricultural prices in 46
   financial administration of 53
   shipbuilding in 49
   social welfare in 56

R

Railroads
   colonial period to 1867 49, 50
   confederation to 1920 75, 76, 77, 82, 83
   land and colonization policies of 88
   nationalization of 23
   1920 to the present 122
   subsidies of 76, 83
   taxation of 82
   See also Electric railroads; names of railroads
Reciprocity 53, 55, 56, 78, 82, 130
Red River Valley 43
Regionalism in economics
   confederation to 1920 62
   government in 27, 28
   history of 9
   1920 to the present 111-12, 128, 135
Rideau Waterway 50
Riel Rebellions 43
Roads, colonial period to 1867 49

S

St. Lawrence Seaway 123, 133
   American shipping in 53
Salmon industry. See Fishing industry
Saskatchewan, economic history of 12
Savings
   employment and 138
   personal 142
Science and technology 29-30, 86, 130, 133, 134-38
   in agriculture 135
   education in 91
   politics and 128
Sea power 54
   lumber industry and 45
Seigneurial system 54, 55, 56, 84
Selkirk, Lord 59
Service industries 121, 122, 123.
      See also Public services and service
Shipbuilding 49
Shipping industry

Subject Index

colonial period to 1867 45-46, 50, 53, 57
confederation to 1920 75, 86
See also Inland water transportation; Steam-navigation
Social Credit movement 130
Social security 127
Social welfare 28
colonial period to 1867 56
See also Public services and service
Soldiers. See Veterans, land settlement and
Speculation, in foreign exchange 108
Steam-navigation 75-76
Steel Company of Canada 20
Steel industry. See Iron and steel industry
Strikes and lockouts
confederation to 1920 79
1920 to the present 124
Subsidies 28
to provincial governments 83
railroad 76, 83
See also Farm products, price supports for
Sudbury, Ontario 74
Sudbury (Ontario) Basin 116
Suffrage, colonial period to 1867 54

T

Tariff 28
colonial period to 1867 55
confederation to 1920 82, 83, 84
1920 to the present 103-6, 127, 131, 132
Taxation 28, 132
of railroads 82
Technology. See Science and technology
Textile industry 120
Toronto 73, 74
Board of Trade 51
Trade. See Commerce
Trade-unions. See Collective bargaining; Labor economics; Labor-management relations; Strikes and lockouts; names of labor unions

Trading companies 51. See also names of trading companies
Trans Canada Air Lines 121
Transportation 22-23, 122
international trade and 105
policies for 131
See also Inland water transportation; Railroads; Roads, colonial period to 1867; Shipping industry
Trusts, industrial 81, 127, 132, 133. See also Monopoly

U

United Farmers of Ontario 78
United Grain Growers Ltd. 78
United Province of Canada (1840-1867) 40, 41
agriculture in 46
financial difficulties. of 54
social welfare in 56
See also Lower Canada; New France; Ontario; Quebec; Upper Canada
United States in Canadian economic history 7, 11, 12, 16, 19, 20, 23, 24, 25, 34
colonial period to 1867 34, 56
confederation to 1920 71, 78, 82
1920 to the present 94, 95, 101, 102, 103, 106, 107, 109, 114, 116, 117, 122, 125, 127, 132
See also Americans in Canada; Frontier thesis in Canadian economic history
Universities and colleges, federal grants to 132
University League of Social Reform 103
Upper Canada (1791-1840) 40, 41
agriculture in 46, 51
capital resources of 59
clergy reserves in 57
commerce in 53
industry in 48
land policies of 54
land tenure in 56
social welfare in 56

Subject Index

statistics 43
See also Ontario
Uranium industry 116
Urban development and urbanization
confederation to 1920 73, 74
1920 to the present 120
Urban history 20

V

Veterans, land settlement and 58
Voting. See Suffrage, colonial period to 1867

W

Wages 136
Water power. See Hydro-electric power
Welland Canal Co. 49, 53
Western provinces
agriculture in 71, 87
economic history of 11-12
colonial period to 1867 42-43
confederation to 1920 65-66
1920 to the present 98
effect of World War II on 129
mineral industries in 117
settlement of 33, 83, 87, 88, 89, 140
tariff burden of 84
See also Alberta; British Columbia; Manitoba, economic history of; Saskatchewan, economic history of
Wheat trade 18
colonial period to 1867 45
confederation to 1920 62, 70, 71, 72, 78, 82
1920 to the present 116, 118, 123, 127, 129, 131
Wildlife, management of 27
Winnipeg General Strike 79
Women, employment of 141
Wood products. See Lumber industry; Pulp and paper industry
Working class. See Labor economics
World War I, finance of 82
World War II, economic aspects of 95, 129

Ref
Z
7165
C2
D5

NOV 27 1978